SCHOLASTIC

GO MATHS

Course Book

Level 5

Published by Scholastic India Pvt. Ltd.
A subsidiary of Scholastic Inc., New York, 10012 (USA).
Publishers since 1920, with international operations in Canada, Australia, New Zealand, the United Kingdom, India, and Hong Kong.

For information regarding permission, write to:
Scholastic India Pvt. Ltd.
A-27, Ground Floor, Bharti Sigma Centre
Infocity-1, Sector 34, Gurgaon (Haryana) - 122001
Email: education@scholastic.co.in

Typeset at Digital Expressions

First edition: 2009
Reprinted: 2009 (thrice), 2010 (twice), 2011 (thrice), 2012 (twice), 2013, 2014 (twice), 2015, 2016 (thrice), 2017, 2018 (4 times), 2019 (twice), 2020, 2023, 2025, 2026

ISBN-13: 978-81-8477-153-4
Printed in India

Contents

Thank You!

The Go Maths books were sent out to approximately sixty schools across the country for primary school principals, departmental heads and teachers to give their feedback on the contents. The publishers would like to thank all those who took the time out of their busy schedules to go through the books and make many valuable suggestions, which have been duly incorporated.

Aloma Das, Seth Anandram Jaipuria School, Kanpur
Anjali Madan, Gyan Bharati School, New Delhi
Anjana Mallick, Bidya Bharati School, Kolkata
Bharati Nabhi, Apeejay School, Kolkata
Jaya Muralidharan, Doon Public School, Delhi
Jayasree.P., Chinmaya Vidyalaya, Annanagar, Chennai
M.Chatelier, St. Xavier Collegiate School, Kolkata
Meera Devi, N.S.N Mat Hr Sec School, Chennai
P.Sharda, Delhi Public School, Visakhapatnam
Priyamvada Rawat, M.G.D Girls School, Jaipur
R.A. Vijaylakshmi, S.I.C.A. Sen.Sec. School, Indore
Shruti Rupani, M.G.D Girls School, Jaipur
Shyama Bihari Mishra, St. John's Whitehall, Shillong
Sonika Garg, Delhi Public School, Dwarka, New Delhi
Tamana Aswani, Delhi Public School, Kolkata
U.A. Issac, Rajkumar College, Rajkot

Special thanks to Apjit Bassi and Sangeeta Kashyap for their assistance and advice.

In addition to the people listed above, there were many teachers who did not want their help to be publicly acknowledged. In deference to their wishes, we have not included their names, but we would once again like to acknowledge their valuable help.

Introduction

Go Maths is a series of graded mathematics course books for the primary classes. These books are designed to help students learn a wide range of mathematical concepts such as addition, subtraction, multiplication, division, fractions, decimals, percentages, measurement, geometry and much more. Each topic has a set of imaginative and challenging activities.

This series has won a national award in Australia. It has been adapted for Indian primary schools by a panel of teachers from reputed school and college teachers and experienced children's publishers, and vetted by school teachers and principals from different parts of India. The approach follows the current national and state curriculum and pedagogical principles.

The *Go Maths* series is comprehensive and rigorous. It has been created based on the following beliefs:

Learning through involvement

Students learn through active involvement and substantive communication between teachers and students, as well as between students and students. This helps students internalise and acquire new skills.

Learning through interaction

Students build their mathematical understanding by interacting with the world around them through a range of engaging learning experiences using real-life contexts to explore mathematical ideas. Quality teaching and learning is required for students to develop a rich conceptual understanding of mathematical ideas.

Learning through thinking critically

Learning should be as much 'minds on' as it is 'hands on'. Students should be encouraged to think critically.

Learning through practice

Skills should be practiced after they have developed from deep conceptual understanding.

Some of the unique features of this series are:

- Easy-to-understand introduction to the concepts.
- Mathematical ideas developed and revisited in related units.
- Fresh and vibrant pages to engage students.
- Developmentally sequenced worksheets for independent learning.
- Clear, open questions to prompt class discussion.
- Emphasis on mental calculations using effective strategies.
- Real-life applications to develop mathematical concepts and skills.
- Revision quizzes to assess mathematical proficiency.
- Additional independent, enrichment activities (marked FF) to encourage fast finishers.
- Teachers' notes (marked TN) to help teachers supplement their teaching strategies.

The *Go Maths* series provides an innovative and interactive approach to learning mathematics. The emphasis on critical thinking ensures that students learn concepts and basic operations with great thoroughness and clarity.

CHAPTER 1

Place Value to Crores

The Place Value Chart

You have already learnt about the place value chart and periods. Starting from the right and moving left in the place value chart, the lakhs place is to the left of the ten thousands place.
It is the beginning of a new period—the lakhs period.

Ten Lakhs Place

When 1 is added to the largest six-digit number 9,99,999 we get:

9,99,999 + 1 = 10,00,000

10,00,000 or ten lakh is the smallest seven-digit number.

Lakhs		Thousands		Ones		
Ten Lakhs (TL)	One Lakh (L)	Ten Thousands (T Th)	One Thousand (Th)	Hundreds (H)	Tens (T)	Ones (O)

The Crores Period

On adding 1 to 99,99,999 (ninety-nine lakh ninety-nine thousand nine hundred and ninety-nine) the smallest eight-digit number is formed.

The smallest eight-digit number is 1,00,00,000 and is read as 1 crore.

This marks the beginning of a new period—the crores period.

Similarly, adding 1 to 9,99,99,999 gives 10,00,00,000, which is the smallest nine-digit number, 10 crore.

Crores		Lakhs		Thousands		Ones		
Ten Crores (TC)	One Crore (C)	Ten Lakhs (TL)	One Lakh (L)	Ten Thousands (T Th)	One Thousand (Th)	Hundreds (H)	Tens (T)	Ones (O)

Remember to put commas to separate the periods.
Start counting from the extreme right moving to the left in the number.
Place the commas after the third digit, fifth digit and the seventh digit.

Example: Put commas in the number 192534768 and place it in the place value chart.

Solution: Starting from the extreme right and moving to the left, place the commas after the third digit (7), fifth digit (3) and the seventh digit (2)

19,25,34,768

Place Value to Crores

Crores		Lakhs		Thousands		Ones		
Ten Crores (TC)	One Crore (C)	Ten Lakhs (TL)	One Lakh (L)	Ten Thousands (T Th)	One Thousand (Th)	Hundreds (H)	Tens (T)	Ones (O)
1	9	2	5	3	4	7	6	8

Word form: Nineteen crore twenty-five lakh thirty-four thousand seven hundred and sixty-eight.
Expanded form: 19,00,00,000 + 20,00,000 + 5,00,000 + 30,000 + 4000 + 700 + 60 + 8

Ordering Numbers

If two numbers have a <u>different number of digits</u>:

The number with more digits is larger.

Example: Compare 96,84,369 and 7,69,523.

96,84,369 has seven digits whereas 7,69,523 has six.

Therefore, 96,84,369 > 7,69,523

If two numbers have the <u>same number of digits</u>:

- Write the numbers lining up the digits in the correct places in the place value chart.
- Compare the digits starting from the left.
- Find the first place where the digits are different; the number with the greater digit is the greater one.

Example: Which is greater 10,35,76,901 or 10,35,76,968?

Both the numbers have eight digits, so we line up the digits in the correct places in the place value chart.

TC	C	TL	L	TTh	Th	H	T	O
1	0	3	5	7	6	9	**0**	1
1	0	3	5	7	6	9	**6**	8

Starting from the left (the ten crore place), compare the digits.

The digits in all the places up to the hundreds place are equal.

The digits in the tens place are unequal.

0 < 6

So 10,35,76,901 < 10,35,76,968.

Locating Large Numbers on a Number Line

Worksheet 1

Write the number that should be shown in the blank boxes.

1.

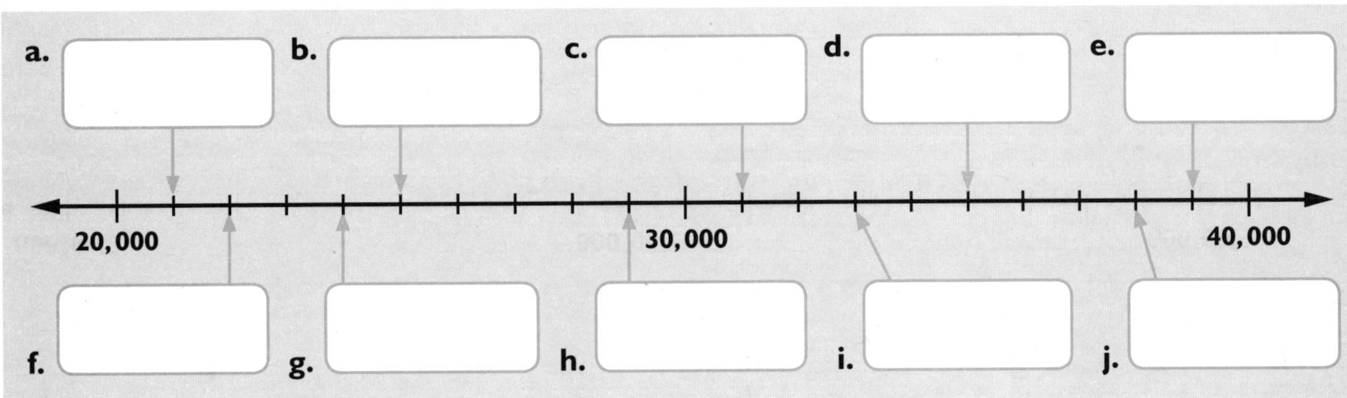

2.

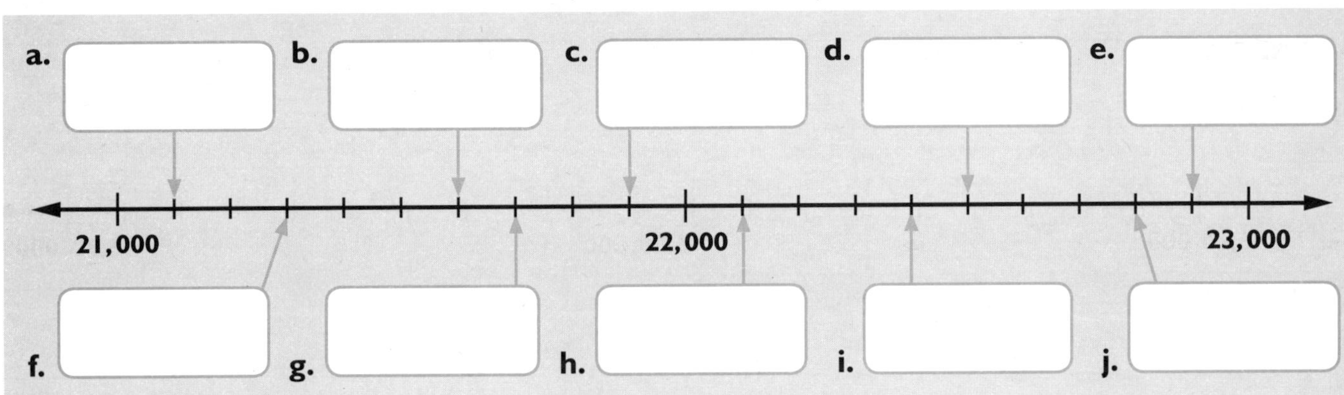

3.

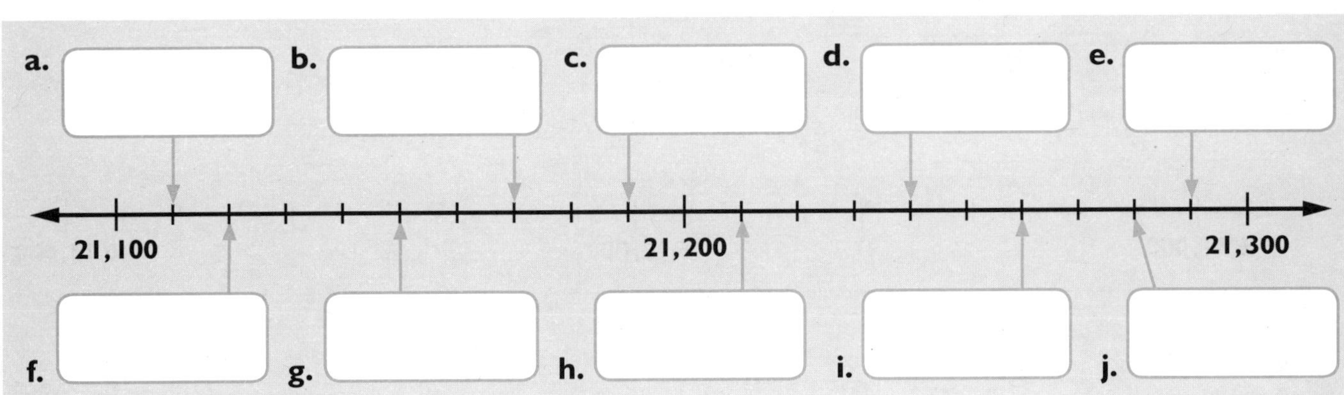

4.

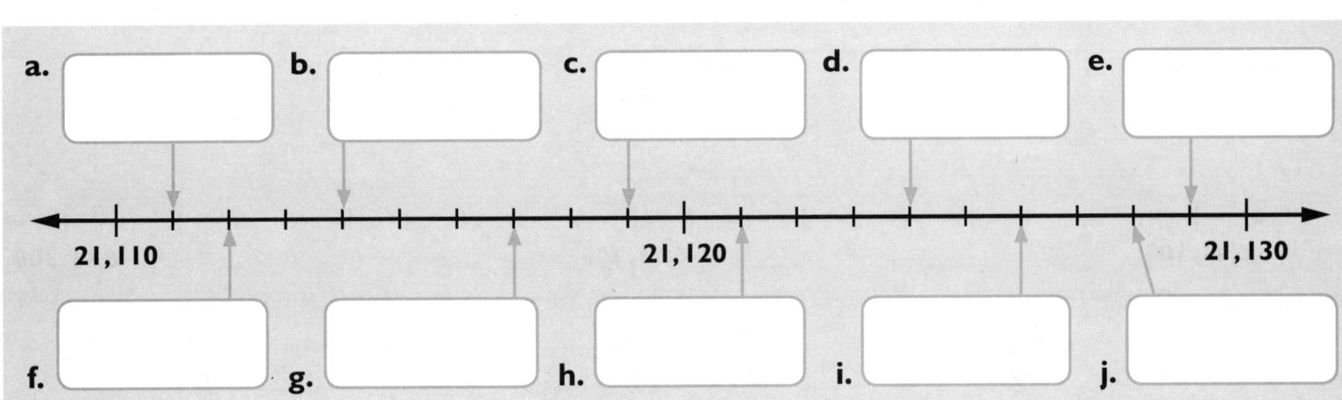

Write the number that is five less than the number shown in part (a) of each number line.

Locating Large Numbers on a Number Line

Worksheet 2

Write the number that should be shown in the blank boxes.

1.

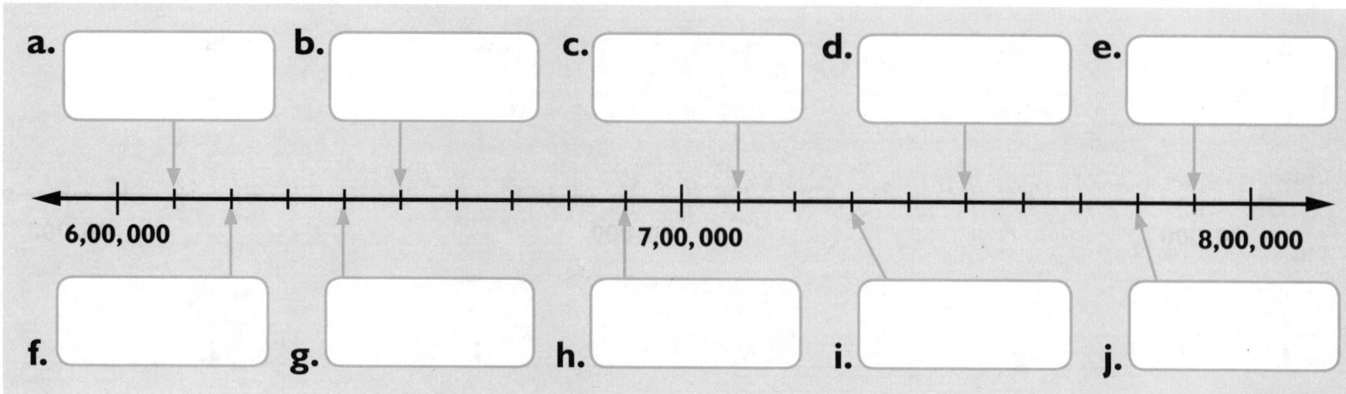

2.

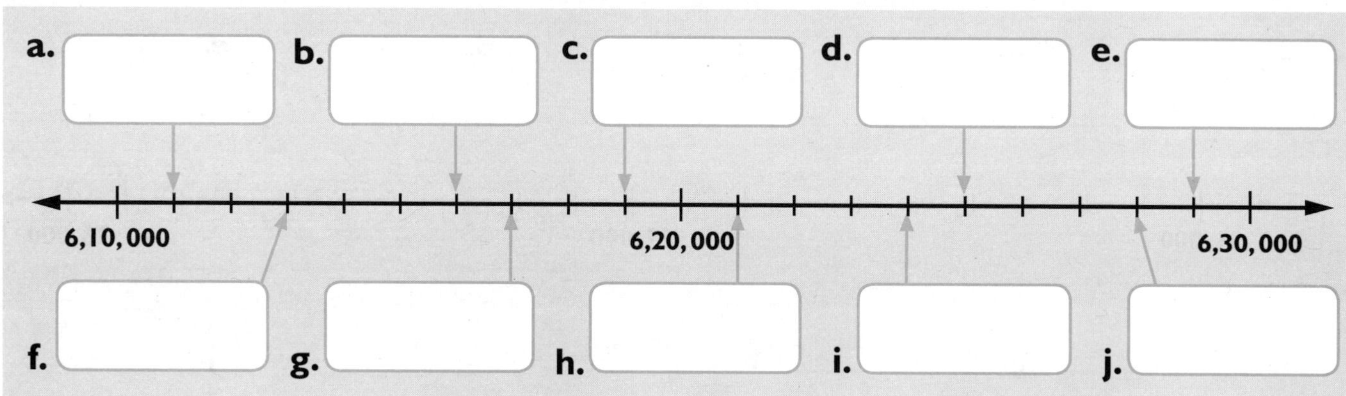

3.

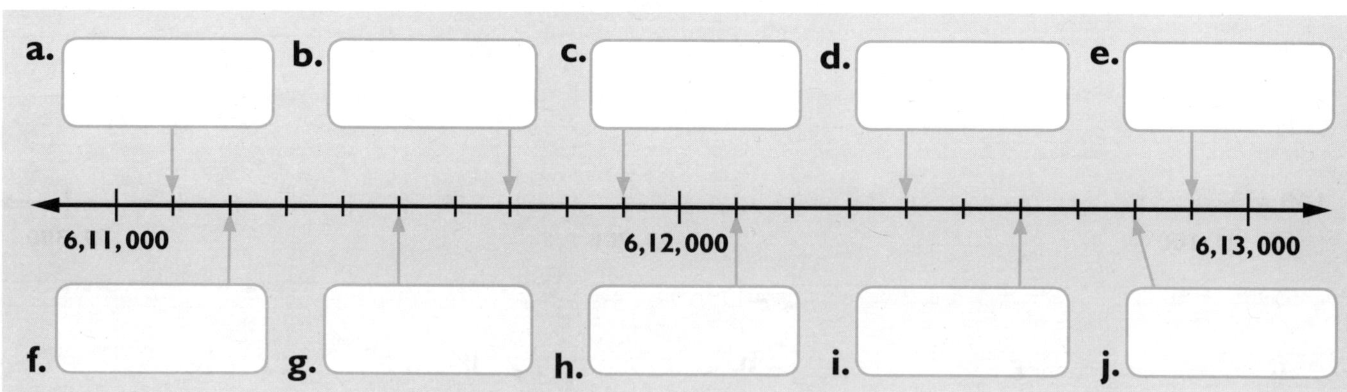

4.

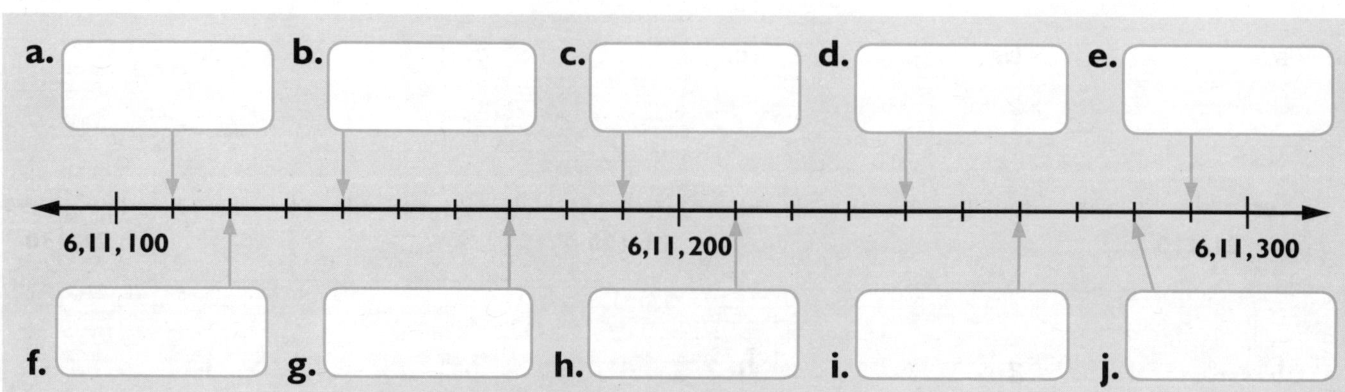

Write the number that is 50 less than the number shown in part (a) on each number line.

1. Write numbers that are 10, 000 less and 10, 000 more than each odometer number.

10,000 less				
Odometer	7,54,190	6,90,517	8,10,200	5,09,720
10,000 more				

2. Write numbers that are 1,000 less and 1,000 more than each odometer number.

1,000 less				
Odometer	3,42,188	6,01,200	3,99,500	4,00,500
1,000 more				

3. Write numbers that are 100 less and 100 more than each odometer number.

100 less				
Odometer	5,65,875	1,09,900	4,10,816	5,02,000
100 more				

4. Write how each odometer number has changed to make the new display.

a.

Odometer	Change
4,50,173	Start
4,51,173	+ 1000
4,51,073	
4,50,073	
4,49,973	

b.

Odometer	Change
9,36,002	Start
9,35,902	− 100
9,36,902	
9,37,902	
9,37,892	

Reading and Writing Six-Digit Numbers

1. Complete the missing parts of each mix-and-match puzzle.

a.

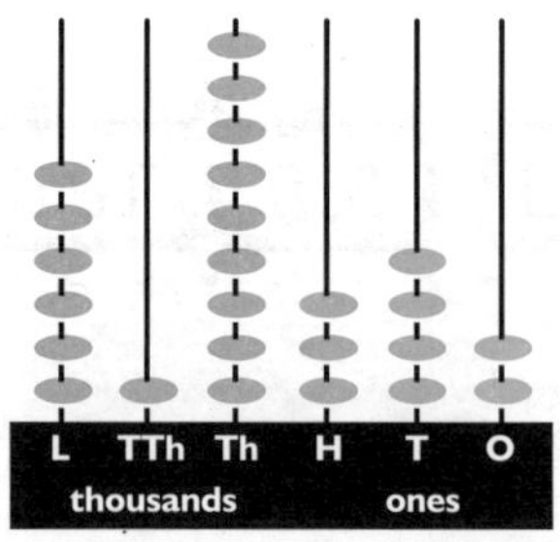

			thousands				ones

b.

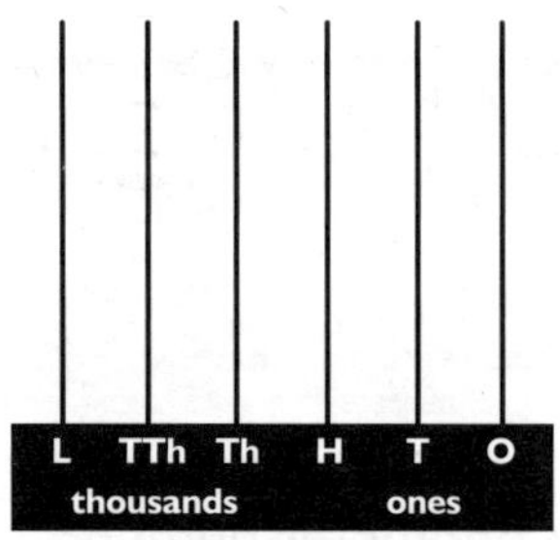

			thousands				ones

seven lakh three thousand

four hundred and fifteen

c.

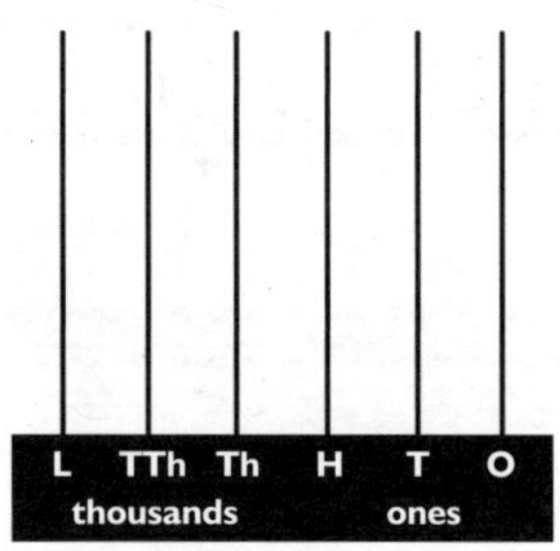

			thousands				ones
2	6	1		5	0	8	

d.

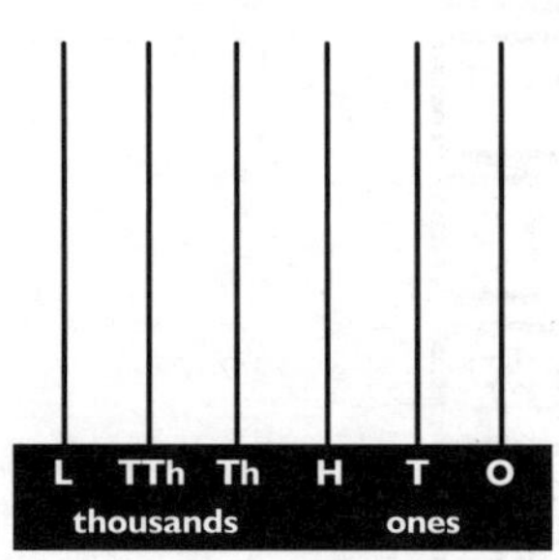

			thousands				ones

three lakh eighteen thousand

and twenty-four

FF **Look at each abacus. Add three beads to each place that has exactly one bead. Write the new number.**

Working with One Crore

1. Write the missing numbers. Then write a matching number sentence.

a. 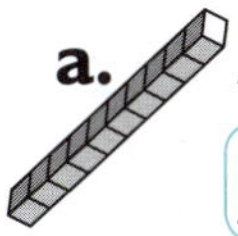 A tens block can be traded for

____ Ones 10 × 1 = ____

b.  A hundreds block can be traded for

____ Tens 10 × ____ = ____

____ Ones 100 × ____ = ____

c. 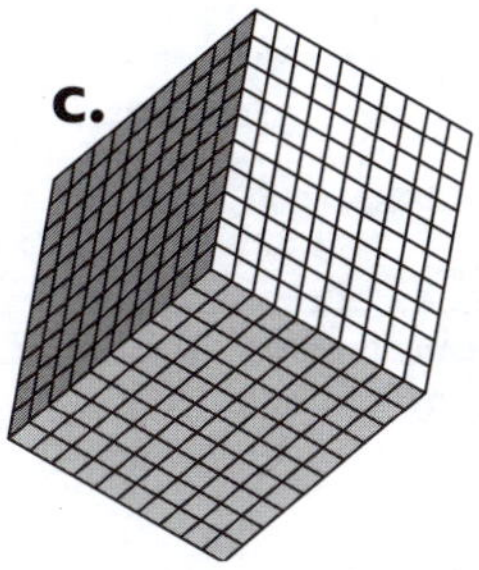 A thousands block can be traded for

____ hundreds 10 × ____ = ____

____ tens 100 × ____ = ____

____ ones 1000 × ____ = ____

2. Imagine you had bigger blocks. Use a pattern to complete each of these.

a. A ten thousand block can be traded for

____ thousands ____ × ____ = ____

____ hundreds ____ × ____ = ____

____ tens ____ × ____ = ____

____ ones ____ × ____ = ____

b. A lakhs block can be traded for

____ ten thousands ____ × ____ = ____

____ thousands ____ × ____ = ____

____ hundreds ____ × ____ = ____

____ tens ____ × ____ = ____

____ ones ____ × ____ = ____

c. A crores block can be traded for

____ lakh ____ × ____ = ____

____ ten thousands ____ × ____ = ____

____ thousands ____ × ____ = ____

____ hundreds ____ × ____ = ____

____ tens ____ × ____ = ____

____ ones ____ × ____ = ____

Look at the number sentences in Question 2c. Write a set of sentences to describe half crore.

Comparing Seven-Digit Numbers

Worksheet 6

Populations

New Delhi	98,17,439	Ahmedabad	42,16,268
Kolkata	45,80,544	Hyderabad	34,49,879
Bangalore	42,92,223	Pune	25,40,069
Chennai	42,16,268	Jaipur	23,24,319
Lucknow	22,07,340	Patna	13,76,950

1. Write the population of each city. Then write < or > to make the number sentence true.

a. New Delhi ____ ☐ ____ Kolkata

b. Ahmedabad ____ ☐ ____ Hyderabad

c. Ahmedabad ____ ☐ ____ Bangalore

d. Hyderabad ____ ☐ ____ Patna

e. Chennai ____ ☐ ____ Kolkata

f. Pune ____ ☐ ____ Kolkata

g. Lucknow ____ ☐ ____ Chennai

h. New Delhi ____ ☐ ____ Jaipur

2. Write the city populations in order from the least to the greatest.

a. ____ **b.** ____ **c.** ____

d. ____ **e.** ____ **f.** ____

g. ____ **h.** ____ **i.** ____

j. ____

Imagine that the population of each city grew by 1,000. Write the new populations.

Writing Numerals Involving Crores

Worksheet 7

1. Read the number. Then write it in the space below.

a. four crore seven hundred fifteen thousand and twenty-nine

b. six crore three hundred eighty thousand two hundred and one

c. twenty-one crore fifty-six thousand nine hundred and thirty

d. ninety-two crore one hundred and eight thousand and five

e. eighteen crore six thousand four hundred and eighty-eight

f. thirty crore fourteen thousand and ninety-seven

2. Read the number. Then write the numeral.

a. six crore eight hundred and three thousand ____________________

b. sixteen crore eight hundred thirty-three thousand four hundred and two ____________________

c. sixty-one crore eighteen thousand three hundred and forty-two ____________________

d. six hundred and one crore eighty-three thousand four hundred and twenty ____________________

Use the words 'ten', 'twenty' and 'thirty' to write an eight-digit number.

Adding Numbers

Addition of large numbers is similar to the addition of smaller numbers.

Example: Add 54,36,289 and 25,86,73,840.

Solution: Write the numbers lining up the digits in the correct places in the place value chart.

TC	C	TL	L	TTh	Th	H	T	O
		5	4	3	6	2	8	9
2	5	8	6	7	3	8	4	0
2	6	4	1	1	0	1	2	9

Add the ones	9 + 0	=	9
Add the tens	8 + 4	=	12 (Carry 1 to hundreds)
Add the hundreds	1+2+8	=	11 (Carry 1 to thousands)
Add the thousands	1+6+3	=	10 (Carry 1 to ten thousands)
Add the ten thousands	1+3+7	=	11 (Carry 1 to lakhs)
Add the lakhs	1+4+6	=	11 (Carry 1 to ten lakhs)
Add the ten lakhs	1+5+8	=	14 (Carry 1 to crores)
Add the crores	1+5	=	6
Add the ten crores	0+2	=	2

54,36,289 + 25,86,73,840 = 26,41,10,129

Subtracting Numbers

To subtract numbers, write the greater number first and subtract the smaller one from it.

Example: Subtract 27,36,874 from 53,42,568.

TC	C	TL	L	TTh	Th	H	T	O
		4	13	3	11	14	16	
		~~5~~	~~3~~	4	~~2~~	~~5~~	6	8
	–	2	7	3	6	8	7	4
		2	6	0	5	6	9	4

53,42,568 – 27,36,874 = 26,05,694

Subtract the ones	8 – 4 = 4
Subtract the tens	6 < 7 So borrow a 100 (10 tens) from the hundreds place, making it 16 (10 + 6) in the tens place. Now, the hundreds place has 4 hundreds left. Now, subtract 7 from 16, which gives 9.

Similarly, continue to subtract the numbers at each place, borrowing from the place to the left, if necessary.

Example:

The table below shows the number of cars manufactured by an automobile company. Look at the table and answer the questions.

Year	Number of cars
1998	2,90,607
2001	5,08,813
2004	36,00,256
2008	4,18,52,349

a. What is the total number of cars manufactured in 2004 and 2008?

b. How many more cars were manufactured in 2001 than in 1998?

c. What is the increase in the number of cars from 1998 to 2008?

Solution:

a. The total number of cars manufactured in 2004 and 2008 = 36,00,256 + 4,18,52,349

C	TL	L	TTh	Th	H	T	O
	1				1	1	
+	3	6	0	0	2	5	6
4	1	8	5	2	3	4	9
4	5	4	5	2	6	0	5

36,00,256 + 4,18,52,349 = 4,54,52,605

1a. To find out how many more cars were manufactured in 2001 than in 1998, we subtract 2,90,607 from 5,08,813

	TL	L	TTh	Th	H	T	O
		4	10			0	13
		~~5~~	~~0~~	8	8	~~1~~	~~3~~
−		2	9	0	6	0	7
		2	1	8	2	0	6

5,08,813 – 2,90,607 = 2,18,206

b. The increase in number of cars from 1998 to 2008 = 4,18,52,349 - 2,90,607

	C	TL	L	TTh	Th	H	T	O
			7	15	1	13		
	4	1	8	5	2	3	4	9
−			2	9	0	6	0	7
	4	1	5	6	1	7	4	2

4,18,52,349 – 2,90,607 = 4,15,61,742

Addition Practice

1. Add.

a. 45609765 + 20098761	**b.** 10985431 + 678540	**c.** 98654300 +65430198
d. 76432009 + 23115700	**e.** 34590817 + 54898001	**f.** 67543200 +13490865

2. Add.

a. 5670916 + 4642390 = ____

b. 1098675 + 346815 = ____

c. 765430 + 12456 = ____

d. 34267230 + 51413289 = ____

e. 3490812 + 4300 = ____

f. 67800189 + 4532190 = ____

3. Fill in the blanks.

```
   _3 4 5 6
+ 5 8 _ 5 _
-----------
  8 2 0 1 3
```

```
   7 2 _ 4 2
+  _ 5 8 _ 9
-------------
 1 4 8 5 0 1
```

Subtraction Practice

Worksheet 9

1. Subtract.

a.
```
  800094
− 654098
________
________
```

b.
```
  654321
−  78960
________
________
```

c.
```
  54332290
− 23470981
__________
__________
```

d.
```
  3470153
− 1727321
_________
_________
```

e.
```
  6467232
− 3987345
_________
_________
```

f.
```
  100895
−  86747
________
________
```

2. Subtract.

a. 234560 − 45600 = ______

b. 56098654 − 2341098 = ______

c. 119870 − 4562 = ______

d. 43890771 − 409875 = ______

e. 67549200 − 32098765 = ______

3. Fill in the boxes.

a.
```
  2 1 4 5 6
− _ _ _ _ _
-----------
    6 9 5 5
```

b.
```
  2 1 4 5 6
− _ _ _ _ _
-----------
  1 6 2 2 8
```

c.
```
  2 1 4 5 6
− _ _ _ _ _
-----------
  1 1 0 4 5
```

d.
```
  2 1 4 5 6
− _ _ _ _ _
-----------
    8 7 1 5
```

Word Problems

Solve the word problems.

1. In a country, 1,75,88,234 women and 6, 54,99,123 men are eligible to vote in an election. What is the total number of voters in that country?
2. Father has Rs 22,54,879 in his bank. He took out Rs 2,98,765 to buy a car. How much money is left in the bank?
3. A farmer produced 5,32,27,421 kilos of wheat, 2,78,12,340 kilos of rice and 1,67,23,456 kilos of maize. What is the total production of foodgrains?
4. Ravi earned Rs 2,93,452 in a year. He spent Rs 1,00,789 on food and clothes. How much did he save?
5. Rs 6,70,65,000 was used to construct a dam. Out of this, 57,92,368 was the cost of land, Rs 2,76,48,530 was the cost of the equipment and the rest was the cost of construction. How much was the cost of construction?
6. What should be added to 54,76,890 to get 1,00,00,000?
7. What should be subtracted from 3,45,88,690 to get 13,34,907?
8. The total population of a city is 3,78,54,000. Out of this 1,23,78,776 are men, 88,97,543 are women and the rest are children? What is the number of children?
9. In the first year of publication, a book sells 1,57,210 copies, in its second year it sells 1,75,378 copies, in its third year it sells 78,680 less than in its second year. How many copies of the book were sold in all?

Multiple Methods to Add and Subtract Mentally

Worksheet 11

Rains

	December	January	February
Cochin	216 mm	255 mm	263 mm
Patna	469 mm	128 mm	539 mm

1. Figure out these totals for Cochin mentally.
Then, write about the strategy you used.

a. The total for December and January is ______ mm.

b. The total for January and February is ______ mm.

c. The total amount of rain is ______ mm.

____

2. Figure out these totals for Patna. Then write about the strategy you used.

a. The total for December and January is ______ mm.

b. The total for January and February is ______ mm.

c. The total amount of rain is ______ mm.

____

3. Mentally calculate the difference in rainfall between Cochin and Patna for each month.
Then, write about the strategy you used.

a. The difference in December is ______ mm.

b. The difference in January is ______ mm.

c. The difference in February is ______ mm.

____

How far short of one metre was Cochin's rainfall?

Subtracting Multiples of 100

Worksheet 12

1. Complete the sentence and then write the answer.

a. **5800 – 600**
is the same as
58 (Hundred) – 6 (Hundred)
5800 – 600 = 5200

b. **7300 – 800**
is the same as
____ (Hundred) – ____ (Hundred)
7300 – 800 = ____

c. **9400 – 1300**
is the same as
____ (Hundred) – ____ (Hundred)
9400 – 1300 = ____

d. **3700 – 1200**
is the same as
____ (Hundred) – ____ (Hundred)
3700 – 1200 = ____

e. **7800 – 6500**
is the same as
____ (Hundred) – ____ (Hundred)
7800 – 6500 = ____

f. **8300 – 6700**
is the same as
____ (Hundred) – ____ (Hundred)
8300 – 6700 = ____

2. Write the answers. Think of the numbers as hundreds.

a. 4900 – 1600 = ____ **b.** 8700 – 5200 = ____

c. 9700 – 6600 = ____ **d.** 2900 – 1400 = ____

e. 5600 – 4300 = ____ **f.** 7300 – 6400 = ____

3. Write some number sentences involving hundreds that you can solve using the same strategy you used in Question 2.

a. ______ – ______ = ______ **b.** ______ – ______ = ______

c. ______ – ______ = ______ **d.** ______ – ______ = ______

Write a story problem for each of the number sentences you wrote in Question 3.

Multiplying Numbers

Example: Find 53478 × 935

Solution: First, multiply 5,3478 by the digit in the ones place, then by the digit in the tens place and finally, by the digit in the hundreds place. Add the partial products.

			5	3	4	7	8	
				x	9	3	5	
		2	6	7	3	9	0	(53478 × 5)
	I	6	0	4	3	4	0	(53478 × 30)
+ 4	8	I	3	0	2	0	0	(53478 × 900)
5	0	0	0	I	9	3	0	

Properties of Multiplication

I. Commutative Property of Multiplication:
The order in which we multiply numbers does not matter; the answer will always be the same.
Example: 7 × 5 = 5 × 7

2. Associative Property of Multiplication:
Changing the grouping of numbers that are being multiplied does not change the answer.
Example: (9 × 2) × 3 = 9 × (2 × 3)

3. Distributive Property of Multiplication with Addition:
When a number is multiplied by the sum of two other numbers, the first number can be multiplied by each of them separately and then the products can be added.
Example: 5 × (9 + 2) = 5 × 9 + 5 × 2

Distributive Property of Multiplication with Subtraction:
When a number is multiplied by the difference of two other numbers, the first number can be multiplied by each of them separately and then the products can be subtracted.
Example: 53 × (99 -82) = 53 × 99 - 53 × 82

A very useful way of using this property is to split a number.
Example: 45 × 12
= 45 × (10 +2)
= 45 × 10 + 45 × 2
= 450 + 90
= 540

4. The product of any number and 1 is the number itself.

Example: $29 \times 1 = 29$

$87239 \times 1 = 87239$

5. The product of any number and 0 is always 0.

Example: $4569 \times 0 = 0$

$75 \times 0 = 0$

Division

Dividing Numbers

Example:

Step 1 Divide 108864 by 4536

Solution:

Since the divisor is a four-digit number, consider the first four digits of the dividend (1088).

1088 < 4536, therefore consider 10886.

See how many times 4536 goes into 10886.

$2 \times 4536 = 9072$, but $3 \times 4536 = 13,608$.
Therefore, 4,536 goes into 10886 two times.

Write 2 in the quotient.

```
         2
4536)1 0 8 8 6 4
    - 9 0 7 2      (Subtract 10886 – 9072 )
      1 8 1 4      (Compare 1814 < 4536)
```

Step 2

Bring down the 4 from 108864 and place it to the right of 1814.

```
         2
4536)1 0 8 8 6 4
      9 0 7 2
      1 8 1 4 4
```

Step 3

Divide 18144 by 4536.

$4536 \times 4 = 18144$

Write 4 in the quotient.

```
         2 4
4536)1 0 8 8 6 4
      9 0 7 2
      1 8 1 4 4
     - 1 8 1 4 4
           0
```

Subtract 18144 from 18144 to get 0.

The remainder is 0 and the quotient 24.

Example: Puneet is building model planes to sell at the fair. He needs 12 m string for each toy. How many planes can he make if he has a 115 m long piece of string? Will there be any string left?

Solution: Puneet can make 115 ÷ 12 model planes

$$\begin{array}{r} 9 \\ 12\overline{)\,115} \\ \underline{108} \\ 7 \end{array}$$

Therefore, Puneet can make 9 model planes and 7 m of string will be left over.

Properties of Division

1. When a number is divided by 1, the quotient is the number itself.
Example: 269 ÷ 1 = 269

2. When a number is divided by itself, the quotient is 1.
Example: 8645 ÷ 8645 = 1

3. When 0 is divided by a number, the quotient is 0.
Example: 0 ÷ 589 = 0

Comparing Strategies for Multiplying Mentally

Worksheet 13

Read how Jyoti and Sumeet mentally calculate 36 × 50.

1. **a.** Use their methods to solve these.

Jyoti's method

16 × 50 = ______ 24 × 50 = ______

27 × 50 = ______ 15 × 50 = ______

Sumeet's method

25 × 50 = ______ 18 × 50 = ______

14 × 50 = ______ 21 × 50 = ______

b. Whose method did you like best? Why? ______________________

____

2. Use either method to mentally calculate these.

a. 72 × 50 = ______ **b.** 34 × 50 = ______ **c.** 64 × 50 = ______

d. 42 × 50 = ______ **e.** 28 × 50 = ______ **f.** 31 × 50 = ______

3. Write how you would mentally figure out 32 × 25.

____

____

4. Use the same method to mentally calculate these.

a. 24 × 25 = ______ **b.** 16 × 25 = ______ **c.** 28 × 25 = ______

d. 44 × 25 = ______ **e.** 12 × 25 = ______ **f.** 36 × 25 = ______

5. Complete number sentences you can solve using your method.

a. ______ × 50 = ______ **b.** 50 × ______ = ______ **c.** ______ × 25 =

Write how you can multiply by 250 and 500.

Extending the Doubling and Halving Strategy

Worksheet 14

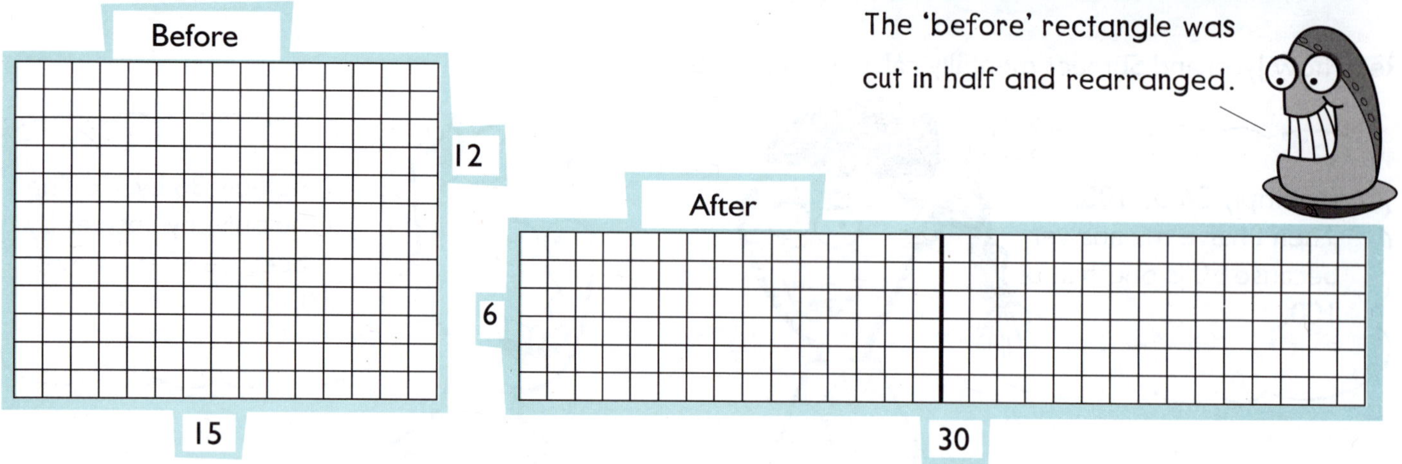

The 'before' rectangle was cut in half and rearranged.

1. **a.** Has the total number of squares in the rectangles changed? ______

b. Write the dimensions of each rectangle and then complete the sentence.

Before: ____ × ____ = ______ **is the same as** After: ____ × ____ = ______

2. Double one factor and halve the other. Then write the answer.

a. 8 × 15 = ______ **is the same as** ____ × ____ = ______

b. 45 × 8 = ______ **is the same as** ____ × ____ = ______

c. 6 × 35 = ______ **is the same as** ____ × ____ = ______

d. 12 × 25 = ______ **is the same as** ____ × ____ = ______

e. 25 × 18 = ______ **is the same as** ____ × ____ = ______

f. 14 × 35 = ______ **is the same as** ____ × ____ = ______

g. 16 × 30 = ______ **is the same as** ____ × ____ = ______

h. 40 × 18 = ______ **is the same as** ____ × ____ = ______

i. 45 × 16 = ______ **is the same as** ____ × ____ = ______

FF **Write two other number sentences you can solve using this strategy.**

Using Place Value to Multiply

1. Use place value to figure out each cost. Then complete the number sentence.

a.

Rs 32 — Buy 12

(32 × 10) + (32 × 2) = ____

b.

Rs 41 — Buy 12

(41 × 10) + (41 × 2) = ____

c.

Rs 23 — Buy 11

(____ × 10) + (____ × 1) = ____

d.

Rs 31 — Buy 13

(____ × 10) + (____ × 3) = ____

e.

Rs 13 — Buy 11

(____ × 10) + (____ × 1) = ____

f.

Rs 42 — Buy 14

(____ × 10) + (____ × 4) = ____

2. Complete each number sentence.

a. 21 × 23 = (____ × ____) + (____ × ____) = ____ + ____ = ____

b. 24 × 12 = (____ × ____) + (____ × ____) = ____ + ____ = ____

c. 41 × 11 = (____ × ____) + (____ × ____) = ____ + ____ = ____

d. 12 × 31 = (____ × ____) + (____ × ____) = ____ + ____ = ____

3. Use the strategy from Question 2 to figure each of these out.

a. 23 × 12 = ____ **b.** 31 × 11 = ____ **c.** 22 × 13 = ____

Write other examples you can solve using the same strategy.

Using Compatible Pairs to Multiply

Worksheet 16

1. Each small box in this stack contains two cans. Use the picture to help you write a number sentence to show the total number of cans.

____ × ____ × ____ × ____ = ____

2. Draw ↔ to connect the pairs you would multiply first. Then, write the total.

a. 5 × 6 × 2 × 11 = ____

b. 3 × 9 × 25 × 4 = ____

c. 15 × 25 × 2 × 4 = ____

d. 4 × 7 × 5 × 3 = ____

e. 5 × 7 × 3 × 8 = ____

f. 2 × 9 × 8 × 5 = ____

3. Use the strategy from Question 2 to calculate the answers to these.

a. 6 × 5 × 3 × 5 = ____

b. 6 × 25 × 2 × 4 = ____

c. 2 × 4 × 75 × 2 = ____

d. 15 × 4 × 2 × 25 = ____

e. 2 × 11 × 2 × 25 = ____

f. 5 × 5 × 15 × 4 = ____

4. Write a number greater than 1 in each space. The number you choose should make it easy to figure out the answer mentally. Then write the answer.

a. ____ × 4 × 2 × ____ = ____

b. 5 × ____ × 3 × ____ = ____

c. 15 × ____ × ____ × 6 = ____

d. ____ × 25 × 7 × ____ =

Write number sentences like those in Question 2.
Make the answers close to 200.

Multiplication Practice

Worksheet 17

1. Complete these multiplication charts.

a.

$217 \times 2 =$ ______

$217 \times 3 =$ ______

$217 \times 4 =$ ______

$217 \times 20 =$ ______

$217 \times 30 =$ ______

$217 \times 40 =$ ______

b.

$388 \times 2 =$ ______

$388 \times 3 =$ ______

$388 \times 4 =$ ______

$388 \times 20 =$ ______

$388 \times 30 =$ ______

$388 \times 40 =$ ______

2. Use the charts in Question 1 to help you figure out each of these.

a. A fun park student ticket costs Rs 382. How much for a class of 24 students?

______

b. A roller-coaster seats 38 passengers. It makes 22 trips each hour. How many people does it carry in an hour?

______

c. A car park has 38 rows. There are 420 spaces in each row. How many spaces does it have?

______

d. A fruit picker can fill 275 boxes of fruit in a day. How many boxes can 32 pickers fill?

______

e. A box of fruit weighs 330 kg. How many kilograms do 27 boxes weigh?

______

f. A farmer makes Rs 402 on each box. How much is made on 27 boxes?

______

FF **Write some 2 × 2-digit multiplication problems you can figure out by using the numbers in the charts above.**

Recording Steps to Multiply

1. Calculate the partial products to figure out each of these. Then write the answers.

a. 403 × 32

403 × 2 = ______

403 × 30 = ______

403 × 32 = ______

b. 62 × 34

____ × 4 = ______

____ × 30 = ______

624 × 34 = ______

c. 785 × 23

____ × 3 = ______

____ × 20 = ______

785 × 23 = ______

d. 324 × 24

____ × ____ = ______

____ × ____ = ______

324 × 24 = ______

e. 412 × 44

____ × ____ = ______

____ × ____ = ______

412 × 44 = ______

f. 253 × 34

____ × ____ = ______

____ × ____ = ______

253 × 34 = ______

2. Record the steps you use to figure out each of these.

a. 546 × 23

______

b. 733 × 32

______

c. 805 × 33

______

d. 214 × 24

______

e. 332 × 34

______

f. 415 × 24

______

FF Write 2, 3, 4, 5 and 6 in this number sentence so that the answer is close to 25,000: ☐☐☐ × ☐☐ = ____

Multiplying Three-Digit Numbers

1. Record the steps you use to figure out each of these. Then write the answer.

a. 164 × 32 = ________

b. 157 × 55 = ________

c. 236 × 47 = ________

d. 274 × 42 = ________

e. 369 × 88 = ________

f. 125 × 23 = ________

g. 350 × 78 = ________

h. 289 × 90 = ________

i. 425 × 18 = ________

j. 126 × 65 = ________

k. 258 × 72 = ________

l. 334 × 57 = ________

Write 2, 3, 4 and 5 in this number sentence so that the answer is close to 1200: ☐☐☐ × ☐ = ____

Working with Three- and Four-Digit Dividends

1. Complete each number sentence. Then write the answer.

a. 654 ÷ 6
is the same as
654 ÷ 6 =
600 ÷ 6 plus 54 ÷ 6
654 ÷ 6 = 109

b. 742 ÷ 7
is the same as
___ ÷ 7 plus ___ ÷ 7
742 ÷ 7 = ___

c. 535 ÷ 5
is the same as
535 ÷ 5 =
500 ÷ 5 plus 35 ÷ 5
535 ÷ 5 = ___

d. 2763 ÷ 3
is the same as
___ ÷ 3 plus ___ ÷ 3
2763 ÷ 3 = ___

e. 3680 ÷ 4
is the same as
___ ÷ 4 plus ___ ÷ 4
3680 ÷ 4 = ___

f. 4249 ÷ 7
is the same as
___ ÷ 7 plus ___ ÷ 7
4249 ÷ 7 = ___

2. Draw an arrow to a matching number sentence. Then write the answer.

a. 168 ÷ 4	900 ÷ 9 plus 72 ÷ 9 = ___
b. 2436 ÷ 6	2800 ÷ 4 plus 12 ÷ 4 = ___
c. 972 ÷ 9	2400 ÷ 6 plus 36 ÷ 6 = ___
d. 3570 ÷ 7	160 ÷ 4 plus 8 ÷ 4 = ___
e. 2812 ÷ 4	3500 ÷ 7 plus 70 ÷ 7 = ___

3. Use the same strategy to help you write the answers to these.

a. 618 ÷ 3 = ___ **b.** 927 ÷ 9 = ___ **c.** 832 ÷ 4 = ___

d. 636 ÷ 6 = ___ **e.** 816 ÷ 8 = ___ **f.** 921 ÷ 3 = ___

List the different divisors you could write in the box so you can mentally calculate the answer to this: 3240 ÷ □ = ___

Splitting Three- and Four-Digit Dividends

Worksheet 21

1. Split each number into two parts you can easily divide by four.

a. 196: ___ + ___

b. 292: ___ + ___

c. 372: ___ + ___

d. 256: ___ + ___

2. Split each number into parts you can easily divide by six.

a. 2520: ___ + ___

b. 2820: ___ + ___

c. 3150: ___ + ___

d. 4506: ___ + ___

3. Figure out the answers to these by splitting the numbers into two smaller parts. Then, write the answers.

a. 810 ÷ 3 **is the same as** 600 ÷ 3 plus 210 ÷ 3 = 270

b. 7020 ÷ 6 **is the same as** ___ ÷ 6 plus ___ ÷ 6 = ___

c. 3680 ÷ 8 **is the same as** ___ ÷ 8 plus ___ ÷ 8 = ___

d. 4550 ÷ 7 **is the same as** ___ ÷ 7 plus ___ ÷ 7 = ___

4. Use the same strategy to help you write the answers to these.

a. 492 ÷ 6 = ___

b. 297 ÷ 9 = ___

c. 228 ÷ 3 = ___

d. 112 ÷ 8 = ___

e. 224 ÷ 7 = ___

f. 216 ÷ 6 = ___

Write 2, 3, 4 and 6 in this number sentence so that the answer is between 250 and 350: □□□ ÷ □ = ___

Using Rules—Multiplication/Division

Worksheet 22

1. A machine packs eight boxes every minute.

a. Complete this table to show the number of boxes it packs in up to eight minutes.

Minutes	1	2	3	4	5	6	7	8
Boxes packed	8	16	24					

b. Write a rule for figuring out the number of boxes the machine can pack if you know the number of minutes.

____

c. Use your rule to figure out the number of boxes the machine will pack in

10 minutes ________ 30 minutes ________ 1 hour ________

2. A coal carriage is loaded every four minutes.

a. Complete this table.

Minutes	4	12	20	28		40		60
Carriages loaded	1	3			8		12	

b. Write a rule for figuring out the number of carriages that have been loaded if you know the number of minutes.

____

c. Use your rule to show the number of minutes it would take to load

20 carriages ________ 25 carriages ________ 32 carriages ________

Try abbreviating the rules you wrote for Questions 1b and 2b.

Exploring Two- and Three-Digit Divisors

For each portion, write how many you can take from the container.
Use the space below to figure out the answers.

Portions	
4 ml	
40 ml	
6 ml	
60 ml	
5 ml	
50 ml	
30 ml	
300 ml	

Portions	
5 ml	
50 ml	
20 ml	
200 ml	
300 ml	
150 ml	
500 ml	
250 ml	

Portions	
500 ml	
250 ml	
1500 ml	
750 ml	
250 ml	
125 ml	
50 ml	
25 ml	

When the size of one portion becomes 10 times greater than the other, what happens to the number of portions?

CHAPTER 4

Factors and Multiples

Factors

The numbers being multiplied are called the factors of the product.

Example: $4 \times 7 = 28$

4 and 7 → **Factors**; 28 → **Product**

Multiples

The products of a number with the natural numbers 1, 2, 3, 4, 5... are called the multiples of the number.

For example:

$3 \times 1 = 3$

$3 \times 2 = 6$

$3 \times 3 = 9$

$3 \times 4 = 12$

$3 \times 5 = 15$ and so on.

3, 6, 9, 12, 15 are called the multiples of 3.

Prime Numbers

A prime number is any number with only two factors—1 and the number itself.

Example: Find all the factors of 11

$11 = 1 \times 11$

11 is a prime number as it has only two factors 1 and 11 itself.

Composite Numbers

A composite number has more than two factors.

Example: Find the factors of 36

Solution: The factors of 36 are 1, 2, 3, 4, 6, 9, 12, 18 and 36

Therefore, 36 is a composite number.

Prime Factorisation

Finding factors of a number is called factorisation and finding factors, which are all prime numbers, is called prime factorisation.

Prime Factorisation by Building a Factor Tree

Example: Factorise 45

Start by thinking of two numbers, which give 45 when multiplied.

For example, $9 \times 5 = 45$.

Write 5 and 9 on the two branches of 45.

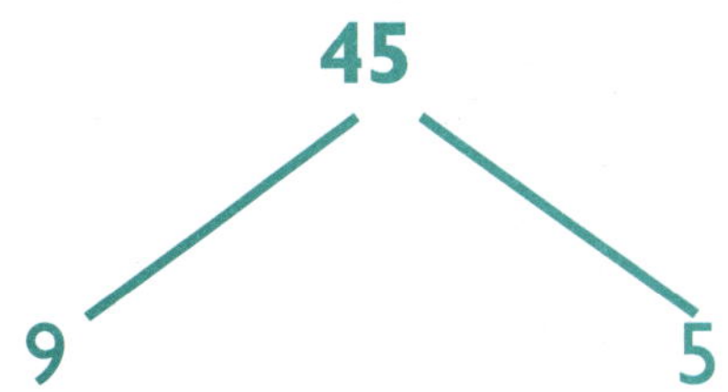

Break down 9.

The factors of 9 are 3 and 3.

The only factors of 5 are 5 and 1(we stop when 1 is needed as a factor).

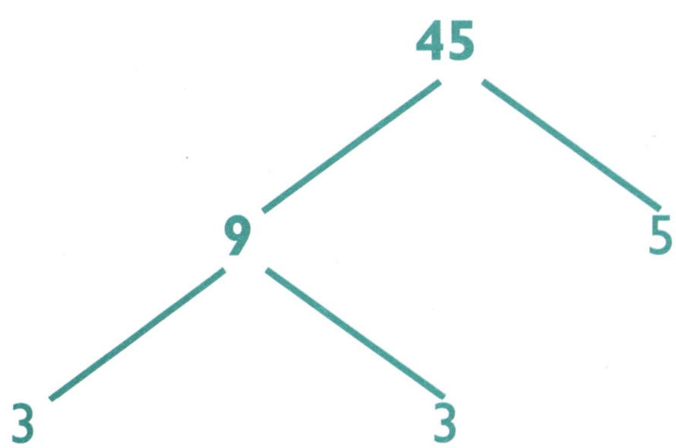

As 3 also has only 1 and 3 as factors, we stop on this branch too.

Therefore, the prime factors of 45 are 5, 3, 3.

Least Common Multiple (LCM)

Example: Find the common multiples of 5 and 8. Also find out the least common multiple.

Solution:

Multiples of 5: 5,10,15,20,25,30,35,40,45,50,55,60,65,70,75,80...

Multiples of 8: 8,16,24,32,40,48,56,64,72,80 ...

Common multiples of 5 and 8 are 40, 80 ...

Least common multiple (LCM) is 40.

LCM by Prime Factorisation

Example: Find the LCM of the numbers 60 and 72.

Solution: Write each number as a product of its prime factors.

$$60 = 2 \times 2 \qquad \times 3 \times 5$$
$$72 = 2 \times 2 \times 2 \times 3 \times 3$$

Write the factors so that all the 2s are above each other, as are the 3s, etc.

60 = 2	× 2		× 3	× 5	
72 = 2	× 2	× 2	×3	× 3	

The LCM is found by multiplying all the factors which appear in either list:

60= 2	× 2		× 3	x 5	
72= 2	× 2	× 2	× 3	× 3	

LCM = $2 \times 2 \times 2 \times 3 \times 3 \times 5$

LCM = 360

So the LCM of 60 and 72 is $2 \times 2 \times 2 \times 3 \times 3 \times 5$, which is 360.

Highest Common Factor (HCF)

Example: Find all the common factors of 9, 12 and 15. Also, find the highest common factor.

Solution:

$9 \times 1 = 9$ and $3 \times 3 = 9$

$12 \times 1 = 12$, $2 \times 6 = 12$ and $3 \times 4 = 12$

$15 \times 1 = 15$, $3 \times 5 = 15$

The factors of 9 are 1, 3 and 9.
The factors of 12 are 1, 2, 3, 4, 6 and 12.
The factors of 15 are 1, 3, 5 and 15.

The common factors are 1 and 3.

The highest common factor is 3.

HCF by Prime Factorisation

Example: Find the HCF of the numbers 60 and 72.

Solution: Write each number as a product of its prime factors.

$$60 = 2 \times 2 \quad \times 3 \times 5$$
$$72 = 2 \times 2 \times 2 \times 3 \times 3$$

Write the factors so that all the 2s are above each other, as are the 3s, etc.

$$60 = 2 \times 2 \qquad \times 3 \qquad \times 5$$
$$72 = 2 \times 2 \times 2 \times 3 \times 3$$

$$60 = 2 \times 2 \qquad \times 3 \qquad \times 5$$
$$72 = 2 \times 2 \times 2 \times 3 \times 3$$

$$\text{HCF} = 2 \times 2 \qquad \times 3$$

$$\text{HCF} = 12$$

The highest common factor is found by multiplying all the factors, which appear in **both** lists.

So, the HCF of 60 and 72 is 12.

1. Find the LCM.

a. 12 and 15

b. 18 and 24

c. 18 and 30

d. 14 and 42

e. 15 and 20

2. Solve the word problems.

a. Mr Patel waters one of his trees every 10 days and the other tree every 14 days. If he waters both trees today, when is the next time both trees will be watered on the same day?

b. One trip around a jogging track is 440 yards. One jogger completes one lap in 8 minutes. The other jogger can complete it in 6 minutes. How long will it take for both joggers to arrive at their starting point together if they start at the same time and maintain their jogging pace?

c. Rita is making a board tile game. The board's dimensions are 16 inches by 24 inches. She wants to use square tiles. What is the largest tile she can use?

LCM and HCF

Worksheet 25

1. Find the HCF of the following.

a. 14 and 28

b. 17 and 23

c. 12 and 18

d. 36 and 28

e. 42 and 72

f. 15 and 69

2. Solve the following word problems.

a. Piyali has two pieces of fabric. One piece is 72 inches wide and the other is 90 inches wide. She wants to cut both pieces into strips of equal width that are as wide as possible. How wide should she cut the strips?

b. Mrs Singh has 120 paint boxes and 30 sheets of paper to give to her class. What is the largest number of students in her class so that each student gets an equal number of paint boxes and equal number of sheets of paper?

Rough Work Sheet

1. Use the colours shown to shade each counter.
2. Draw coloured counters on the track to show where each counter can land.

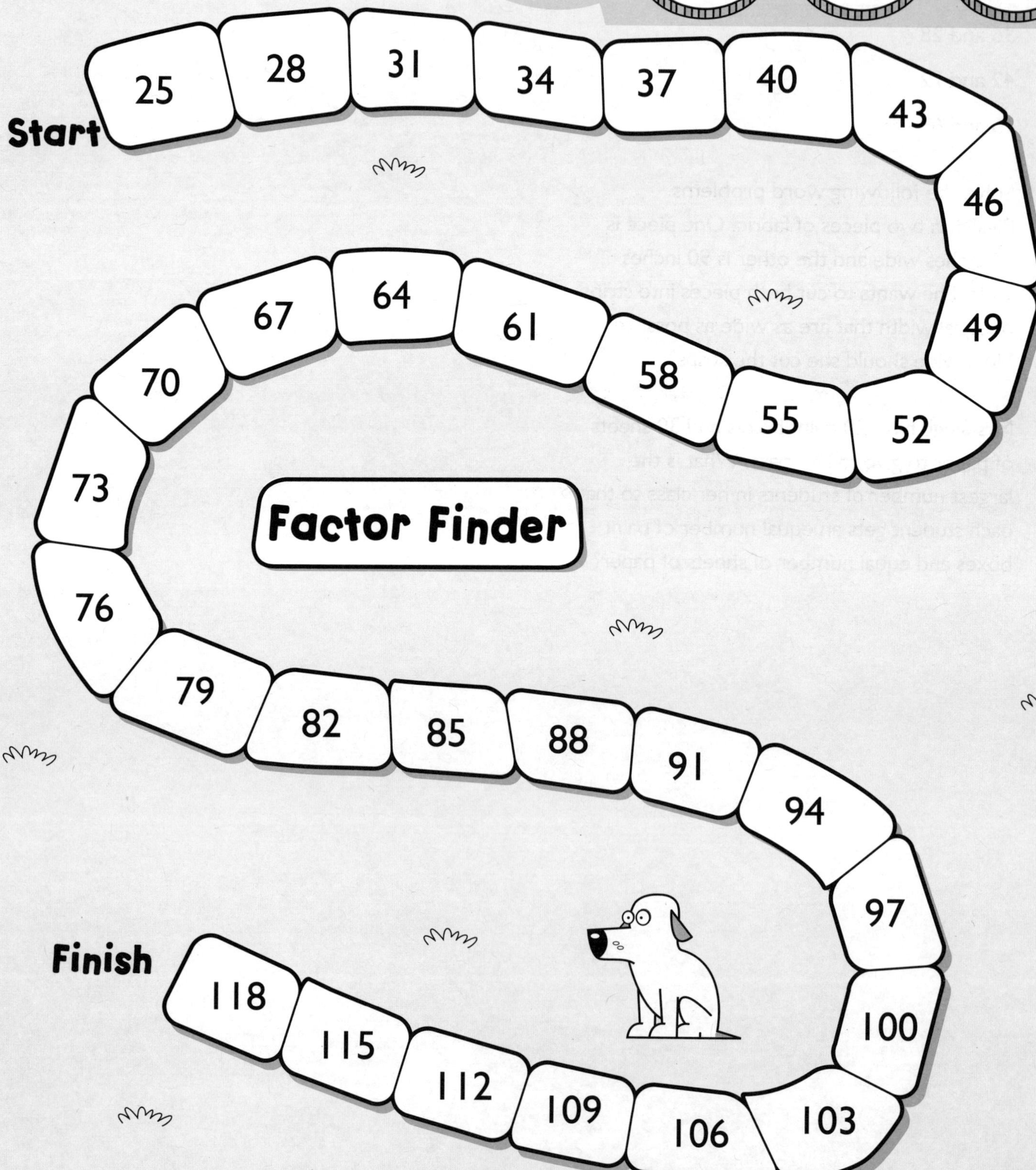

What do you notice about the numbers that have factors of 2, 4 and 5?

1. Complete these factor trees.

a.

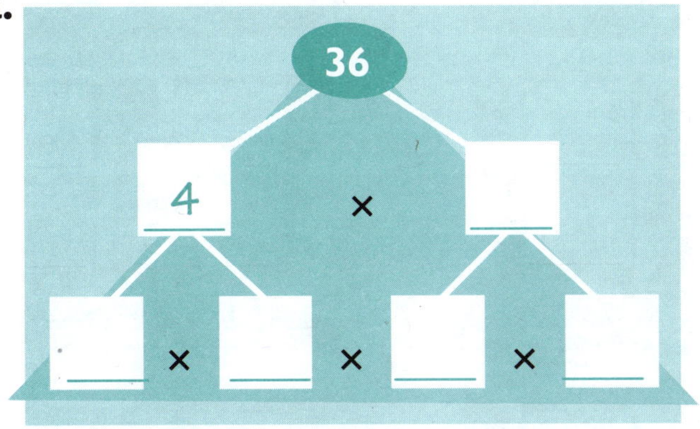

b.

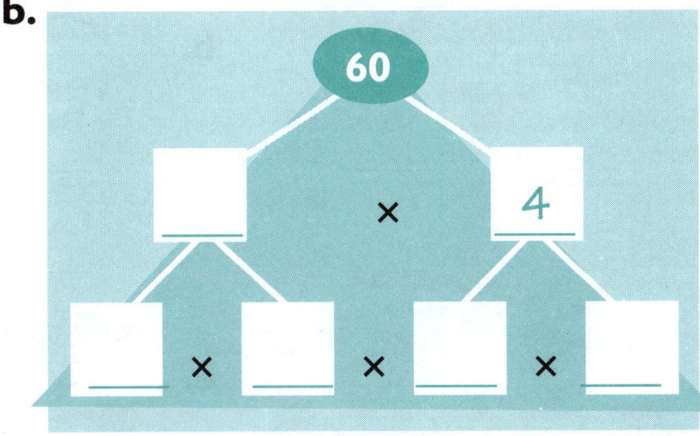

c.

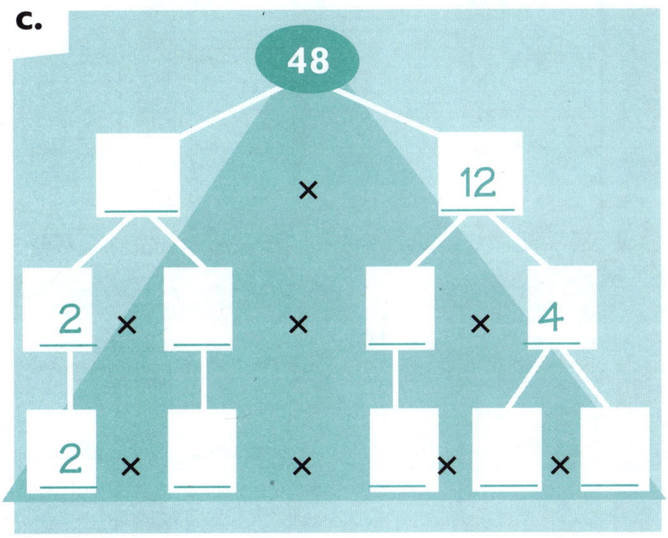

d.

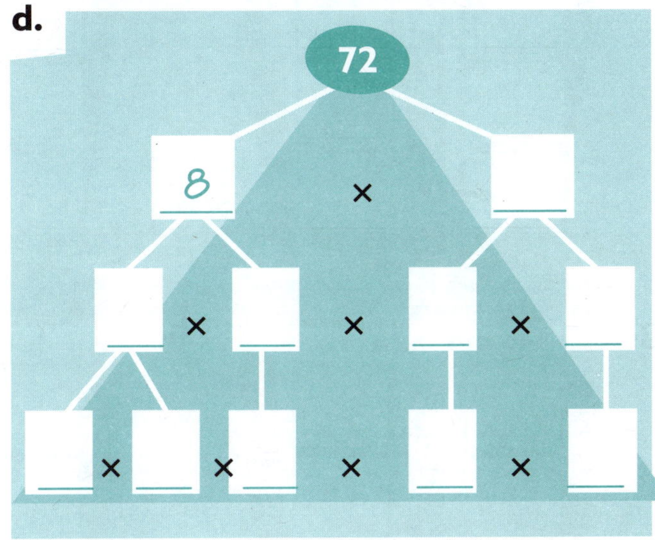

2. Draw a factor tree for each of these numbers.

a.

b.

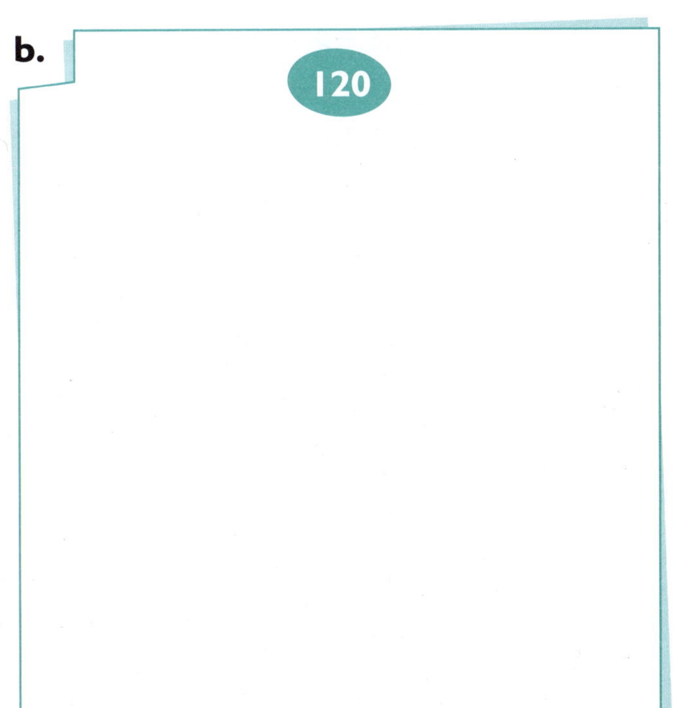

Use the trees above to help you list all the factors of 36 and 60.

Finding Factors

Worksheet 28

1. Write all the factors of each number.

a. 15 is the same as ___ × ___, ___ × ___

b. 25 is the same as ___ × ___, ___ × ___

c. 14 is the same as ___ × ___, ___ × ___

d. 16 is the same as ___ × ___, ___ × ___, ___ × ___

e. 28 is the same as ___ × ___, ___ × ___, ___ × ___

f. 18 is the same as ___ × ___, ___ × ___, ___ × ___

g. 24 is the same as ___ × ___, ___ × ___, ___ × ___, ___ × ___

h. 64 is the same as ___ × ___, ___ × ___, ___ × ___, ___ × ___

i. 30 is the same as ___ × ___, ___ × ___, ___ × ___, ___ × ___

j. 36 is the same as ___ × ___, ___ × ___, ___ × ___, ___ × ___, ___ × ___

k. 80 is the same as ___ × ___, ___ × ___, ___ × ___, ___ × ___, ___ × ___

l. 100 is the same as ___ × ___, ___ × ___, ___ × ___, ___ × ___, ___ × ___

FF Write another pair of factors for 80 and 100.

Factoring Two-Digit Numbers

Worksheet 29

1. Write the missing numbers to show factors greater than 1.

a. 16 is equal to
___ × ___
___ × ___

b. 28 is equal to
___ × ___
___ × ___

c. 18 is equal to
___ × ___
___ × ___

d. 24 is equal to
___ × ___
___ × ___
___ × ___

e. 42 is equal to
___ × ___
___ × ___
___ × ___

f. 30 is equal to
___ × ___
___ × ___
___ × ___

g. 100 is equal to
___ × ___
___ × ___
___ × ___
___ × ___

h. 80 is equal to
___ × ___
___ × ___
___ × ___
___ × ___

i. 48 is equal to
___ × ___
___ × ___
___ × ___
___ × ___

j. 60 is equal to
___ × ___
___ × ___
___ × ___
___ × ___
___ × ___

k. 84 is equal to
___ × ___
___ × ___
___ × ___
___ × ___
___ × ___

l. 96 is equal to
___ × ___
___ × ___
___ × ___
___ × ___
___ × ___

What number between 100 and 108 can be written as a product of two factors in the greatest number of different ways?

Using Factors to Multiply

Worksheet 30

1. Split one number into two factors to make it easier to figure out. Then, complete the number sentence.

a. 6 × 45 is the same as ___ × ___ × ___ = ______

b. 24 × 25 is the same as ___ × ___ × ___ = ______

c. 55 × 4 is the same as ___ × ___ × ___ = ______

d. 25 × 32 is the same as ___ × ___ × ___ = ______

2. Split both numbers into two factors. Then complete the number sentence.

a. 12 × 45 is the same as ___ × ___ × ___ × ___ = ______

b. 35 × 22 is the same as ___ × ___ × ___ × ___ = ______

c. 15 × 18 is the same as ___ × ___ × ___ × ___ = ______

d. 18 × 55 is the same as ___ × ___ × ___ × ___ = ______

e. 36 × 15 is the same as ___ × ___ × ___ × ___ = ______

f. 45 × 16 is the same as ___ × ___ × ___ × ___ = ______

3. Use the same strategy to figure out each of these.

a. 25 × 16 = ______ **b.** 15 × 28 = ______ **c.** 45 × 24 = ______

d. 18 × 45 = ______ **e.** 35 × 18 = ______ **f.** 25 × 22 = ______

FF **Use the strategy on this page to figure out 120 × 35.**

Using Factors to Divide by Multiples of 10

Worksheet 31

1. Write the numbers to show the equal monthly payments for this computer.

Rs 2430 ÷ 30 **is the same as** 2430 ÷ 3 =

÷ 10 =

2. Complete each of these.

a. 1260 ÷ 30

is the same as

1260 ÷ 3 =

÷ 10 =

b. 3550 ÷ 50

is the same as

3550 ÷ 5 =

÷ 10 =

c. 3280 ÷ 40

is the same as

3280 ÷ 4 =

÷ 10 =

d. 3660 ÷ 60

is the same as

3660 ÷ 6 =

÷ 10 =

e. 1470 ÷ 70

is the same as

1470 ÷ 7 =

÷ 10 =

f. 2460 ÷ 60

is the same as

2460 ÷ 6 =

÷ 10 =

3. Use the same thinking to complete these.

a. 1290 ÷ 30

is the same as

1290 ÷ 3 ÷ 10 =

b. 5050 ÷ 50

is the same as

5050 ÷ 5 ÷ 10 =

c. 1860 ÷ 60

is the same as

1860 ÷ 6 ÷ 10 =

d. 4840 ÷ 40

is the same as

4840 ÷ 4 ÷ 10 =

e. 4970 ÷ 70

is the same as

4970 ÷ 7 ÷ 10 =

f. 2760 ÷ 30

is the same as

2760 ÷ 3 ÷ 10 =

Write two other ways that you can use to calculate the answer to Question 1 mentally.

Using Factors to Divide by Two-Digit Numbers

Worksheet 32

1. Complete these to show different ways of using factors to calculate 576 ÷ 12.

a. 576 → ÷ 3 → ____ → ÷ 4 → ____ (576 ÷ 12)

b. 576 → ÷ 4 → ____ → ÷ 3 → ____ (576 ÷ 12)

c. 576 → ÷ 2 → ____ → ÷ 6 → ____ (576 ÷ 12)

d. 576 → ÷ 6 → ____ → ÷ 2 → ____ (576 ÷ 12)

2. Use factors to help you figure these out.

a. 636 → ÷ ___ → ____ → ÷ ___ → ____ (÷ 12)

b. 525 → ÷ ___ → ____ → ÷ ___ → ____ (÷ 15)

c. 648 → ÷ ___ → ____ → ÷ ___ → ____ (÷ 18)

d. 854 → ÷ ___ → ____ → ÷ ___ → ____ (÷ 14)

e. 848 → ÷ ___ → ____ → ÷ ___ → ____ (÷ 16)

f. 1224 → ÷ ___ → ____ → ÷ ___ → ____ (÷ 24)

Write how you can use three steps to solve the last two examples.

Solving Number Puzzles

1. Use this hundred chart to help figure out the mystery numbers from the clues below.

1	2	3	4	5	6	7	8	9	10
11	12	13	14	15	16	17	18	19	20
21	22	23	24	25	26	27	28	29	30
31	32	33	34	35	36	37	38	39	40
41	42	43	44	45	46	47	48	49	50
51	52	53	54	55	56	57	58	59	60
61	62	63	64	65	66	67	68	69	70
71	72	73	74	75	76	77	78	79	80
81	82	83	84	85	86	87	88	89	90
91	92	93	94	95	96	97	98	99	100

a.

It is a multiple of 5.
The sum of the digits is 7.
It is not a square number.

It is ________.

b.

It is an odd number.
The difference between its digits is 0.
It is a multiple of 9.

It is ________.

c.

It is a multiple of 5.
It is an odd number.
It has 11 as a factor.

It is ________.

d.

It is an odd number.
It is a multiple of 1, 3 and 13.
The difference between its digits is 6.

It is ________.

e.

It is greater than 20 but less than 50.
It has exactly 2 factors.
The sum of its digits is 10.

It is ________.

f.

It is less than 30.
Some of its factors are 14, 7, 4 and 2.

It is ________.

g.

It is a multiple of 2 and 3.
The sum of its digits is 12.
It is between 50 and 70.

It is ________.

h.

It is less than 50.
It is a multiple of 7.
It has exactly 3 factors.

It is ________.

Choose a number between 100 and 200. Write some clues about your number and give them to your partner to solve.

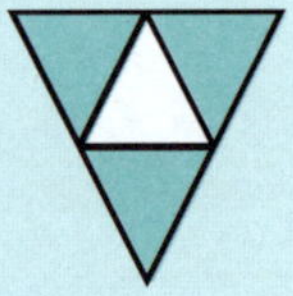

Fractions are parts of a whole.

Example: $\frac{1}{4}$ of the triangle is white, $\frac{3}{4}$ of the triangle is blue.

Building Equivalent Fractions

Fractions that have the same value are called equivalent fractions.

To build a fraction equivalent to the given fraction, multiply the numerator and denominator by the same number.

Example:

Find two fractions that are equivalent to the fraction $\frac{1}{5}$

$$\frac{1}{5} \xrightarrow{\times 2} \frac{2}{10} \qquad \frac{1}{5} \xrightarrow{\times 3} \frac{3}{15}$$

If you multiply the numerator and denominator by 2, you get the equivalent fraction $\frac{2}{10}$

Similarly, if the numerator and denominator are multiplied by 3, you get $\frac{3}{15}$

Therefore,

$\frac{1}{5} = \frac{2}{10} = \frac{3}{15}$

How to Find Out if Two Fractions are Equivalent?

Two fractions are equivalent only if the product of the numerator of the first fraction and the denominator of the other fraction is equal to the product of the denominator of the first fraction and the numerator of the other fraction.

Example: Are the fractions $\frac{2}{7}$ and $\frac{6}{21}$ equivalent?

Solution: Multiply the numerator of the first fraction (2) by the denominator of the second (21) and then multiply the denominator of the first fraction (7) by the numerator of the second (6)

$$\frac{2}{7} \quad \frac{6}{21}$$

$2 \times 21 = 42$

$7 \times 6 = 42$

$42 = 42$

Therefore, $\frac{2}{7}$ is equivalent to $\frac{6}{21}$.

Fractions

Reducing Fractions to their Lowest Terms

Reducing fractions is another way of saying, 'finding the lowest equivalent fraction'.

When reducing a proper fraction, follow these steps:

- Factor the numerator.
- Factor the denominator.
- Cancel out the common factors in the numerator and the denominator.
- Rewrite your answer as the reduced fraction.

Example: Reduce $\frac{24}{56}$ to its lowest term.

Solution:

Factors of the numerator 24 $= 2 \times 2 \times 2 \times 3$

Factors of the denominator 56 $= 2 \times 2 \times 2 \times 7$

$$\frac{24}{56} = \frac{\cancel{2} \times \cancel{2} \times \cancel{2} \times 3}{\cancel{2} \times \cancel{2} \times \cancel{2} \times 7}$$

The reduced fraction $= \frac{3}{7}$

Proper Fractions

A fraction whose numerator is less than the denominator is called a **proper fraction**.

Example: $\frac{4}{5}$, $\frac{2}{7}$, $\frac{5}{9}$ are proper fractions as the denominators are more than the numerators.

Improper Fractions

A fraction whose numerator is more than the denominator is called an **improper fraction**.

Example: $\frac{13}{5}$, $\frac{23}{7}$, $\frac{14}{9}$ are improper fractions as the denominators are less than the numerators.

Mixed Numbers

When an improper fraction is written as a combination of a whole number and a proper fraction, it is called a **mixed number**.

Example: $10\frac{1}{2}$, $12\frac{3}{4}$ are mixed numbers.

Changing an Improper Fraction into a Mixed Number

Example: Change $\frac{25}{2}$ to a mixed number.

Solution: Divide 25 by 2

When 25 is divided by 2, the quotient is 12 and the remainder is 1.

Write the quotient as the whole number part of the mixed number.

Write the remainder as the numerator of the fractional part.

The denominator of the fractional part is the same as the improper fraction.

$$\frac{25}{2} = 12\,\frac{1}{2}$$

Remainder (1); Quotient (12)

Changing a Mixed Number to an Improper Fraction

Example: Write the mixed number $3\,\frac{4}{7}$ as an improper fraction.

Solution:

Multiply the whole part 3 by the denominator 7.

$3 \times 7 = 21$

Add the numerator 4 to 21

$21 + 4 = 25$

The improper fraction's numerator is 25 and the denominator is 7.

$$3\,\frac{4}{7} = \frac{25}{7}$$

Comparison of Fractions

> If the denominators are the same, just compare the numerators.
> The fraction with the bigger numerator is the bigger fraction.

Example: Compare $\frac{5}{8}$ and $\frac{7}{8}$

Since $7 > 5$,

$$\frac{5}{8} < \frac{7}{8}$$

> If the numerators are the same, compare the denominators.
> The fraction with the bigger denominator is the smaller fraction.

Example: Compare $\frac{5}{9}$ and $\frac{5}{6}$

Since $9 > 6$,

$$\frac{5}{9} < \frac{5}{6}$$

If both the numerator and the denominator are different:

- Find a common denominator by finding the least common multiple (LCM) of the denominators.
- Rewrite each as an equivalent fraction using this new denominator.
- Compare the equivalent fractions.

Example: **1.** Compare $\frac{3}{5}$ and $\frac{2}{3}$

Solution:

a. To find the common denominator, list the multiples of 5 and 3

Multiples of 5: 5, 10,15,20,25, 30 …

Multiples of 3: 3, 6, 9, 12, 15, 18, 21, 24, 27, 30 …

Some of the common multiples are 15, 30 …

LCM of 5 and 3 is 15.

b. Find the equivalent fraction of $\frac{3}{5}$ with the denominator 15.

$$\frac{3 \times 3}{5 \times 3} = \frac{9}{15}$$

Find the equivalent fraction of $\frac{2}{3}$ with the denominator 15

$$\frac{2 \times 5}{3 \times 5} = \frac{10}{15}$$

c. Compare $\frac{9}{15}$ and $\frac{10}{15}$

So, $9 < 10$

$$\frac{9}{15} < \frac{10}{15}$$

Therefore, $\frac{3}{5} < \frac{2}{3}$

For mixed numbers, just look at the whole number part. The mixed number with the smaller whole number part is the smaller mixed number.

If the whole number parts are the same, then compare the fraction parts.

Example: **1a.** Compare $3\frac{2}{3}, 4\frac{2}{3}$

Since $3 < 4$,

$$3\frac{2}{3} < 4\frac{2}{3}$$

b. Compare $3\frac{2}{3}$ and $3\frac{1}{3}$.

The whole number parts are equal.

Therefore, compare the fractions $\frac{2}{3}$ and $\frac{1}{3}$.

$$\frac{2}{3} > \frac{1}{3}$$

Therefore, $3\frac{2}{3} > 3\frac{1}{3}$

Representing Fractions

Worksheet 34

1. Follow these steps to show each fraction.

- Read the fraction.
- Think about how you would draw lines to show equal parts.
- Draw the lines and shade the parts to show the fraction.

a. $\frac{1}{3}$

b. $\frac{1}{4}$

c. $\frac{3}{4}$

d. $\frac{4}{6}$

e. $\frac{9}{12}$

f. $\frac{4}{12}$

g. $\frac{2}{5}$

h. $\frac{1}{4}$

i. $\frac{3}{10}$

j. $\frac{4}{10}$

k. $\frac{5}{20}$

l. $\frac{3}{5}$

Write the pairs of fractions shown above that are equivalent.

Write the common fraction or mixed numeral in the blank boxes.

1.

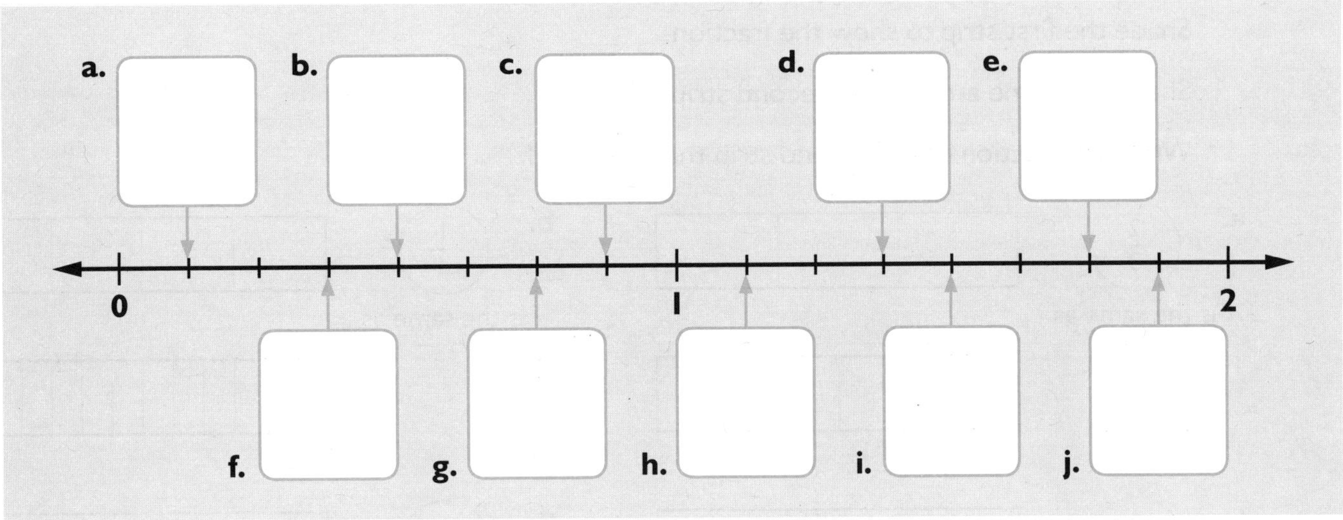

2.

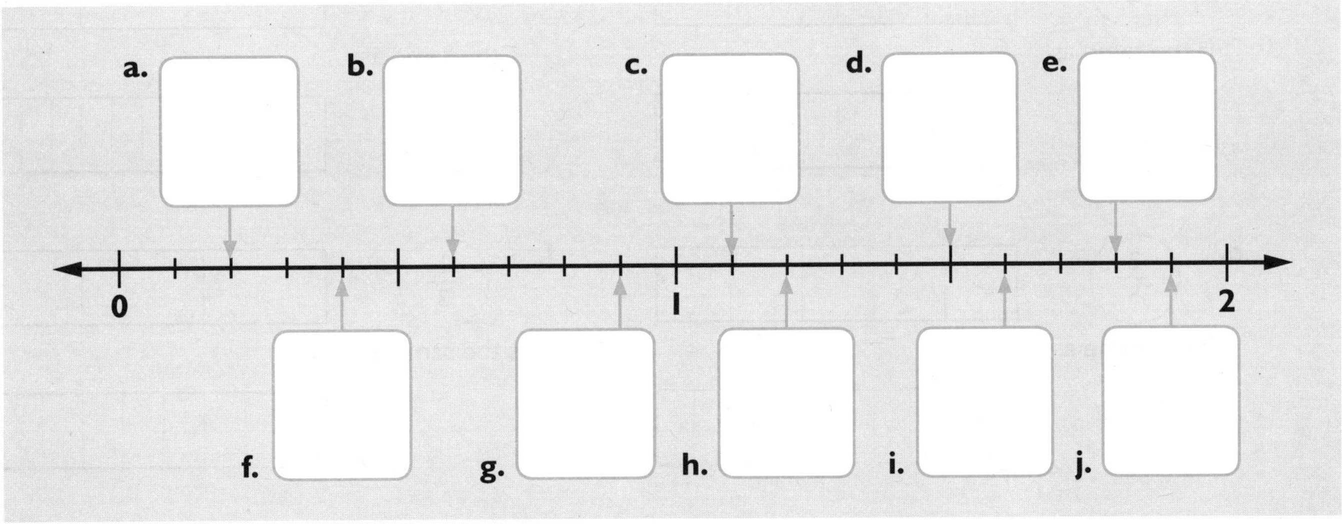

3.

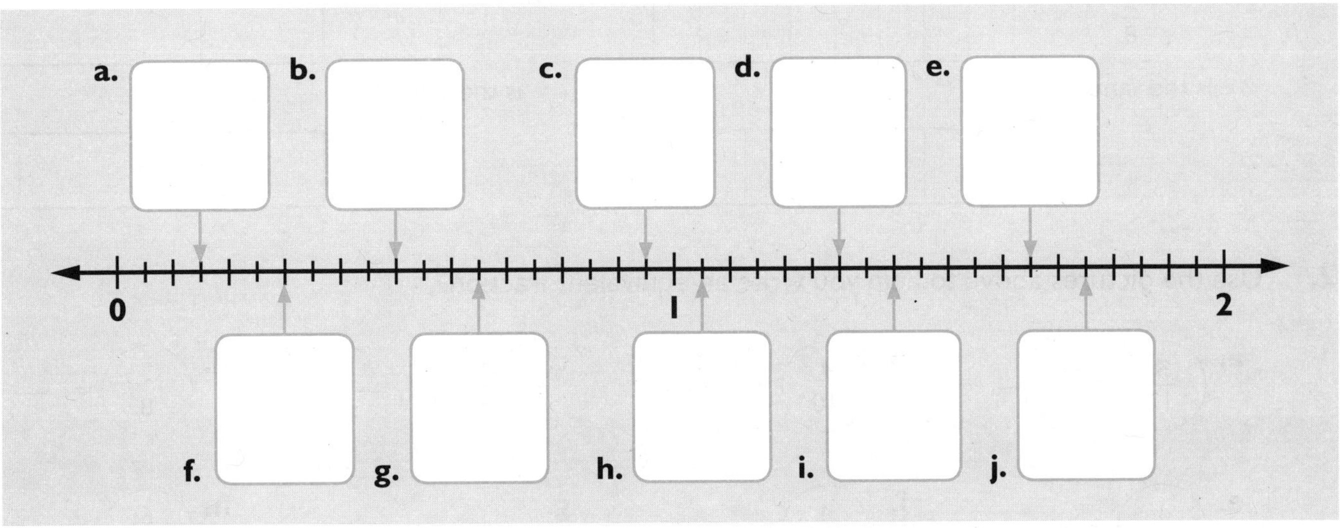

Write the fractions that are between 1 and $1\frac{1}{2}$.

Exploring Equivalent Fractions

Worksheet 36

1. Follow these steps to find equivalent fractions.

- Shade the first strip to show the fraction.
- Shade the same area on the second strip.
- Write the fraction of the second strip that is shaded.

a. $\frac{2}{3}$ is the same as ☐

b. $\frac{1}{4}$ is the same as ☐

c. $\frac{3}{4}$ is the same as ☐

d. $\frac{1}{3}$ is the same as ☐

e. $\frac{2}{5}$ is the same as ☐

f. $\frac{1}{3}$ is the same as ☐

g. $\frac{2}{8}$ is the same as ☐

h. $\frac{1}{3}$ is the same as ☐

2. Use the pictures above to help you write an equivalent fraction.

a. $\frac{4}{12} = \frac{\square}{3}$

b. $\frac{4}{10} = \frac{\square}{5}$

c. $\frac{2}{6} = \frac{\square}{3}$

d. $\frac{2}{8} = \frac{\square}{4}$

e. $\frac{1}{4} = \frac{\square}{\square}$

f. $\frac{4}{6} = \frac{\square}{\square}$

g. $\frac{3}{9} = \frac{\square}{\square}$

h. $\frac{6}{8} = \frac{\square}{\square}$

Write all the fractions on this page that are equivalent to one-third.

Relating Fractions to Tenths and Hundredths

1. Shade the fraction. Then write an equivalent fraction.

a. $\frac{1}{5} = \frac{\quad}{10}$

b. $\frac{3}{5} = \frac{\quad}{100}$

c. $\frac{1}{4} = \frac{\quad}{100}$

d. $\frac{3}{10} = \frac{\quad}{100}$

e. $\frac{3}{4} = \frac{\quad}{100}$

f. $\frac{7}{10} = \frac{\quad}{100}$

2. Shade the fraction. Then write two equivalent fractions.

a. $\frac{2}{5} = \frac{\quad}{10} = \frac{\quad}{100}$

b. $\frac{4}{5} = \frac{\quad}{10} = \frac{\quad}{100}$

c. $\frac{1}{2} = \frac{\quad}{10} = \frac{\quad}{100}$

Write five fractions that are equivalent to

a. one-quarter **b. three-quarters**

Expressing Fractions as Hundredths

1. Write the fraction shown by the arrows on each side of the strip.

a. b. c. d.

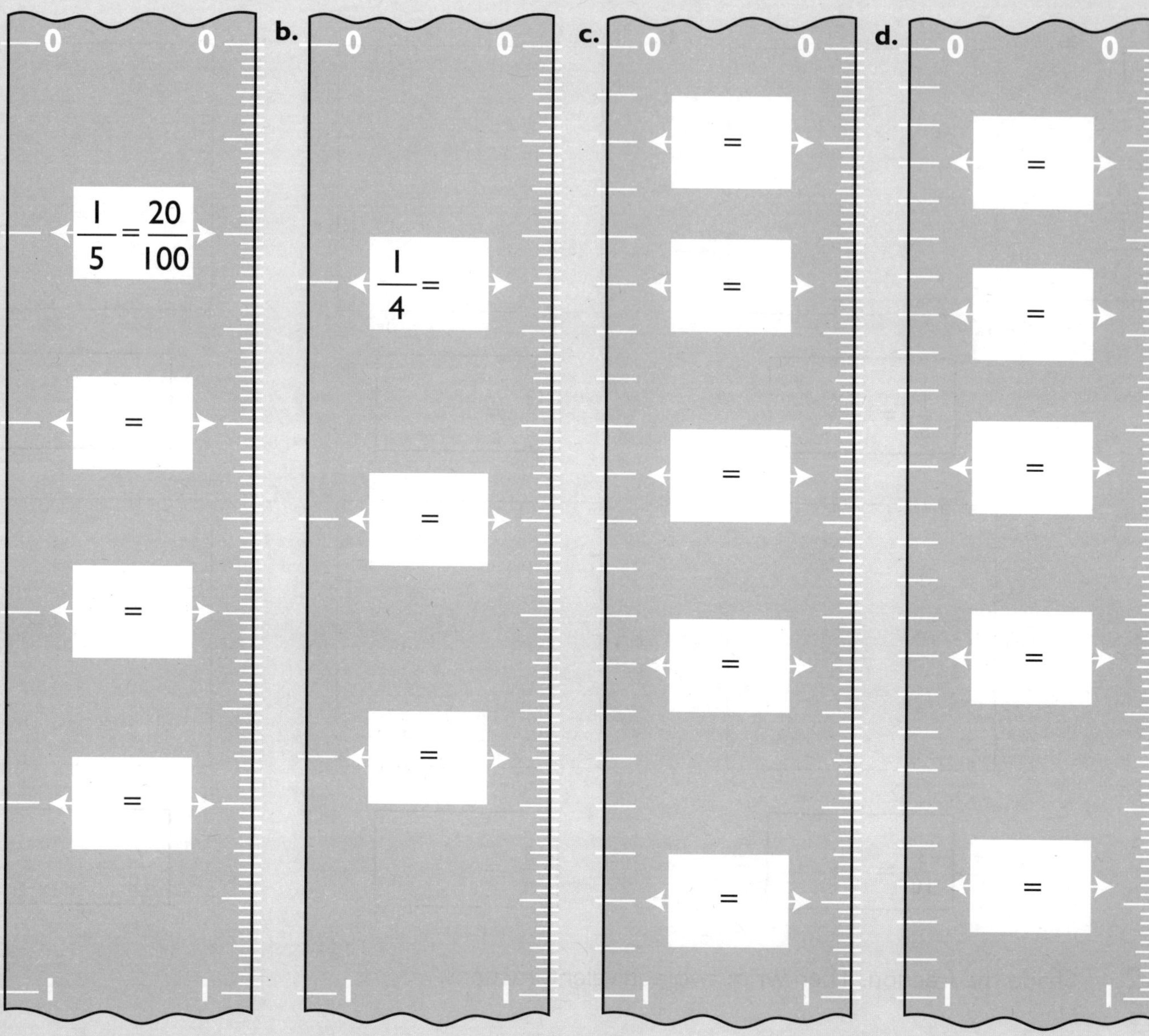

2. Complete each of these. Use the strips above to help you.

a. $\frac{4}{20} = \frac{\quad}{100}$

b. $\frac{8}{20} = \frac{\quad}{100}$

c. $\frac{10}{20} = \frac{\quad}{100}$

d. $\frac{15}{20} = \frac{\quad}{100}$

e. $\frac{5}{25} = \frac{\quad}{100}$

f. $\frac{9}{25} = \frac{\quad}{100}$

g. $\frac{15}{25} = \frac{\quad}{100}$

h. $\frac{20}{25} = \frac{\quad}{100}$

FF **Write the fractions on this page that are the same as**

a. 0.5 **b. 0.8**

Relating Improper Fractions and Mixed Numerals

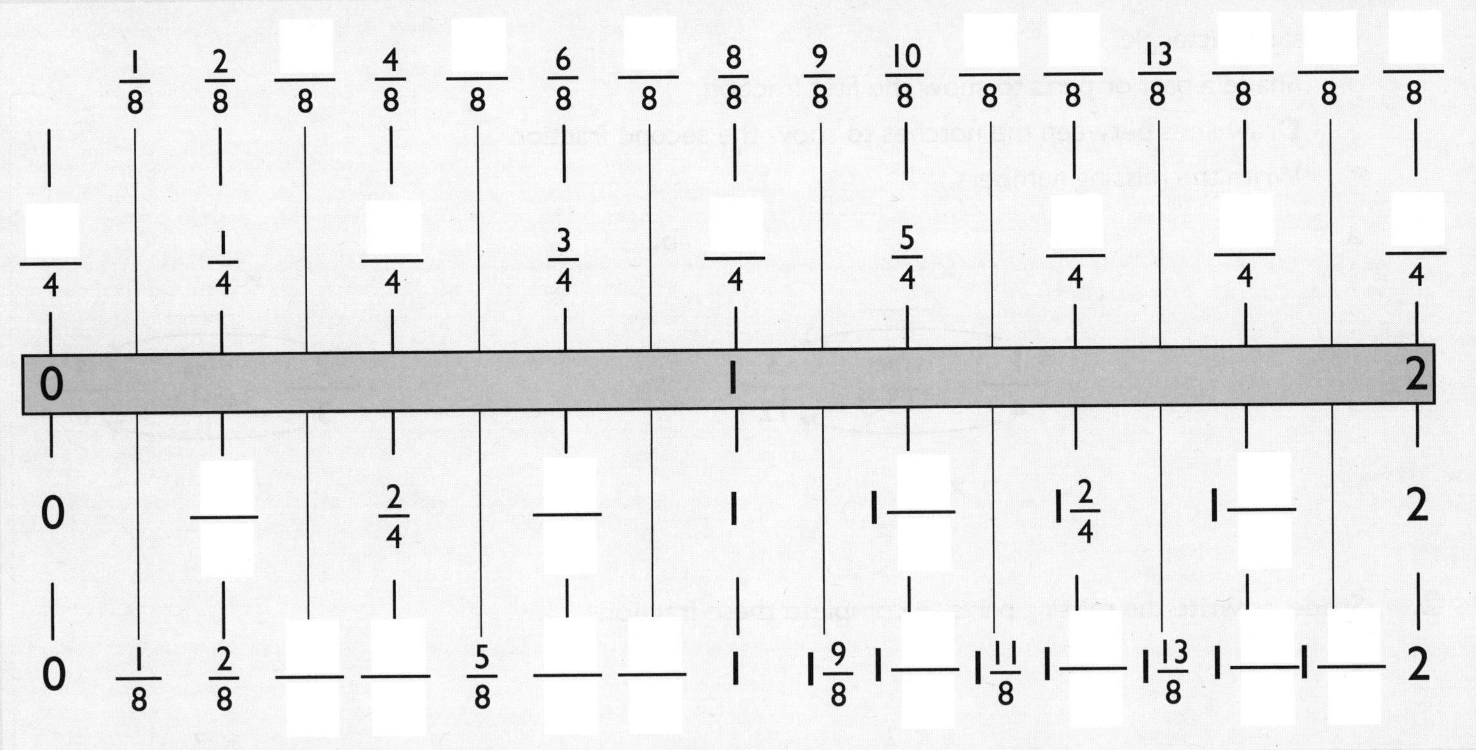

1. Look above the number line.
   a. Count by eighths. Write the missing fractions.
   b. Count by quarters. Write the missing fractions.
2. Look below the number line. Write the missing numbers.
3. Write each of these improper fractions as a mixed numeral.

   a. $\frac{15}{8} =$ b. $\frac{5}{4} =$ c. $\frac{17}{8} =$ d. $\frac{11}{4} =$

4. Write each of these mixed numeral as an improper fraction.

   a. $1\frac{3}{8} =$ b. $1\frac{3}{4} =$ c. $2\frac{7}{8} =$ d. $3\frac{1}{4} =$

5. Write each of these improper fractions as a mixed numeral.

   a. $\frac{15}{10} =$ b. $\frac{26}{10} =$ c. $\frac{115}{100} =$ d. $\frac{126}{100} =$

   e. $\frac{18}{10} =$ f. $\frac{80}{10} =$ g. $\frac{190}{100} =$ h. $\frac{270}{100} =$

Write a rule you could use to convert a mixed numeral to an improper fraction. Reverse your rule.

Finding Equivalent Fractions

1. For each rectangle
- Shade a part or parts to show the first fraction.
- Draw lines between the notches to show the second fraction.
- Write the missing numbers.

a.

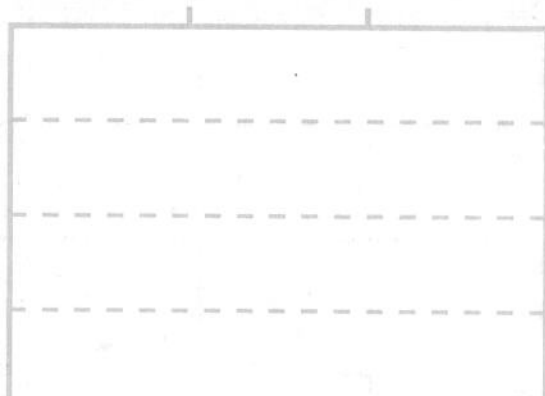

× ___

$\frac{1}{4}$ is the same as $\frac{3}{12}$

× ___

b.

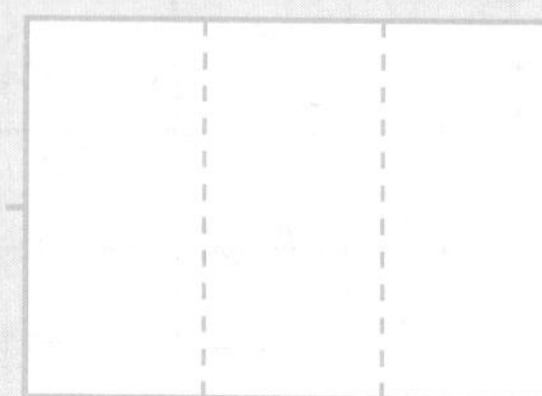

× ___

$\frac{2}{3}$ is the same as $\frac{4}{6}$

× ___

2. Shade or write the missing parts to complete these fractions.

a.

× 2

$\frac{1}{4}$ is the same as $\frac{\square}{\square}$

× 2

b.

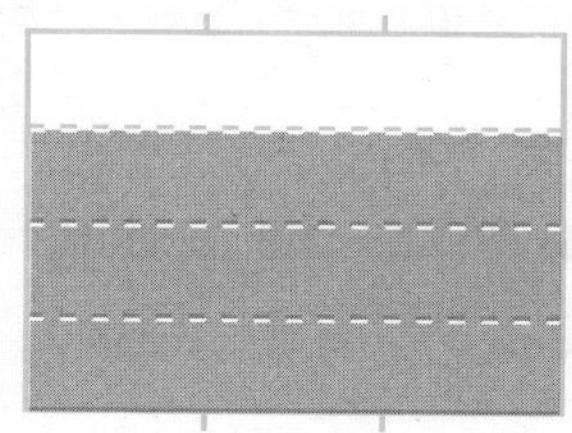

× 3

$\frac{\square}{\square}$ is the same as $\frac{\square}{\square}$

× 3

c.

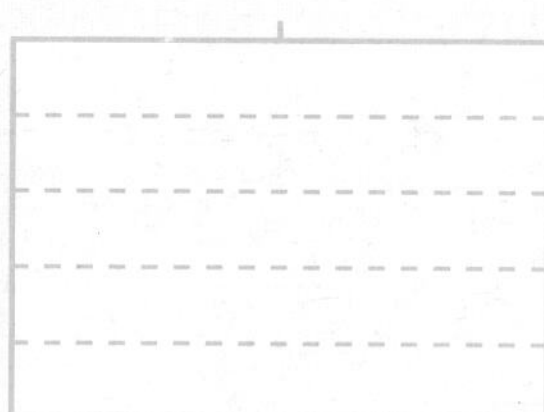

× ___

$\frac{3}{5}$ is the same as $\frac{\square}{\square}$

× ___

d.

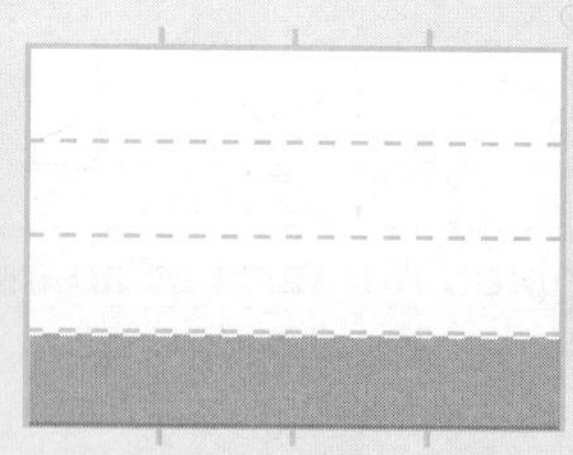

× ___

$\frac{\square}{\square}$ is the same as $\frac{\square}{\square}$

× 4

3. Complete each of these.

a. × ___ $\quad \frac{1}{5} = \frac{}{20} \quad$ × ___

b. × ___ $\quad \frac{2}{5} = \frac{}{100} \quad$ × ___

c. × ___ $\quad \frac{7}{20} = \frac{}{100} \quad$ × ___

d. × ___ $\quad \frac{9}{25} = \frac{}{100} \quad$ × ___

FF Write three common fractions that are equivalent to $\frac{3}{5}$.

Adding Fractions

Adding Like Fractions

You have already learnt how to **add like fractions**. To add like fractions:

1. Add the numerators of the fractions.
2. Write the sum of the numerators over the same denominator.

Example: Add $\frac{5}{7}$ and $\frac{8}{7}$

Solution: $\frac{5}{7} + \frac{8}{7}$

$$= \frac{5+8}{7}$$

$$= \frac{13}{7}$$

$$= 1\frac{6}{7}$$

Adding Unlike Fractions:

If the fractions being added are unlike fractions:

- Find a common denominator by finding the least common multiple of the denominators.
- Rewrite each fraction as an equivalent fraction using this new denominator.
- Now, add the numerators and keep the denominator of the equivalent fractions.

Example: Find the sum of $\frac{2}{9}$ and $\frac{3}{12}$

Solution:

- Multiples of 9: 9, 18, 27, 36, 45, 54, 63, 72, 81, 90 …
  Multiples of 12: 12, 24, 36, 48, 60, 72, 84 …
  Least common multiple (LCM) is 36
  So, the common denominator is 36
- Equivalent fraction of 2/9 with denominator 36 is

$$\frac{2 \times 4}{9 \times 4} = \frac{8}{36}$$

- Equivalent fraction of 3/12 with denominator 36 is

$$\frac{3 \times 3}{12 \times 3} = \frac{9}{36}$$

- Add the numerators and put the sum over the lowest common denominator.

$$\frac{8}{36} + \frac{9}{36} = \frac{8 \times 9}{36}$$

$$= \frac{17}{36}$$

Subtracting Fractions

Subtracting Like Fractions

To subtract like fractions:

1. Subtract the numerators of the fractions.

2. Write the difference of the numerators over the same denominator.

Example: Find $\frac{11}{17} - \frac{5}{17}$

Solution: $\frac{11}{17} - \frac{5}{17}$

$= \frac{11-5}{17}$

$= \frac{6}{17}$

Subtracting Unlike Fractions

If the fractions being subtracted are unlike fractions:

- Find a common denominator by finding the least common multiple of the denominators.
- Rewrite each fraction as an equivalent fraction using this new denominator.
- Now, subtract the numerators, and keep the denominator of the equivalent fractions.

Example: Find $\frac{3}{4} - \frac{2}{5}$

Solution:

- Multiples of 4: 4, 8, 12, 16, 20, 24, …

  Multiples of 5: 5, 10, 15, 20, 25, 30, 35, …

  Least common multiple (LCM) is 20

  So, the common denominator is 20
- Equivalent fraction of $\frac{3}{4}$ with denominator 20 is $\frac{3 \times 5}{4 \times 5} = \frac{15}{20}$

  Equivalent fraction of $\frac{2}{5}$ with denominator 20 is $\frac{2 \times 4}{5 \times 4} = \frac{8}{20}$
- Subtract the numerators and put the difference over the lowest common denominator.

  $\frac{15}{20} - \frac{8}{20} = \frac{15-8}{20} = \frac{7}{20}$

Remember to change a mixed number into an improper fraction before adding or subtracting it.

Example: $1\frac{1}{3} + 2\frac{1}{3}$

Solution: $1\frac{1}{3} = \frac{4}{3}$ $\quad 2\frac{1}{3} = \frac{7}{3}$

$\frac{4}{3} + \frac{7}{3} = \frac{11}{3} = 3\frac{2}{3}$

Adding and Subtracting Fractions

Worksheet 41

1. Colour boxes to show both fractions. Write the fraction of the total that you coloured.

a. $\frac{3}{8} + \frac{4}{8} =$ ____

b. $\frac{1}{6} + \frac{3}{6} =$ ____

c. $\frac{4}{10} + \frac{3}{10} =$ ____

d. $\frac{3}{8} + \frac{2}{8} =$ ____

e. $\frac{3}{5} + \frac{1}{5} =$ ____

f. $\frac{5}{12} + \frac{6}{12} =$ ____

2. Colour boxes to show the first fraction. Cross out coloured boxes to show the second fraction. Then write the fraction that the remaining coloured boxes show.

a. $\frac{5}{6} - \frac{2}{6} =$ ____

b. $\frac{7}{10} - \frac{4}{10} =$ ____

c. $\frac{6}{8} - \frac{4}{8} =$ ____

d. $\frac{11}{12} - \frac{7}{12} =$ ____

e. $\frac{7}{8} - \frac{5}{8} =$ ____

f. $\frac{9}{12} - \frac{6}{12} =$ ____

Rewrite the answers that can be expressed in a simpler form.

Adding and Subtracting Fractions

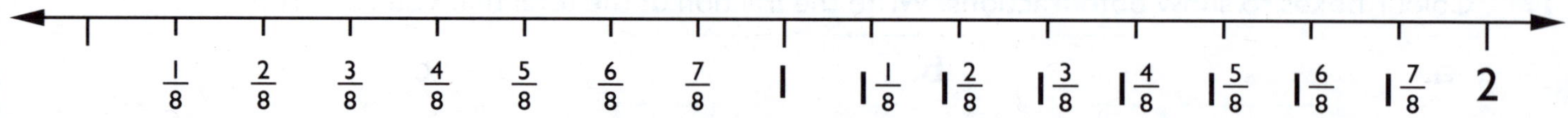

1. Use the number line above to help you write the answers.

a. $\frac{4}{8} + \frac{2}{8} =$

b. $\frac{3}{8} + \frac{1}{8} =$ ____

c. $\frac{5}{8} + \frac{2}{8} =$ ____

d. $\frac{7}{8} - \frac{3}{8} =$

e. $1\frac{2}{8} - \frac{4}{8} =$ ____

f. $1\frac{5}{8} - \frac{1}{8} =$ ____

2. Use this number line to help you write the answers.

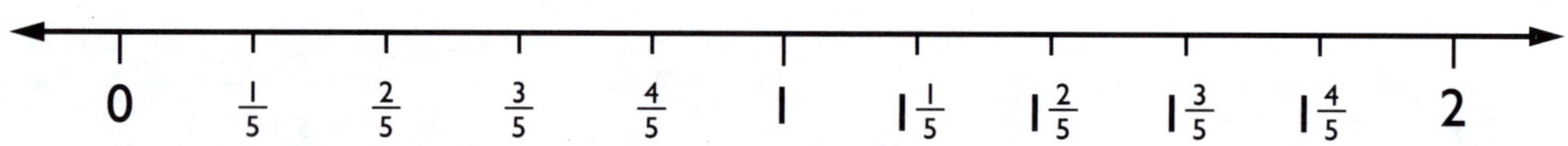

a. $\frac{3}{5} + \frac{4}{5} =$

b. $\frac{1}{5} + 1\frac{2}{5} =$

c. $\frac{2}{5} + 1\frac{3}{5} =$

d. $1\frac{3}{5} - \frac{4}{5} =$ ____

e. $1\frac{4}{5} - 1\frac{1}{5} =$ ____

f. $1\frac{1}{5} - \frac{2}{5} =$ ____

3. Write the answers to these.

a. $\frac{5}{8} + 1\frac{2}{8} =$ ____

b. $5\frac{1}{8} + 2\frac{7}{8} =$ ____

c. $4\frac{2}{5} + 1\frac{3}{5} =$ ____

d. $3\frac{1}{5} + 2\frac{3}{5} =$ ____

e. $2\frac{3}{8} - 1\frac{1}{8} =$ ____

f. $4\frac{5}{8} - 2\frac{7}{8} =$ ____

g. $\frac{6}{8} - \frac{3}{8} =$ ____

h. $1\frac{2}{5} - \frac{3}{5} =$ ____

i. $3\frac{3}{5} - 1\frac{4}{5} =$ ____

Calculate these: **a.** $1\frac{2}{4} + 3\frac{3}{4}$ **b.** $\frac{6}{10} + 1\frac{5}{10}$

Adding and Subtracting Fractions

1. Use the grid to help you rewrite the number sentence. Then write the answer.

a. $\frac{1}{2} + \frac{3}{8} =$ ____

____ + ____ = ____

b. $\frac{1}{4} + \frac{5}{8} =$ ____

____ + ____ = ____

c. $\frac{1}{3} + \frac{1}{6} =$ ____

____ + ____ = ____

d. $\frac{3}{16} + \frac{3}{8} =$ ____

____ + ____ = ____

e. $\frac{1}{3} + \frac{3}{12} =$ ____

____ + ____ = ____

f. $\frac{1}{2} - \frac{3}{8} =$ ____

____ − ____ = ____

g. $\frac{7}{10} - \frac{1}{2} =$ ____

____ − ____ = ____

h. $\frac{5}{6} - \frac{2}{3} =$ ____

____ − ____ = ____

i. $\frac{3}{5} - \frac{3}{10} =$ ____

____ − ____ = ____

Imagine you had to change $\frac{1}{4}$. What fraction can you change it to?

Adding Common Fractions

Worksheet 44

$\frac{1}{2}$ $\frac{1}{2}$

$\frac{1}{3}$ $\frac{1}{3}$ $\frac{1}{3}$

$\frac{1}{4}$ $\frac{1}{4}$ $\frac{1}{4}$ $\frac{1}{4}$

$\frac{1}{5}$ $\frac{1}{5}$ $\frac{1}{5}$ $\frac{1}{5}$ $\frac{1}{5}$

$\frac{1}{6}$ $\frac{1}{6}$ $\frac{1}{6}$ $\frac{1}{6}$ $\frac{1}{6}$ $\frac{1}{6}$

$\frac{1}{8}$ $\frac{1}{8}$ $\frac{1}{8}$ $\frac{1}{8}$ $\frac{1}{8}$ $\frac{1}{8}$ $\frac{1}{8}$ $\frac{1}{8}$

$\frac{1}{10}$ $\frac{1}{10}$ $\frac{1}{10}$ $\frac{1}{10}$ $\frac{1}{10}$ $\frac{1}{10}$ $\frac{1}{10}$ $\frac{1}{10}$ $\frac{1}{10}$ $\frac{1}{10}$

$\frac{1}{12}$ $\frac{1}{12}$ $\frac{1}{12}$ $\frac{1}{12}$ $\frac{1}{12}$ $\frac{1}{12}$ $\frac{1}{12}$ $\frac{1}{12}$ $\frac{1}{12}$ $\frac{1}{12}$ $\frac{1}{12}$ $\frac{1}{12}$

1. Use the fraction strips to help you rewrite one of the fractions. Then calculate the total.

a. $\frac{3}{6} + \frac{1}{3}$

$= \frac{3}{6} + \frac{2}{6} = \underline{\quad}$

b. $\frac{3}{8} + \frac{2}{4}$

$= \frac{3}{8} + \frac{\quad}{8} = \underline{\quad}$

c. $\frac{1}{2} + \frac{2}{8}$

$= \frac{\quad}{8} + \frac{2}{8} = \underline{\quad}$

2. Rewrite both fractions so the denominators are the same. Then calculate the total.

a. $\frac{3}{5} + \frac{2}{10} = \underline{\quad} + \underline{\quad} = \underline{\quad}$

b. $\frac{2}{4} + \frac{5}{12} = \underline{\quad} + \underline{\quad} = \underline{\quad}$

c. $\frac{1}{3} + \frac{4}{12} = \underline{\quad} + \underline{\quad} = \underline{\quad}$

d. $\frac{6}{12} + \frac{1}{4} = \underline{\quad} + \underline{\quad} = \underline{\quad}$

e. $\frac{5}{12} + \frac{2}{6} = \underline{\quad} + \underline{\quad} = \underline{\quad}$

f. $\frac{1}{2} + \frac{3}{8} = \underline{\quad} + \underline{\quad} = \underline{\quad}$

FF How would you add $\frac{1}{4}$ and $\frac{1}{3}$?

Subtracting Common Fractions

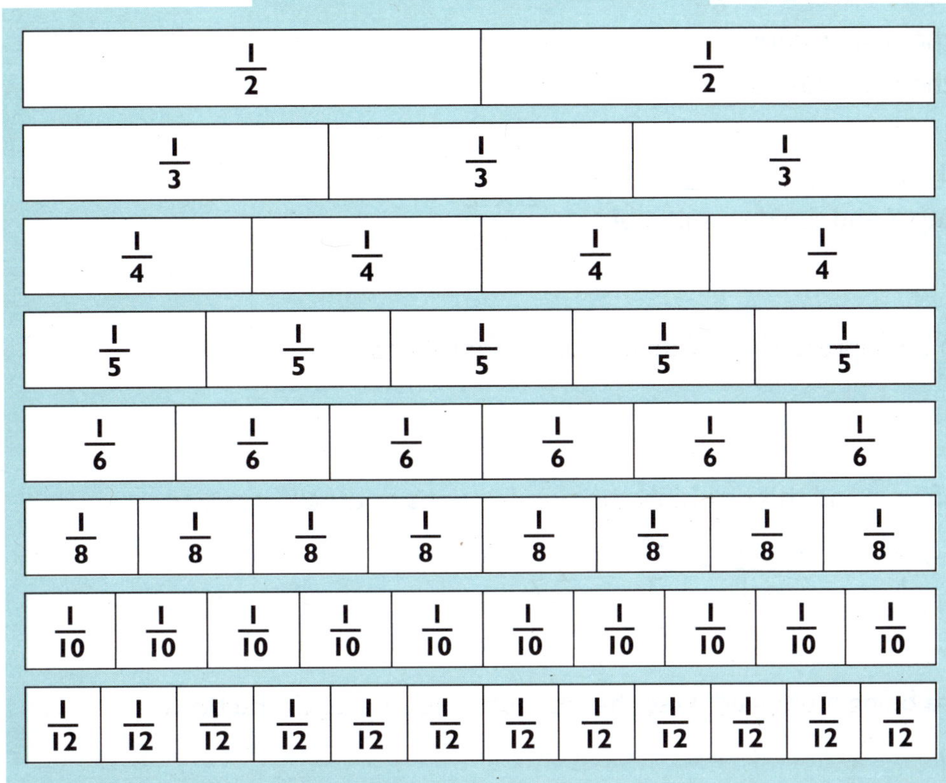

1. Use the fraction strips to help you rewrite one of the fractions. Then calculate the difference.

a. $\frac{2}{3} - \frac{1}{6}$

$= \frac{4}{6} - \frac{1}{6} = \_\_\_$

b. $\frac{1}{4} - \frac{1}{12}$

$= \frac{\_\_}{12} - \frac{1}{12} = \_\_\_$

c. $\frac{3}{4} - \frac{3}{8}$

$= \frac{\_\_}{8} - \frac{3}{8} = \_\_\_$

2. Rewrite both fractions so the denominators are the same. Then calculate the difference.

a. $\frac{5}{8} - \frac{1}{4} = \_\_\_ - \_\_\_ = \_\_\_$

b. $\frac{2}{4} - \frac{5}{12} = \_\_\_ - \_\_\_ = \_\_\_$

c. $\frac{3}{4} - \frac{7}{12} = \_\_\_ - \_\_\_ = \_\_\_$

d. $\frac{11}{12} - \frac{2}{3} = \_\_\_ - \_\_\_ = \_\_\_$

e. $\frac{7}{12} - \frac{1}{4} = \_\_\_ - \_\_\_ = \_\_\_$

f. $\frac{7}{8} - \frac{3}{4} = \_\_\_ - \_\_\_ = \_\_\_$

How would you find the difference between $\frac{2}{3}$ and $\frac{3}{4}$?

Multiplying Fractions

To multiply fractions, do the following:

- Multiply the numerators.
- Multiply the denominators.

Example: Multiply $\frac{2}{3}$ and $\frac{2}{5}$

Multiply the numerators and the denominators $\frac{2 \times 2}{3 \times 5}$

Multiplying a Fraction and a Whole Number

Whole numbers can be expressed as a fraction with denominator 1

Example: $\frac{4}{7} \times 5$

Solution: Write 5 as $\frac{5}{1}$ and then multiply the two fractions as usual!

$$\frac{4}{7} \times \frac{5}{1} = \frac{4 \times 5}{7 \times 1} = \frac{20}{7} = 2\frac{6}{7}$$

Multiplying Mixed Numbers

If mixed numbers are being multiplied, first change them into improper fractions.

Example: $1\frac{1}{2} \times 2\frac{1}{5}$

Solution:

$$1\frac{1}{2} = \frac{3}{2}$$

$$2\frac{1}{5} = \frac{11}{5}$$

$$1\frac{1}{2} \times 2\frac{1}{5} = \frac{3}{2} \times \frac{11}{5} = \frac{33}{10} = 3\frac{3}{10}$$

Fraction of a Fraction

The 'of' means that we are taking a part of something.
The word 'of' is frequently used to indicate multiplying fractions.

Example: Find 1/5th of 10

Solution:

$\frac{1}{5}$ th of 10 means a fifth part of 10

$\frac{1}{5} \times 10 = \frac{1}{5} \times \frac{10}{1}$ (10 can be written as $\frac{10}{1}$)

$= \frac{10}{5}$

$= 2$

Multiplication of Fractions

1. Multiply the following fractions and express the answer in the lowest terms.

a. $\frac{3}{5} \times \frac{5}{8}$

b. $\frac{6}{13} \times \frac{5}{9}$

c. $\frac{6}{8} \times 12$

d. $\frac{5}{10} \times \frac{7}{18}$

e. $\frac{10}{16} \times \frac{5}{11}$

f. $\frac{14}{4} \times 7$

g. $\frac{6}{13} \times \frac{4}{9}$

h. $\frac{8}{9} \times 7$

Rough Work Sheet

1. Word Problems

a. Mr Mallik bought 250 acres of land in his village. He gave one-eighth of his land to his father. How many acres did he have left?

b. Rahul and Ratan went to eat pizza. The pizza was divided into eight slices. Ratan ate half of the pizza. Rahul ate the rest. How many slices of pizza did Ratan eat?

c. Fahid bought five flavours of ice-cream: chocolate chip, strawberry, vanilla, butterscotch and mango. He asked 78 friends to choose their favourite flavour. Two-thirteenths of the students liked chocolate chip the best. Three-thirteenths of the students preferred mango ice-cream. Vanilla was the favourite of $\frac{7}{39}$ of the students. $\frac{8}{39}$ of the students just loved butterscotch and the rest of the students liked strawberry best. How many students preferred the strawberry flavour?

Rough Work Sheet

CHAPTER 6

Decimals

The word 'decimal' means 'based on 10'.
476.52 is a decimal.

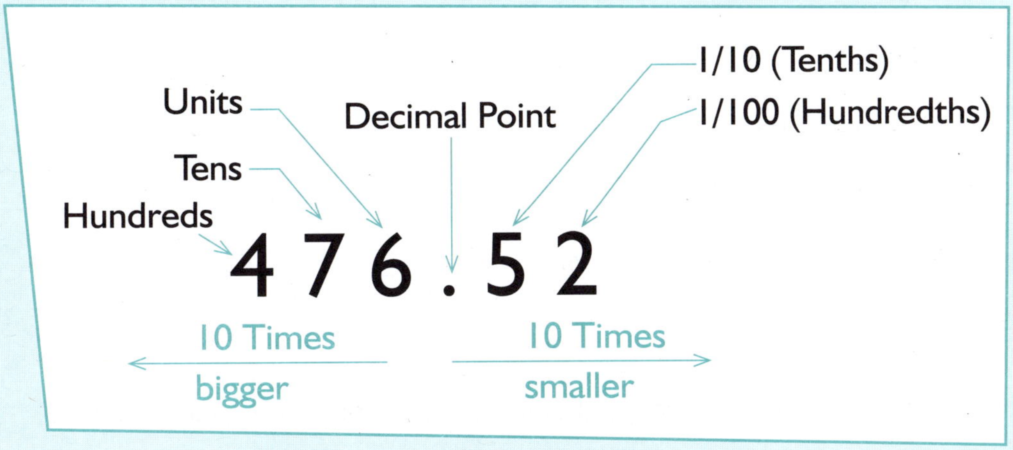

The dot in the decimal representation is called the decimal point.
A decimal number has two parts. The part before the decimal point is called the whole number part.
As we move further left, every number place gets 10 times bigger.
The part after the decimal point is called the decimal part.
As we move further right, every number place gets 10 times smaller

Example: In 325.89, 325 is the whole number part and .89 is the decimal part.

A whole number can also be written as a decimal by putting zeroes in the decimal places.

Example: 69 is same as 69.0

Decimal in the Place Value Chart

Thousands	Hundreds	Tens	Ones	.	Tenths	Hundredths	Thousandths
1000	100	10	1		$\frac{1}{10}$ (0.1)	$\frac{1}{100}$ (0.1)	$\frac{1}{1000}$ (0.1)

The first place to the right of the decimal point is called Tenths and its value is $\frac{1}{10}$.
The place after that is Hundredths with a value $\frac{1}{100}$ etc.
We can arrange the decimal fraction 476.52 in the place value chart as follows:

Hundreds	Tens	Ones	.	Tenths	Hundredths
4	7	6	.	5	2

The place value of 4 is 400 (4 hundreds).

The place value of 7 is 70 (7 tens).

The place value of 6 is 6 (6 ones).

The place value of 5 is $\frac{5}{10}$ or 0.5 (5 tenths).

The place value of 2 is $\frac{2}{100}$ or 0.02 (2 hundredths).

Therefore, we can write 476.52 in expanded form as:

$$400 + 70 + 6 + \frac{5}{10} + \frac{2}{100}$$

In word form, 476.52 is written as four hundred and seventy-six and fifty-two hundredths.

Decimals and Fractions

You can think of a decimal number as a decimal fraction.
A decimal fraction is a fraction where the denominator is 10, 100, 1000, etc.

This is one whole. 

If we divide it into 10 equal parts, it will look like 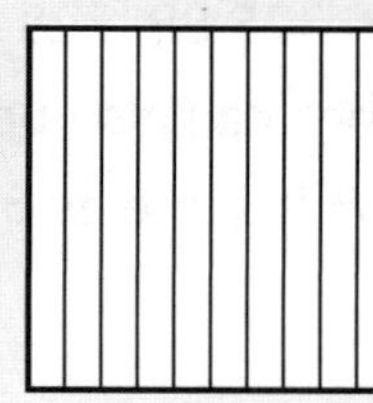

Each part is one tenth ($\frac{1}{10}$) of the whole or 0.1— zero wholes and one tenth.

Example: 0.4 is 4 tenths or 4 parts of a whole

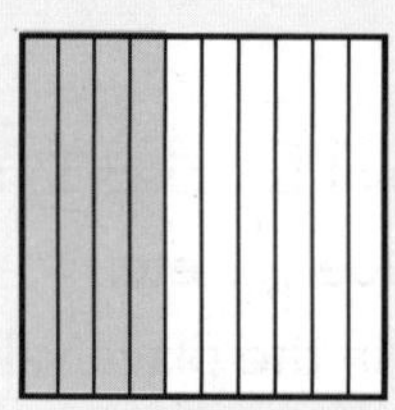

Example: 3.5 is 3 and $\frac{5}{10}$ or 3 wholes and 5 tenths.

and

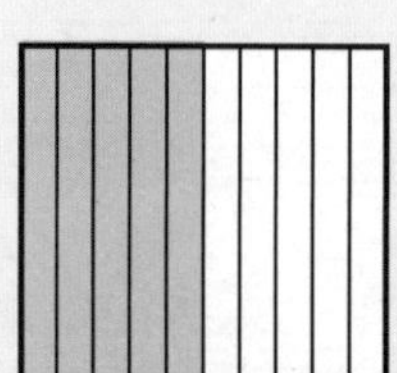

Decimals

Like and Unlike Decimals

Decimals that have the same number of decimal places are called like decimals.

Example: 5.128, 0.757, 89,760.056 are like decimals as all have three decimal places.

Decimals that have a different number of decimal places are called unlike decimals.

Example: 23.04, 0.123 and 498.8 are unlike decimals.

To convert unlike decimals to like ones, add zeroes to the extreme right of the decimal part.

$0.5 = \frac{5}{10}$

$0.50 = \frac{5}{10} + \frac{0}{100} = \frac{5}{10} = 0.5$

Similarly, $0.500 = 0.5$

Therefore, putting zeroes to the extreme right of the decimal part does not change the number.

Example: To make 23.04, 0.123 like decimals; we add a 0 at the end of 23.04

Now, 23.040 and 0.123 are like decimals (both have 3 decimal places).

Ordering Decimal Numbers

To compare two decimal numbers, follow these simple rules:

- Convert the numbers into like decimals.
- Compare the whole number parts. The decimal with a greater whole number part is greater.
- If the whole parts are equal, compare the tenths digits. The decimal with the greater tenths digit is greater.
- If the tenths digits are equal, compare the hundredths digits and so on.

Example: Which is greater, 25.76 or 26.98?

Solution: Comparing the whole parts, we find:

$25 < 26$, therefore 25.76 is smaller than 26.98.

$25.76 < 26.98$

Example: Compare 248.5 and 248.05.

Solution: The two decimals are unlike. Therefore, we add a zero to the end of 248.5 to get 248.50.

The whole parts of the two decimals are equal, so we compare the tenths digits.

5 tenths $>$ 0 tenths

Therefore, $248.5 > 248.05$

Decimals and Fractions

Converting Decimals to Fractions

To convert a decimal into a fraction:

- Write the given decimal without the decimal point. This is the numerator of the fraction.
- Count the decimal places in the given number. The denominator will be 1 followed by zeroes equal to the number of digits after the decimal point. If there is one number after the decimal, use 10 as the denominator. If there are two numbers after the decimal, use 100 as the denominator and so on.
- Reduce the fraction to the lowest form.

Example: Write 7.5 as a fraction.

Solution: The numerator of the fraction is 75.

There is one decimal place in 7.5.

The denominator will therefore be 10.

So, the fraction is $\frac{75}{10}$

Reducing $\frac{75}{10}$ to the lowest form we get

$$\frac{\cancel{75}^{15}}{\cancel{10}_{2}} = \frac{15}{2}$$

Therefore, $7.5 = \frac{15}{2}$

Converting Fractions to Decimals

To convert a fraction into a decimal:

- Find a number you can multiply the denominator by to make it 10, or 100, or 1,000 and so on.
- Multiply both the numerator and denominator by that number.
- Then write down just the numerator, putting the decimal place in the correct spot (one place left for every zero in the denominator).

The decimal fraction with 10 as the denominator has one digit after the decimal point (one zero in the denominator means one decimal place).

The decimal fraction with 100 as the denominator has two digits after the decimal point (two zeroes in the denominator means two decimal places, and so on).

Example: Convert $\frac{2}{5}$ into a decimal.
Solution: Multiplying 5 by 2 gives 10.

$$\frac{2}{5} \underset{\times 2}{\overset{\times 2}{=}} \frac{4}{10}$$

Multiply both numerator and denominator by 2

$\frac{4}{10}$ can be written as 0.4 (move the decimal one place to the left of 4 as 10 has one zero).

Example: Write $\frac{61}{1000}$ as a decimal.
Solution: The denominator has three zeroes so the decimal will have three decimal places.

00.061 — Add zeroes at the beginning of the number to get the correct number of decimal places.

In the number 61, count three places from the right and put the decimal point.

So, $\frac{61}{1000}$ can be written as 0.061.

Each arrow is pointing to a number. Write it as a common fraction above the line and as a decimal fraction below the line.

1.

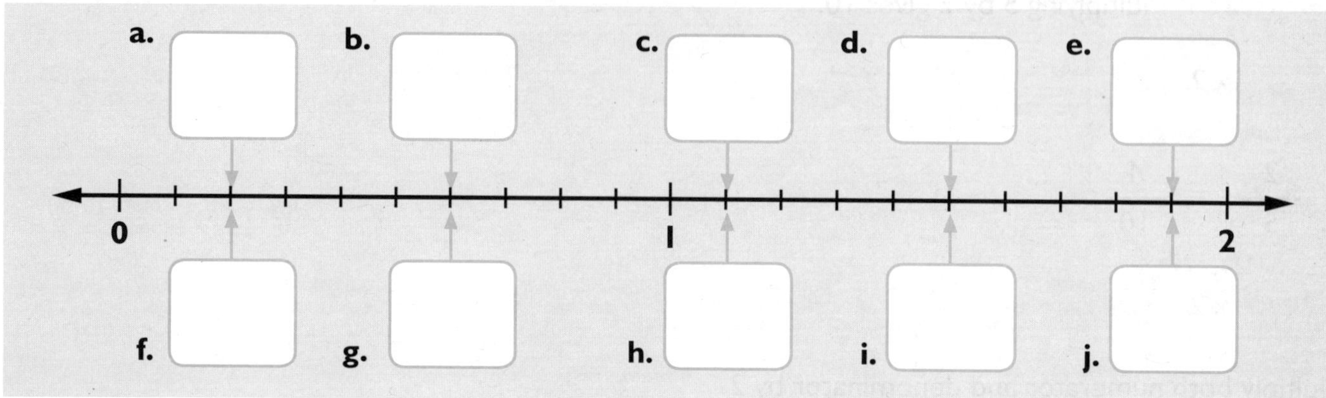

2.

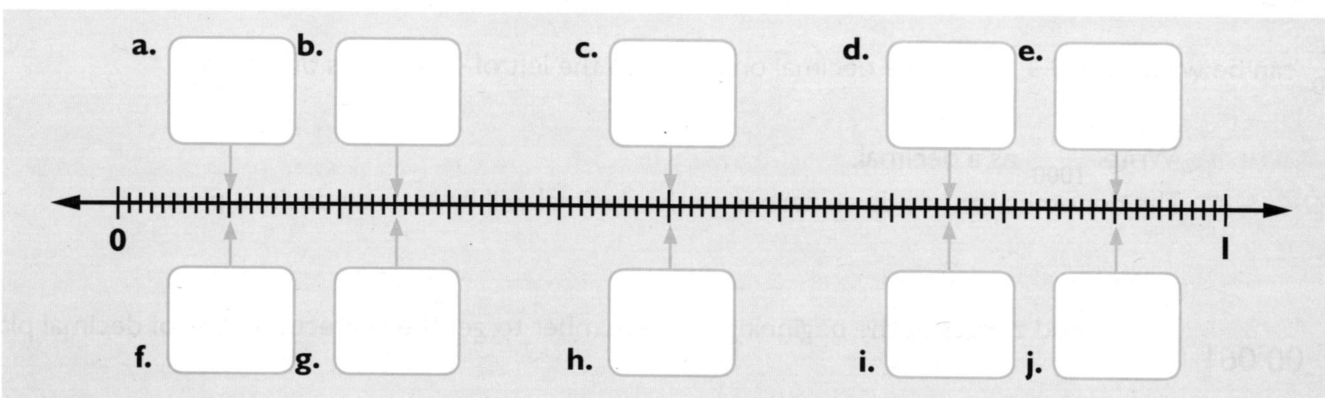

3.

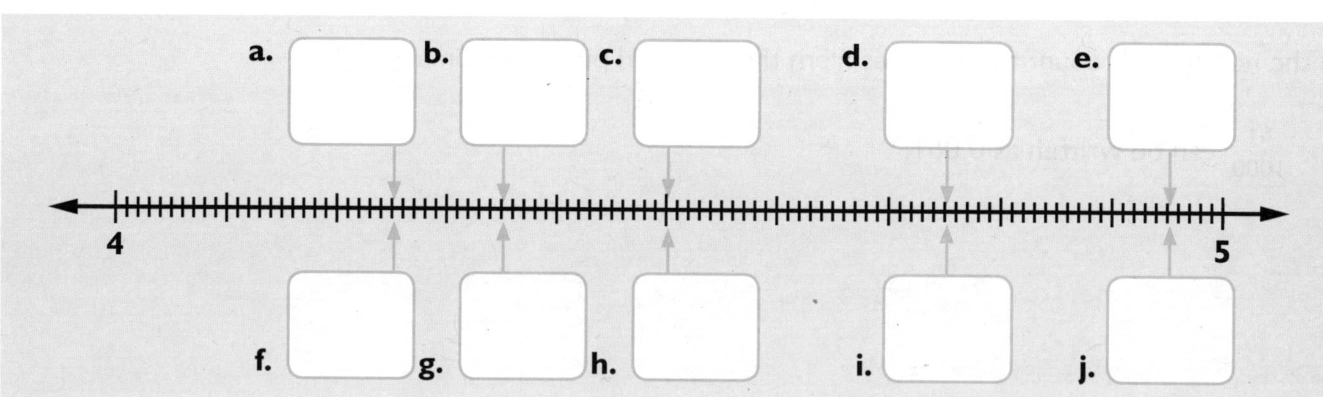

4.

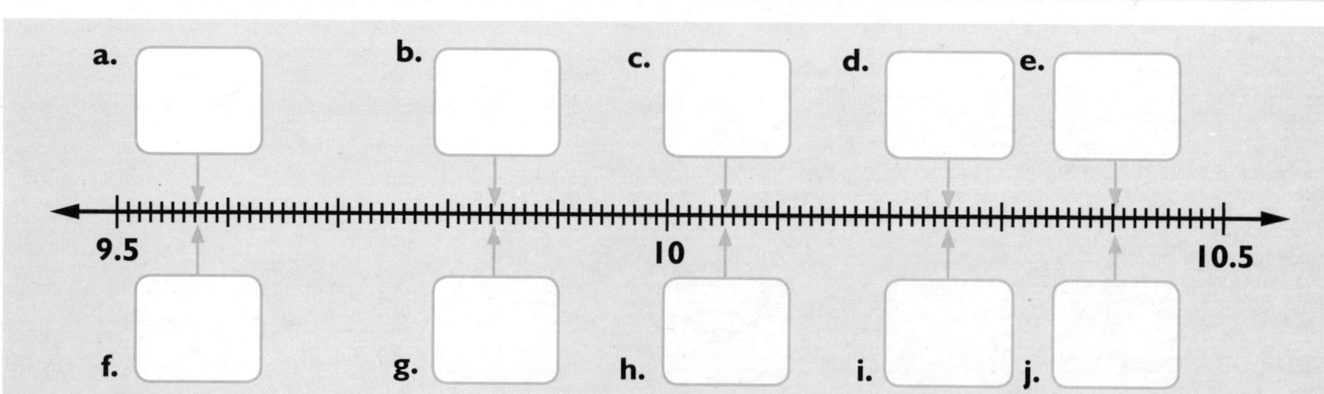

Place a ✓on the fractions you wrote in Questions 1 and 2 that you could round to 1.

Relating Common and Decimal Fractions

1. Colour each square to show the fraction. Then complete the sentences.

a. Colour $\frac{1}{2}$ of each

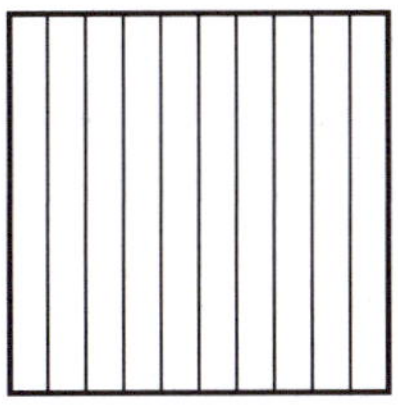

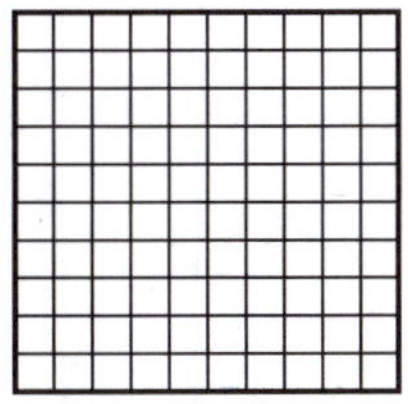

$\frac{1}{2}$ is the same as $\frac{\quad}{100}$

$\frac{1}{2}$ is the same as **0.**____

b. Colour $\frac{1}{10}$ of each

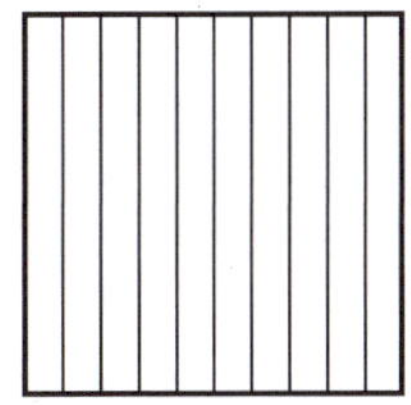

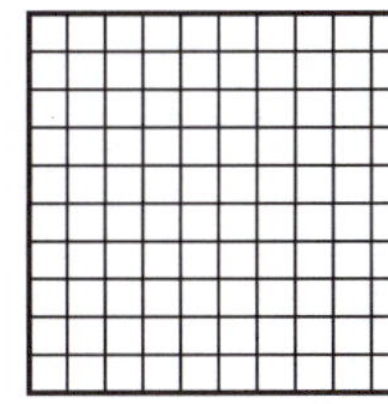

$\frac{1}{10}$ is the same as $\frac{\quad}{100}$

$\frac{1}{10}$ is the same as **0.**____

c. Colour $\frac{1}{5}$ of each

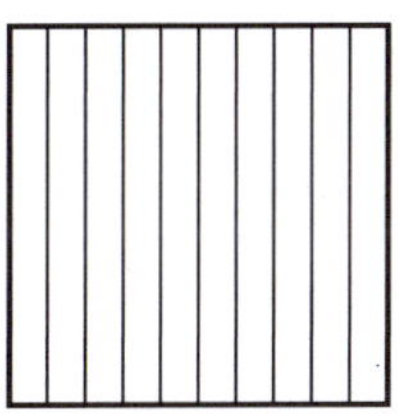

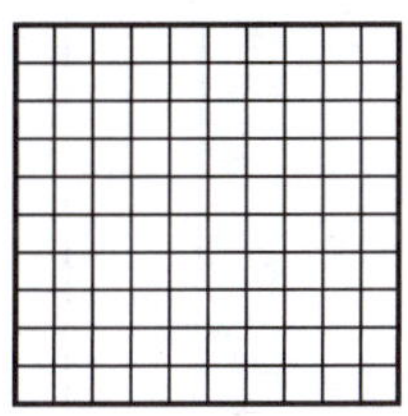

$\frac{1}{5}$ is the same as $\frac{\quad}{100}$

$\frac{1}{5}$ is the same as **0.**____

d. Colour $\frac{4}{5}$ of each

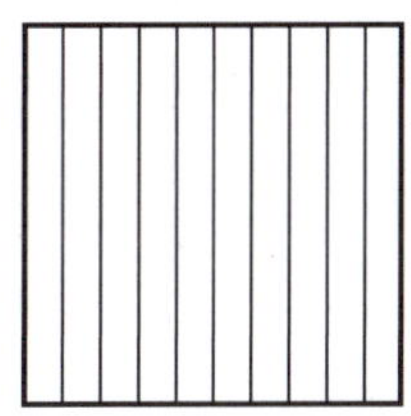

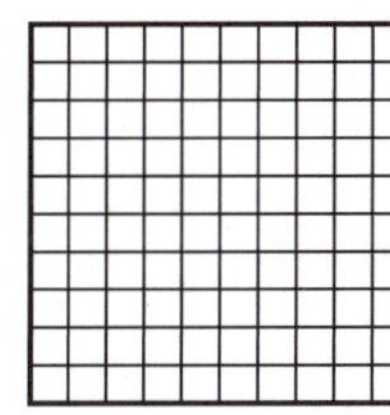

$\frac{4}{5}$ is the same as $\frac{\quad}{100}$

$\frac{4}{5}$ is the same as **0.**____

2. Colour the square to show the fraction. Then complete the sentences.

a. Colour $\frac{1}{4}$

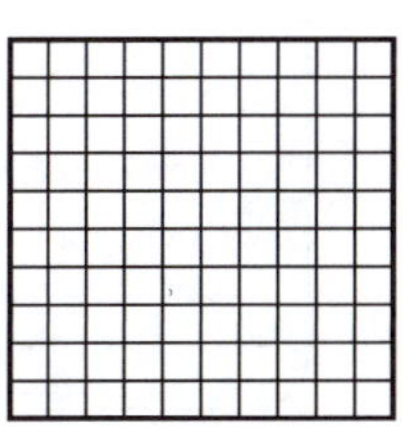

$\frac{1}{4}$ is the same as $\frac{\quad}{100}$

$\frac{1}{4}$ is the same as **0.**____

b. Colour $\frac{3}{4}$

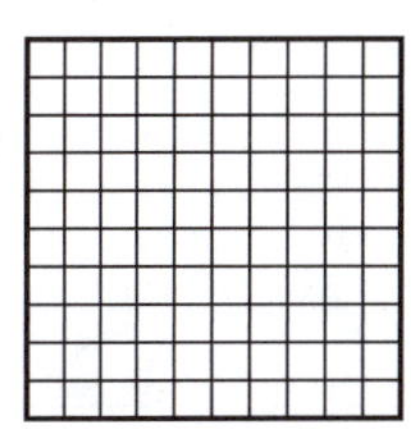

$\frac{3}{4}$ is the same as $\frac{\quad}{100}$

$\frac{3}{4}$ is the same as **0.**____

Look at Question 1. Write as decimal fractions the fractions involving fifths that are not shown on this page.

Relating Common and Decimal Fractions

1. Shade the decimal fraction. Then write the common fraction.

a. 0.05 $\frac{5}{100}$

b. 0.8

c. 0.45

d. 0.55

e. 0.95

f. 0.15

2. Shade the common fraction. Then write the decimal fraction.

a. $\frac{65}{100}$

b. $\frac{10}{100}$

c. $\frac{35}{100}$

3. Write a decimal fraction that is either equal or close to

a. $\frac{1}{3}$ ________ **b.** $\frac{3}{4}$ ________ **c.** $\frac{1}{2}$ ________ **d.** $\frac{1}{4}$ ________

For each square, write the decimal fraction that is not shaded.

1. Draw arrows to show where each decimal fraction is positioned on the number line.

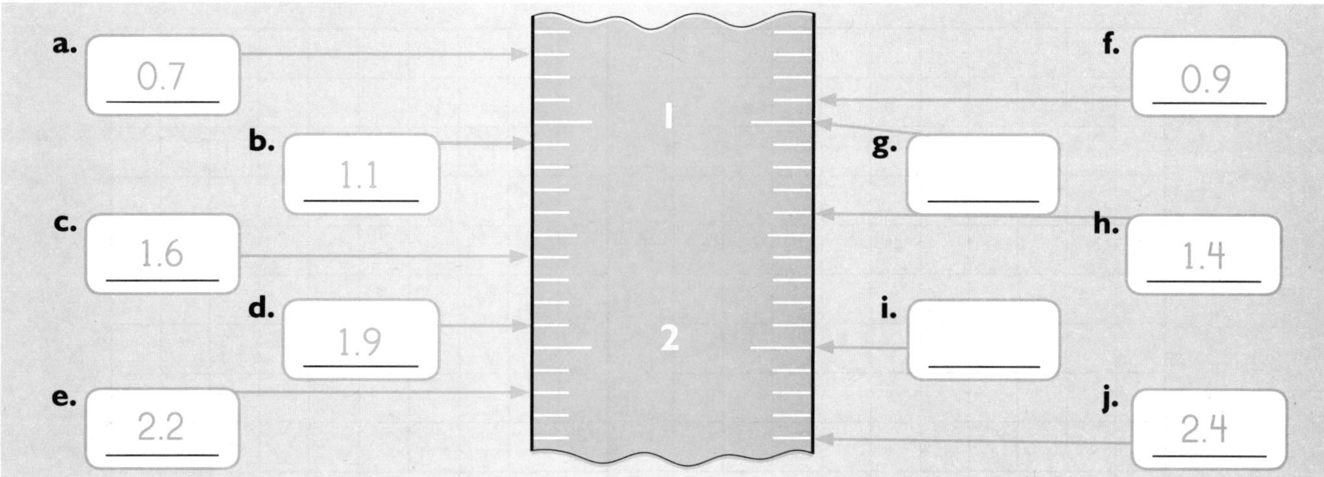

2. Write the decimal fraction in the box or draw an arrow to show where the number is located on the number line.

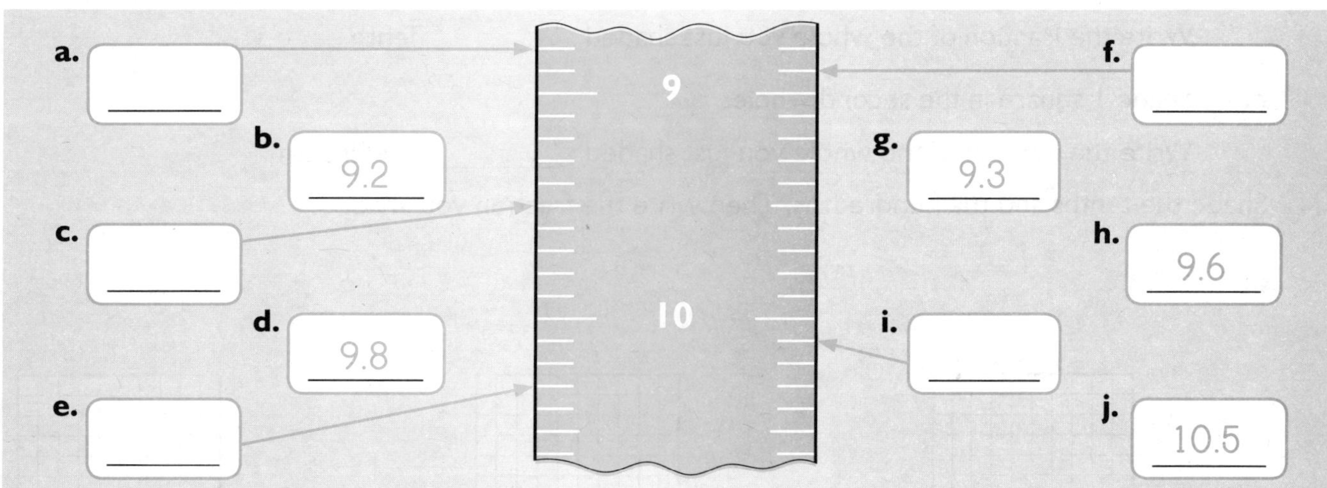

3. Write the decimal fraction in the box or draw an arrow to show where the number is located on the number line.

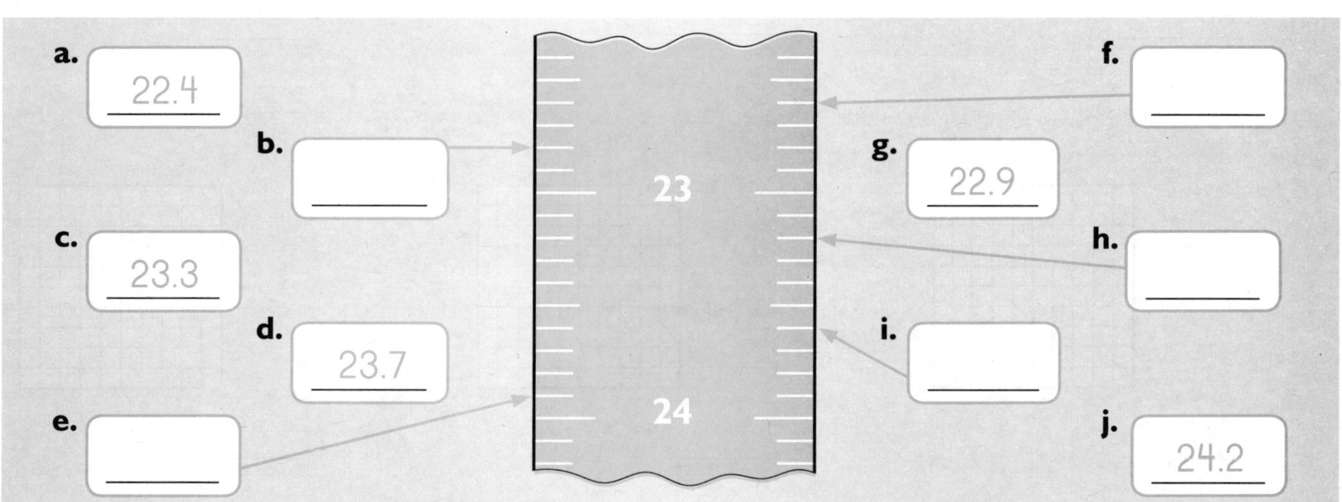

Look at the number line in Question 1. Write the number of Tenths that are missing between 0 and 1.

Working with Hundredths

1. **a.** This picture shows 2 wholes. Shade 1 whole.

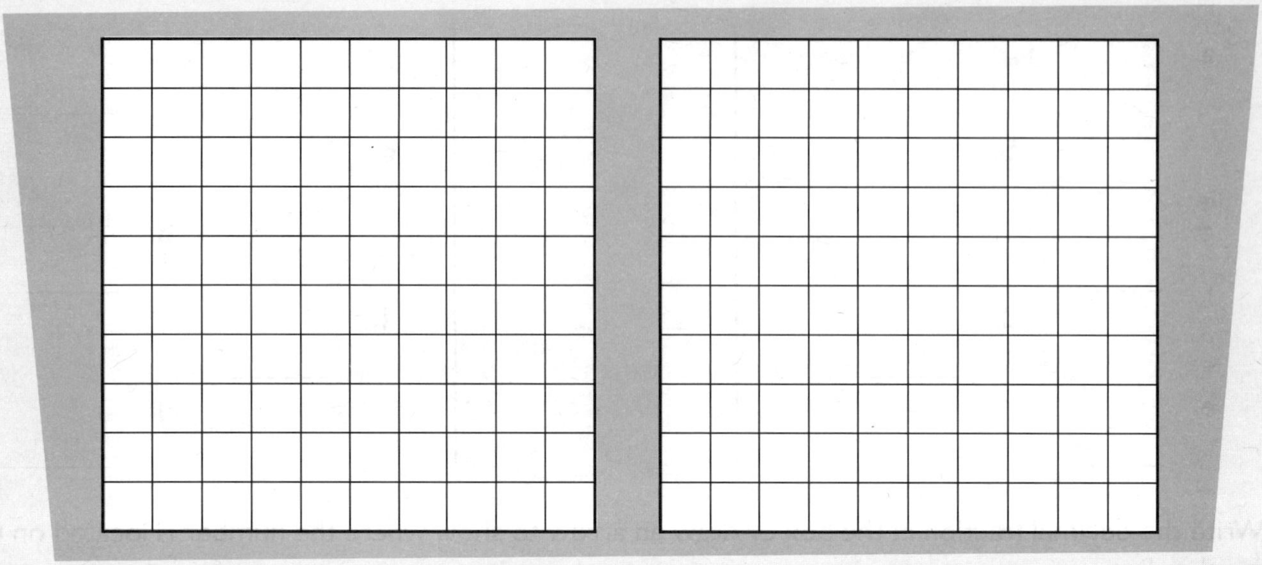

b. Shade 1 column in the second whole.

Write the fraction of the whole you just shaded. ______ Tenth

c. Shade 1 square in the second whole.

Write the fraction of the whole you just shaded. ______ Hundredth

2. Shade the tenths and the hundredths. Then write the fraction you shaded.

a. 2 Tenths
4 Hundredths

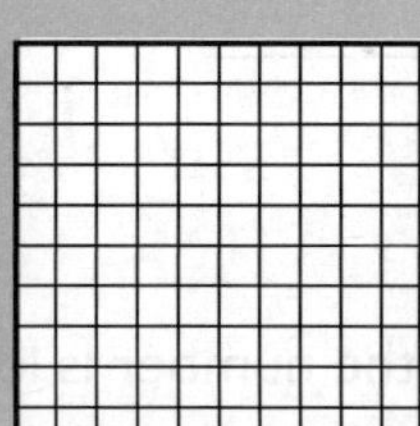

______ Hundredths

b. 6 Tenths
1 Hundredth

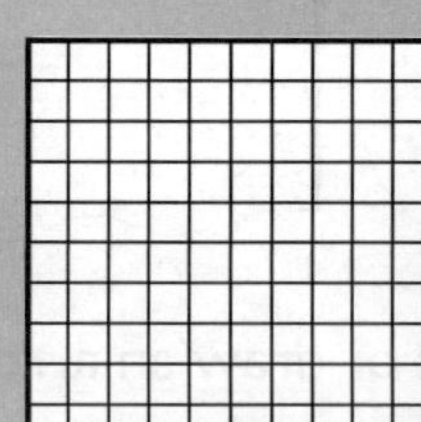

______ Hundredths

c. 3 Tenths
7 Hundredths

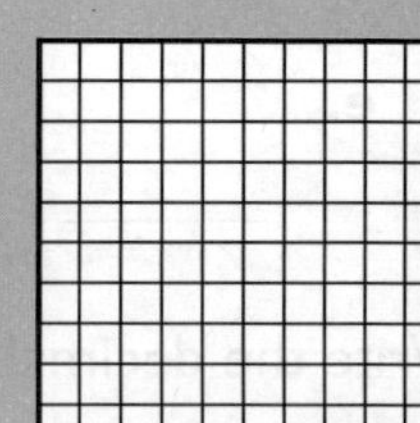

______ Hundredths

d. 5 Tenths
9 Hundredths

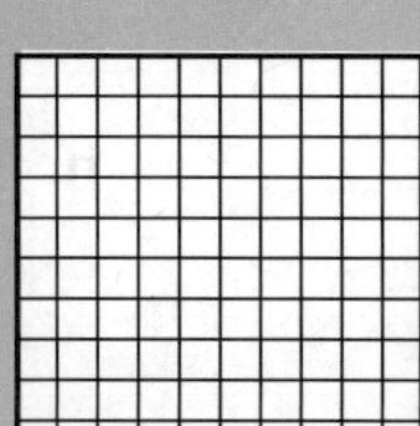

______ Hundredths

e. 9 Tenths
2 Hundredths

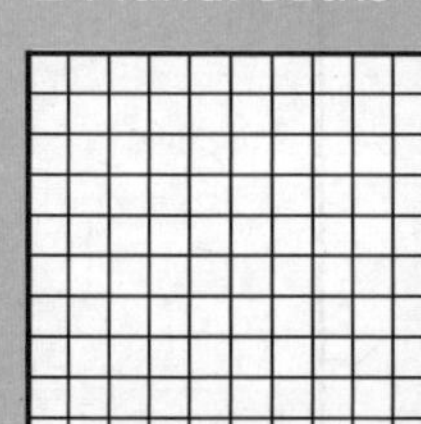

______ Hundredths

f. 1 Tenth
5 Hundredths

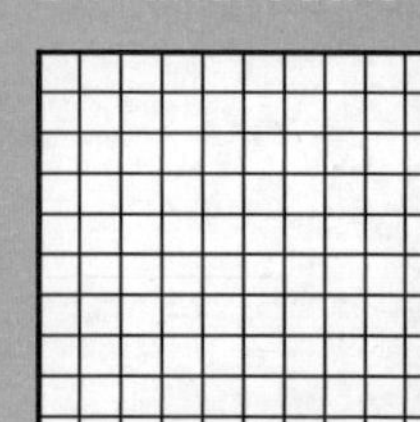

______ Hundredths

For each picture in Question 2, write the fraction that is not shaded.

Locating Tenths and Hundredths on a Number Line

Each arrow points to a number. Write each number as a decimal fraction.

1.

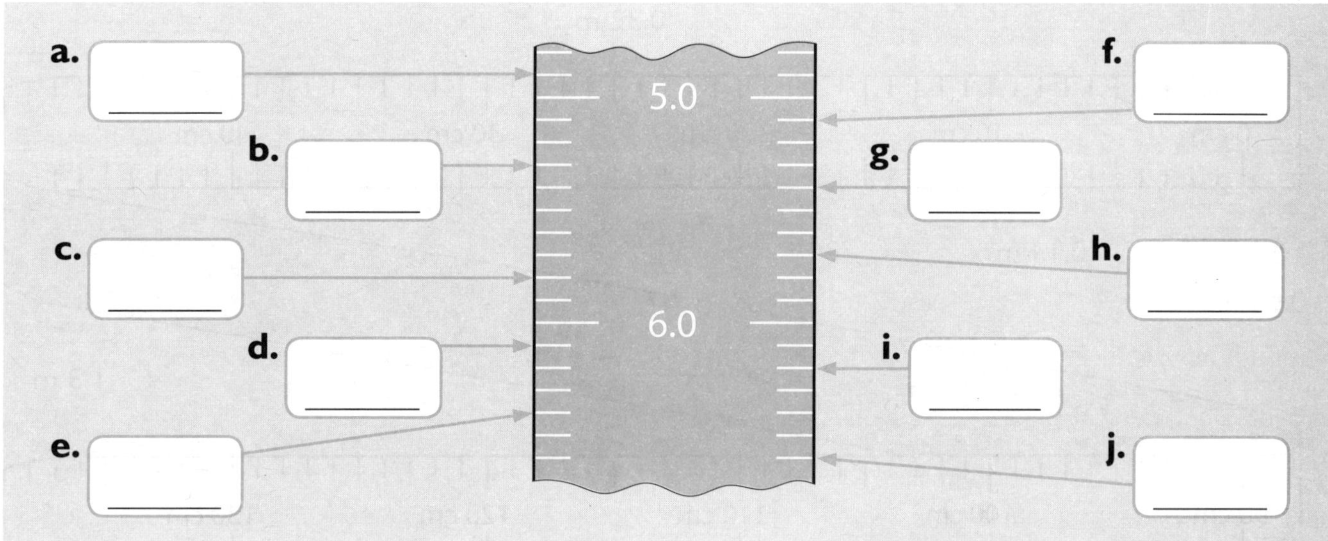

2.

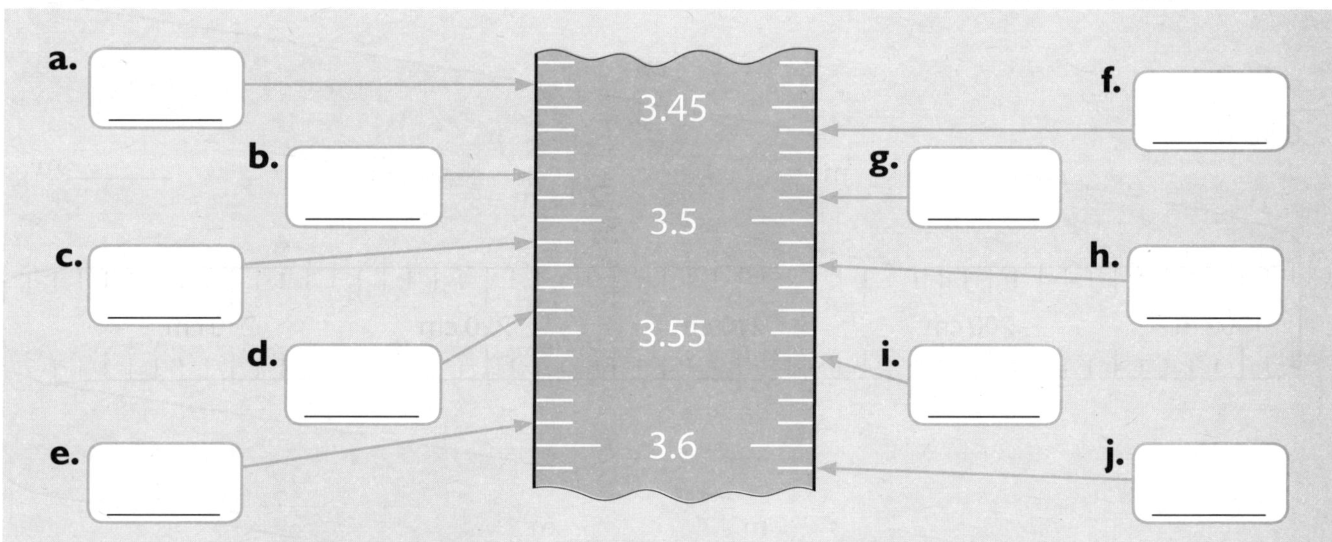

3.

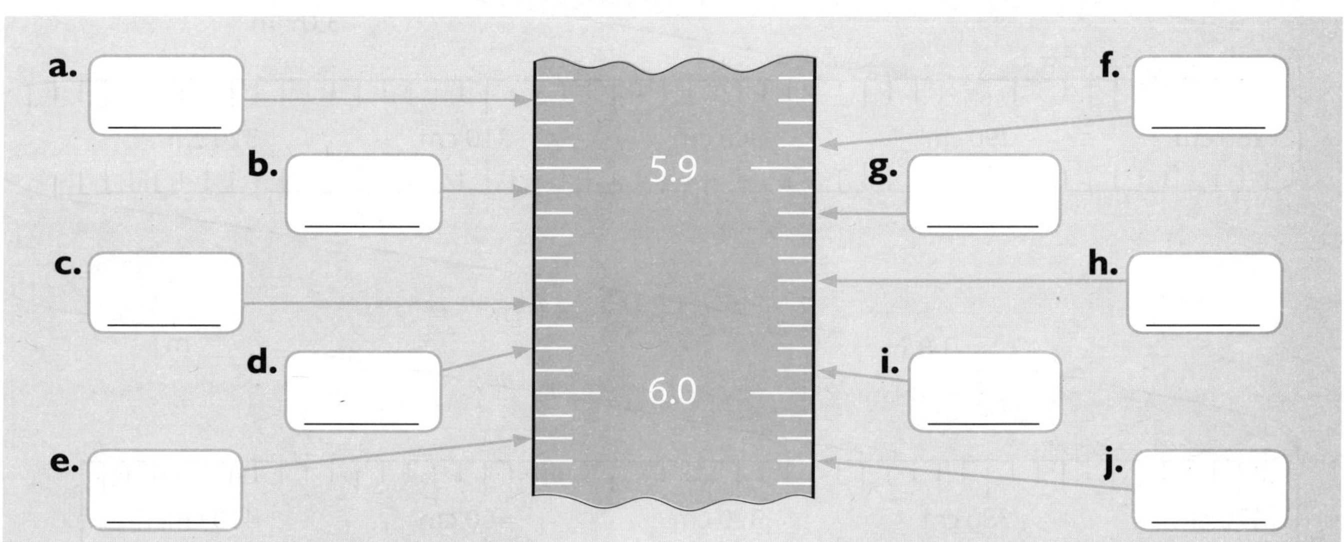

Write the two numbers that are one-tenth more than and less than 7. Then write two numbers that are between 7 and each of those numbers.

Locating Hundredths on a Number Line

Worksheet 54

1. Write the decimal fraction in the box or draw an arrow to show where the number is located on the number strip.

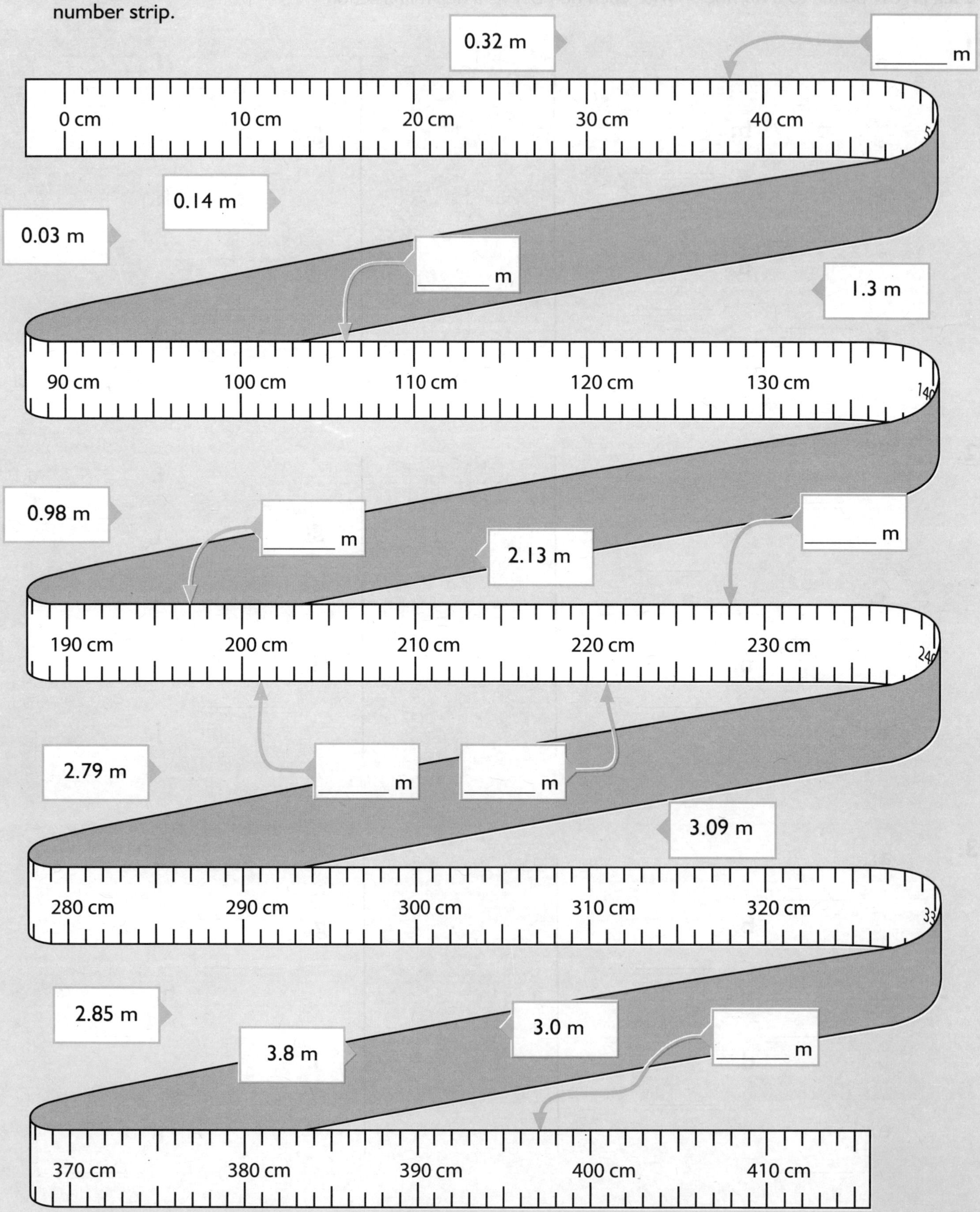

Write each of these lengths in metres:

a. 120 centimetres b. 375 centimetres

Reading and Writing Hundredths

1. Read the number words. Write the number on the expander and then, write the numeral.

a. three and seventeen-hundredths — ones . hundredths

b. three and seven-hundredths — ones . hundredths

c. seven and three-hundredths — ones . hundredths

2. Read the number. Then write the numeral.

a. three and five-hundredths

b. six and twenty-hundredths

c. seven and five-hundredths

d. fifty-three hundredths

e. two and sixty-one hundredths

f. seven and thirteen-hundredths

3. Read the numeral. Then write the numeral in words.

a. 7.06

b. 9.5

c. 1.6

d. 0.43

e. 12.8

f. 3.11

Use combinations of 6, 0 and 1 to write 3 different numbers that are less than 2. Write each number in words.

Shade the squares to show the number.

Then write the number on the expanders.

The first two are shaded for you.

a. two and thirty-five hundredths

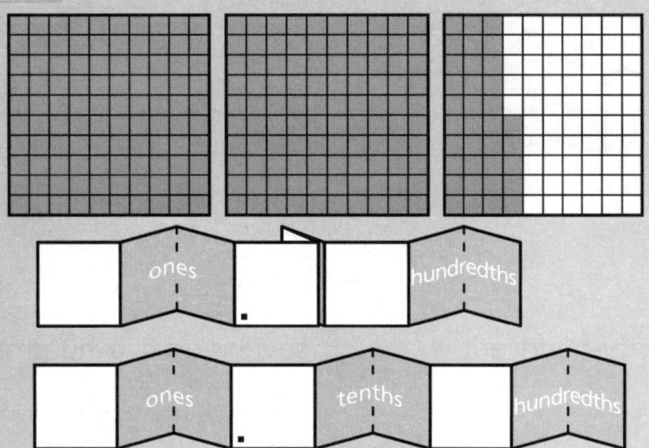

b. one and twenty-nine hundredths

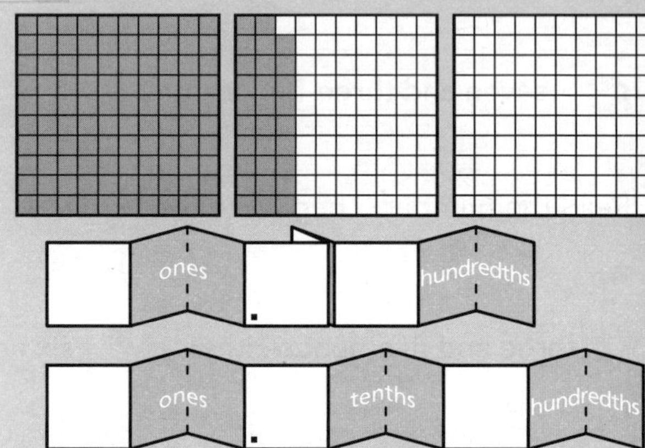

c. two and twenty-six hundredths

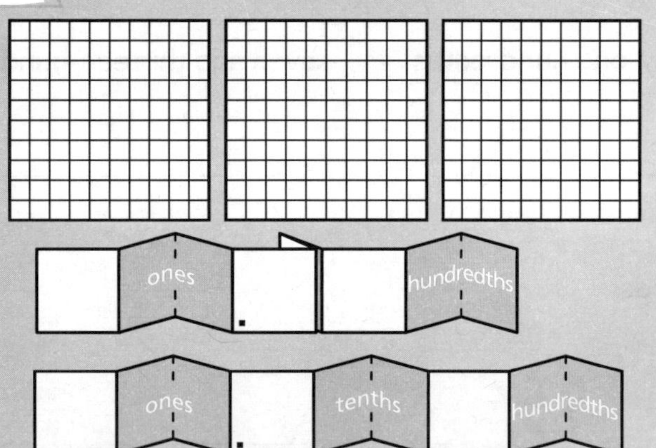

d. one and forty-two hundredths

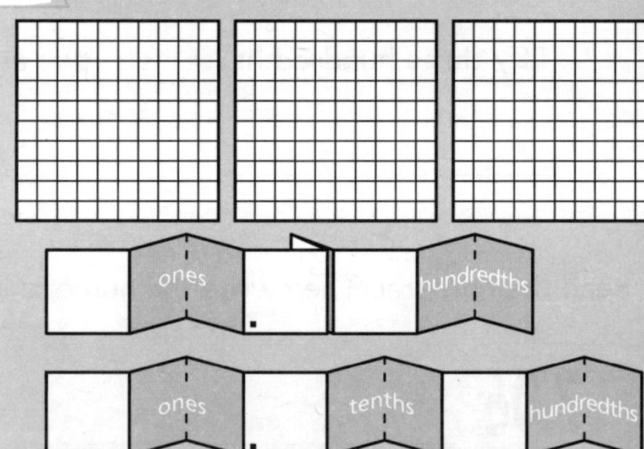

e. one and seventy-three hundredths

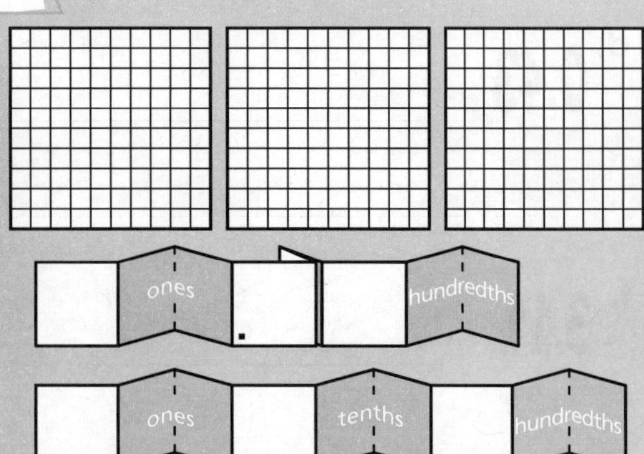

f. two and fifty-eight hundredths

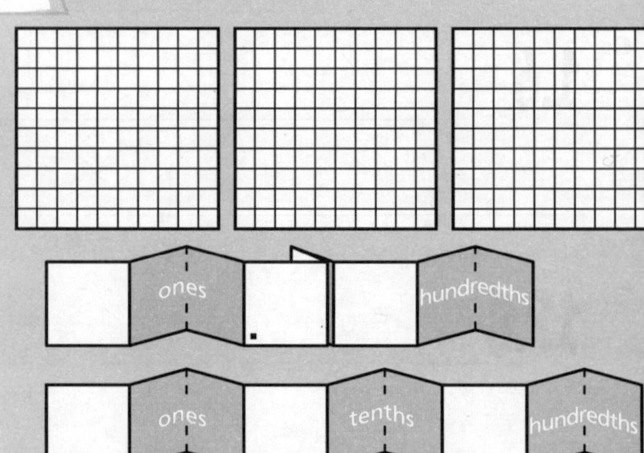

Which number shown above is closest to 2? How did you decide?

Working with Thousandths

1. a. This picture shows two wholes. Shade one whole.

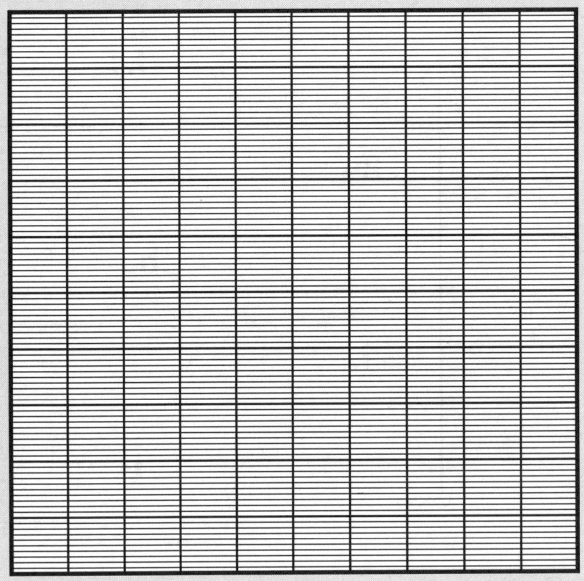

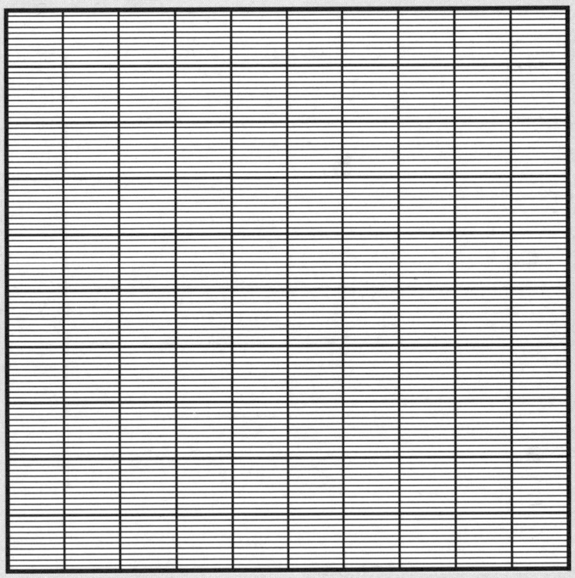

b. Shade these parts of the unshaded whole. Write the decimal fraction of the whole you shaded.

Shade 1 column. ______ Shade 1 square. ______ Shade 1 row of a square. ______

2. Shade parts of the whole to show the fraction on the expander.
Then, write the decimal fraction.

a.

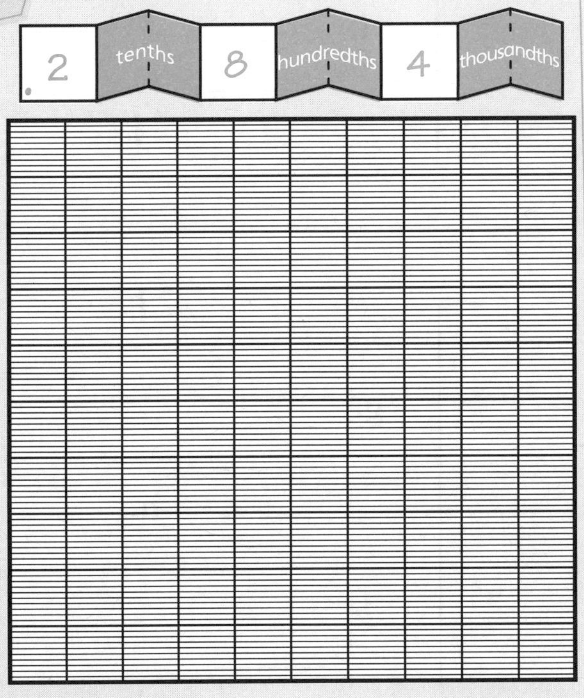

______

b.

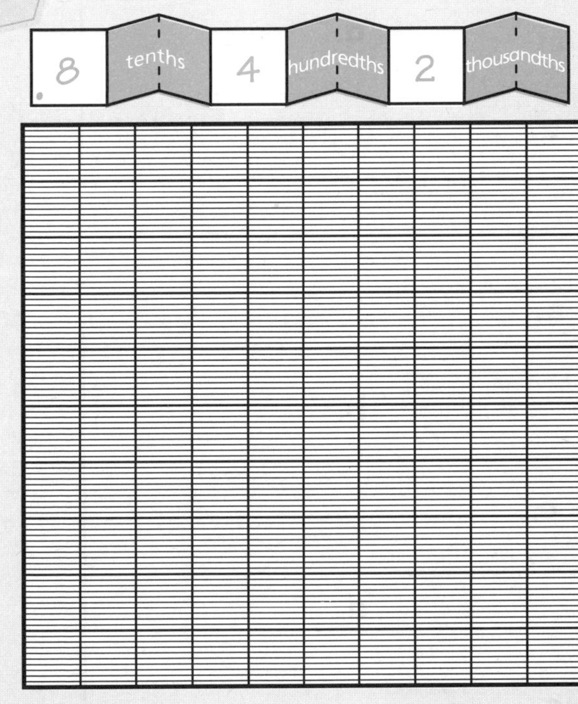

______

For each picture in Question 2, write the decimal fraction that is not shaded.

Locating Thousandths on a Number Line

Each arrow points to a number. Write each number as a decimal fraction.

1

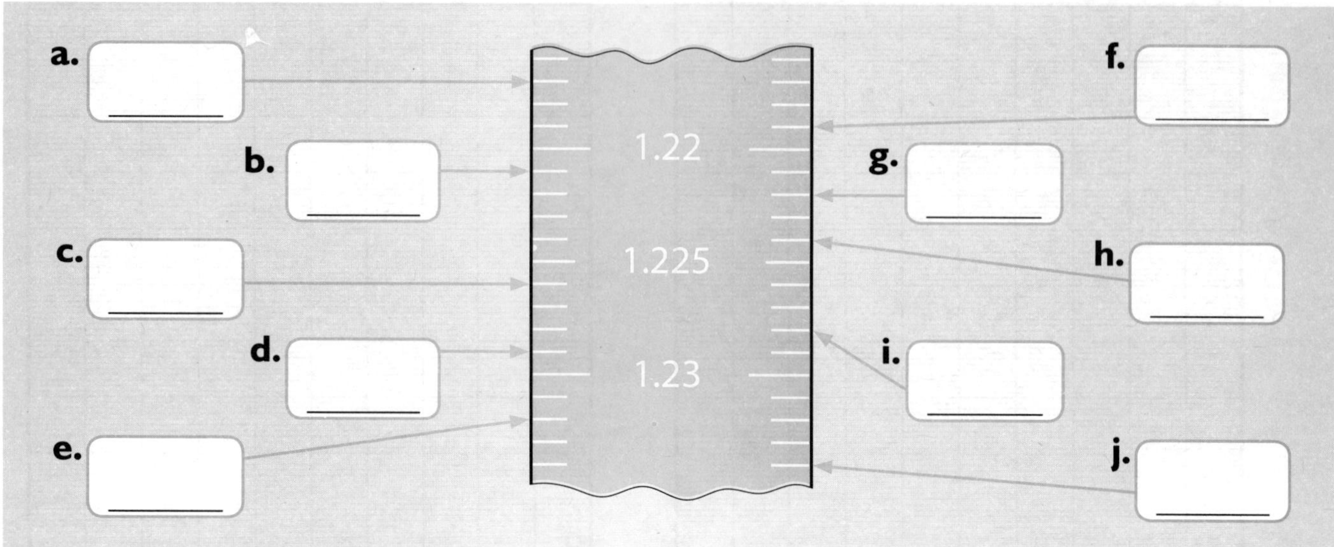

2

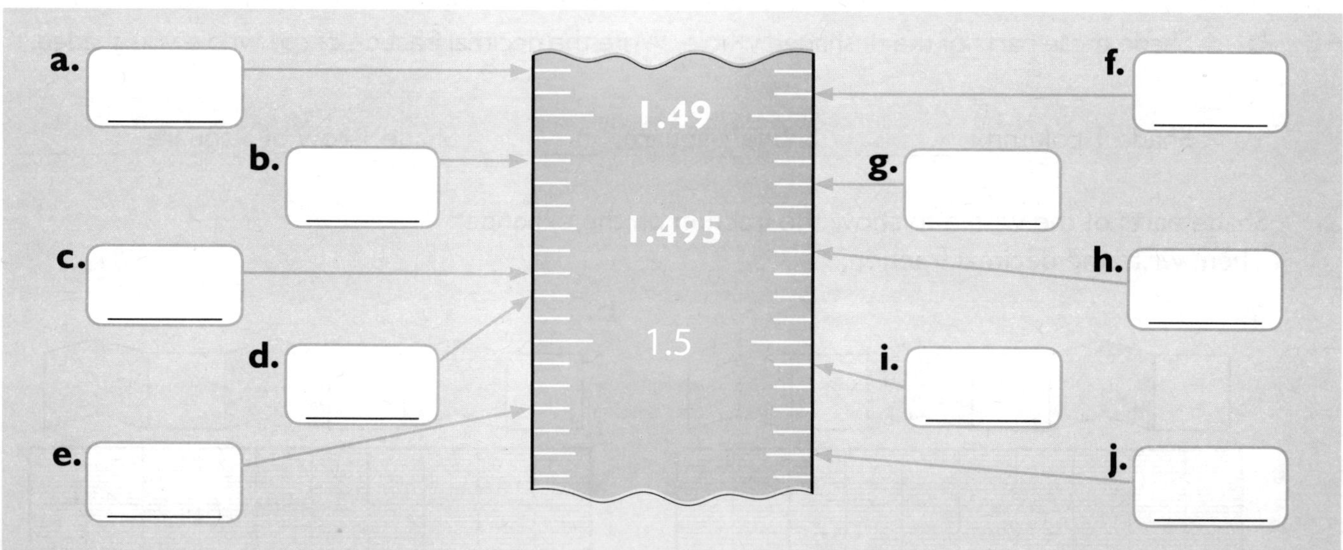

3

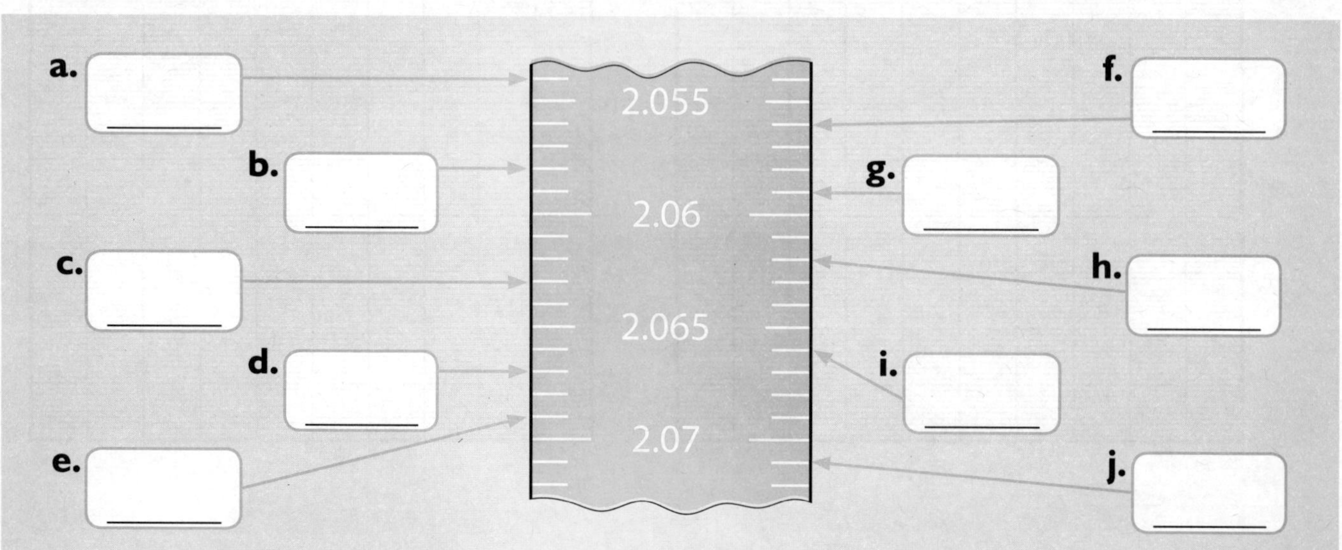

Write the two numbers that are one-hundredth more than and less than 4.5. Then write two numbers that are between 4.5 and each of those numbers.

Locating Thousandths on a Number Line

Each arrow points to a number. Write each number as a decimal fraction.

1.

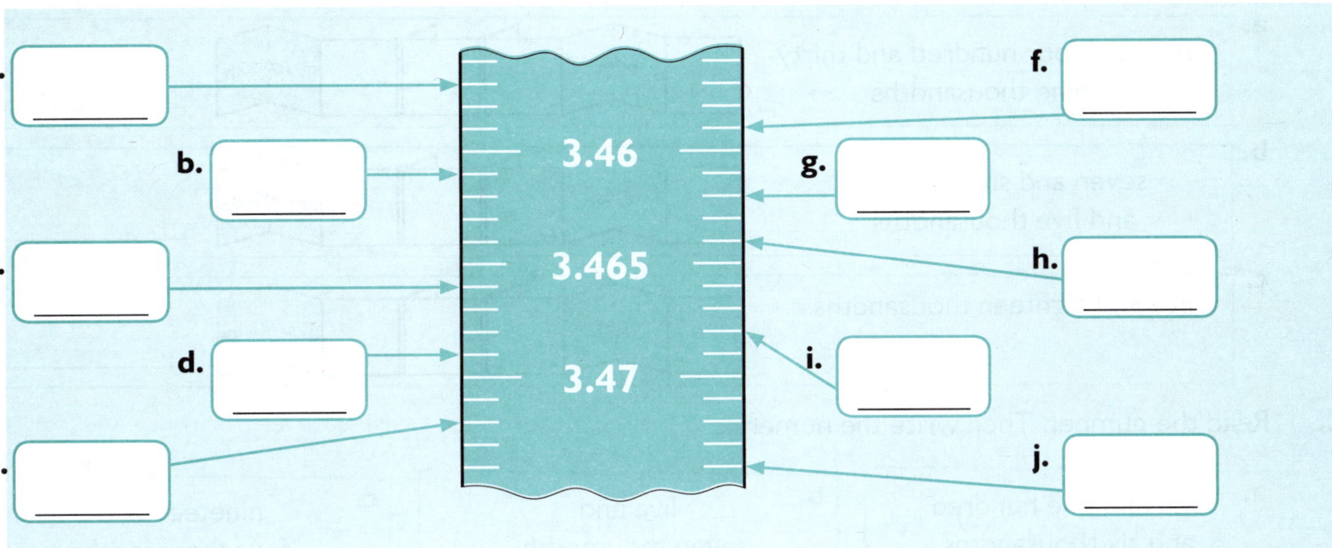

2.

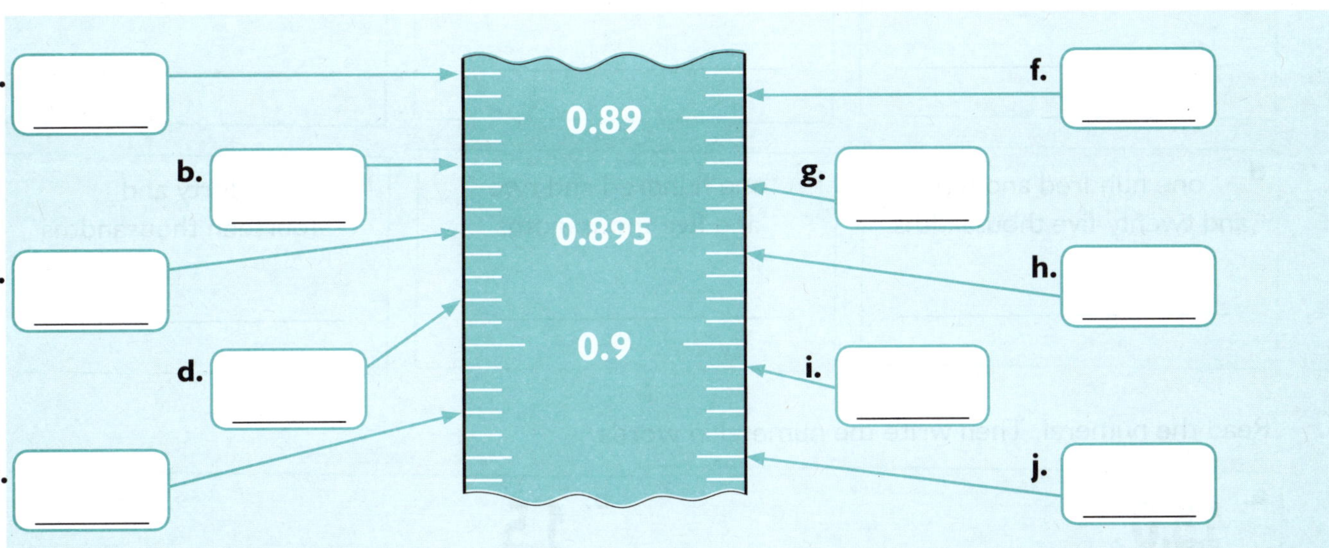

3.

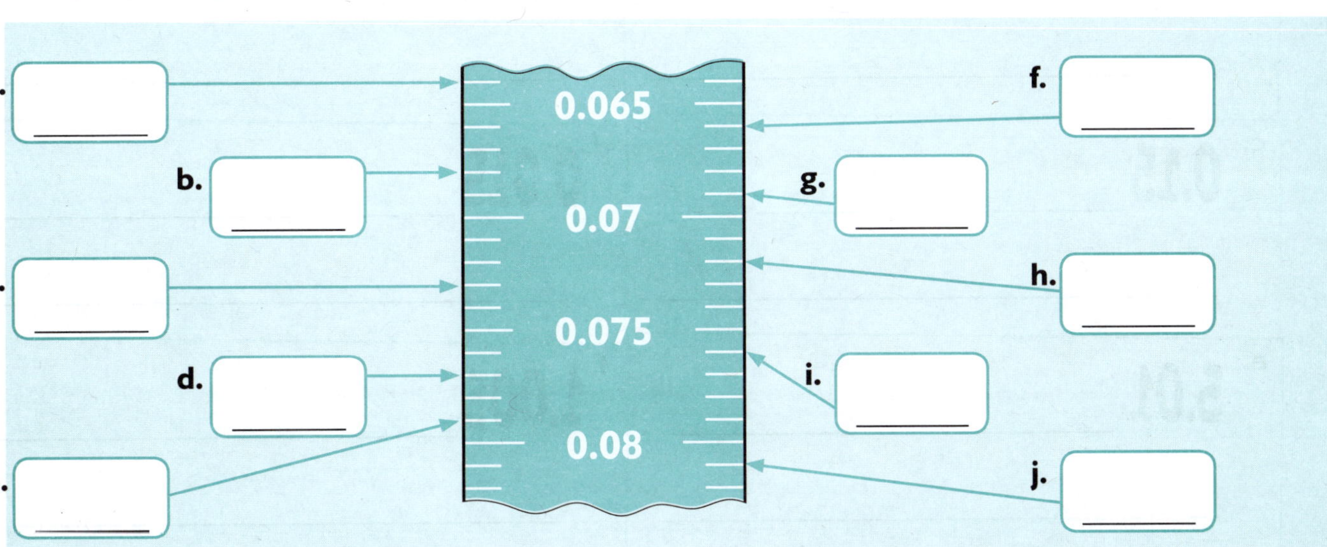

Write a number that is one-hundredth more than and less than 3.7.
Then write a number that is between 3.7 and each of those numbers.

Reading and Writing Thousandths

Worksheet 60

1. Read the number. Write the digits on the expander and then write the numeral.

a. two and four hundred and thirty-nine thousandths

	ones	.			thousandths

______

b. seven and six hundred and five thousandths

	ones	.			thousandths

______

c. five and eighteen thousandths

	ones	.			thousandths

______

2. Read the number. Then write the numeral.

a. one and one hundred and six thousandths ______

b. five and seven thousandths ______

c. nineteen and four thousandths ______

d. one hundred and ten and twenty-five thousandths ______

e. one hundred and two and five thousandths ______

f. forty and fourteen thousandths ______

3. Read the numeral. Then write the numeral in words.

a. **15.0** ______

b. **1.5** ______

c. **0.15** ______

d. **0.015** ______

e. **5.01** ______

f. **1.005** ______

FF **Look at the numerals in Question 3. Write some other numerals you can make using the digits 0, 1 and 5.**

Relating Tenths, Hundredths and Thousandths

Worksheet 61

1. Write the numerals on the expanders. Then write the number in words.

a. Write 3.2

3	ones	. 2	tenths

three and two-tenths

	ones	.		hundredths

	ones	.			thousandths

b. Write 5.7

	ones	.	tenths

	ones	.		hundredths

	ones	.			thousandths

2. Read the number names. Write the numerals on the expander and then write the number.

a. four and six hundred and fifty-two thousandths

	ones	.			thousandths

b. nine and two hundred and thirty-one thousandths

	ones	.			thousandths

c. five and three hundred and sixty-one thousandths

	ones	.			thousandths

d. seven and eighty-five thousandths

	ones	.			thousandths

e. two and four hundred and eleven thousandths

	ones	.			thousandths

Use combinations of 2, 4, 5 and 9 to write 3 different numbers that are greater than 2 but less than 3. Write each number in words.

Sequencing Tenths and Hundredths

Worksheet 62

1. This is a chunk of a number board. Complete the next row.

3.01	3.02	3.03	3.04	3.05	3.06	3.07	3.08	3.09	3.1
3.11	3.12	3.13	3.14	3.15	3.16	3.17	3.18	3.19	3.2
____	____	____	____	____	____	____	____	____	____

2. Complete the missing numbers from these pieces of the same board.

a.

	____	
____	3.48	____
	____	

b.

	____	
____	3.15	____
	____	

c.

	____	
____	3.49	____
	____	

d.

	____	
____	3.59	____
	____	

e.

	____	
____	3.95	____
	____	

f.

	____	
____	3.98	____
	____	

g.

	____	
____	6.09	____
	____	

h.

	____	
____	7.02	____
	____	

i.

	____	
____	7.99	____
	____	

j.

	____	
____	5.19	____
	____	

k.

	____	
____	5.89	____
	____	

l.

	____	
____	5.99	____
	____	

Draw a piece of a number board like those above.
Write 9.999 in the centre. Then write the missing numbers.

Long Jump

	1st jump	2nd jump	3rd jump
Chaman	3.45 m	3.87 m	3.18 m
Bunty	4.06 m	4.15 m	4.27 m
Sujata	3.38 m	3.5 m	3.42 m
Vani	3.21 m	3.86 m	2.97 m
Akul	4.3 m	4.51 m	4.04 m

1. Write the greatest distance that each student jumped.

a. Chaman	**b.** Bunty	**c.** Sujata	**d.** Vani	**e.** Akul

2. Write the distances for these students' second and third jumps.
Then write **is greater than** or **is less than** to make each one true.

a.

2nd	Vani	3rd

b.

2nd	Sujata	3rd

3. Write each student's jumps in order from longest to shortest.

	Longest		Shortest
a. Chaman			
b. Bunty			
c. Sujata			
d. Vani			
e. Akul			

4. Who recorded

a. the longest jump? ___________

b. the shortest jump? ___________

Look at the first column of numbers in Question 3. Write the numbers in order from greatest to least.

1. For each number below:

- Draw a line to show where you think it is on the number line.
- Write the whole number that is closest.

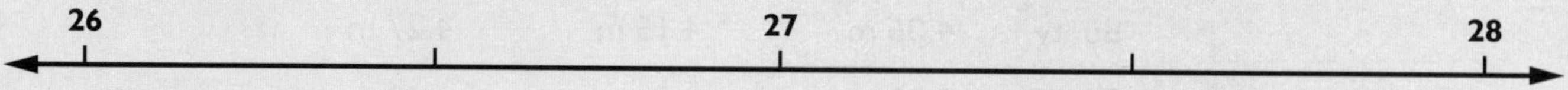

a. **26.4** _____ b. **26.2** _____ c. **26.8** _____ d. **27.3** _____ e. **27.6** _____ f. **27.9** _____

2. Repeat the same steps for this number line.

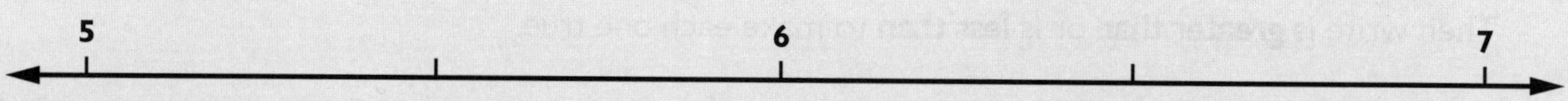

a. **5.27** _____ b. **5.48** _____ c. **5.76** _____ d. **6.09** _____ e. **6.35** _____ f. **6.70** _____

3. For each number below:

- Draw a line to show where you think it is on the number line.
- Round each number to the nearest tenth and write that number.

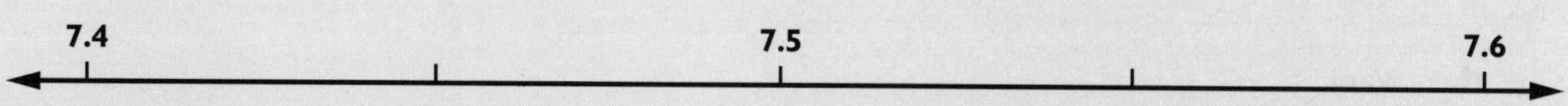

a. **7.43** _____ b. **7.46** _____ c. **7.48** _____ d. **7.51** _____ e. **7.54** _____ f. **7.57** _____

Write five numbers you would round to 9.8.

Ordering Decimal Fractions

Draw arrows to show the relative position of these numbers on the empty number line.
Then, rewrite the numbers in order from least to greatest.

a. 0.24 0.32 0.27

______ ______ ______

b. 0.56 0.7 0.6

______ ______ ______

c. 0.213 0.425 0.356

______ ______ ______

d. 0.782 0.728 0.756

______ ______ ______

e. 0.25 0.275 0.205

______ ______ ______

f. 0.356 0.4 0.23

______ ______ ______

g. 0.5 0.425 0.475 0.45 0.54 0.505

______ ______ ______ ______ ______ ______

FF Write the numbers on this page that are between one-hundredth more and one-hundredth less than 0.5.

Working with Relative Position

1. Write how far away each number is from the nearest **tenth**. You can draw arrows to help.

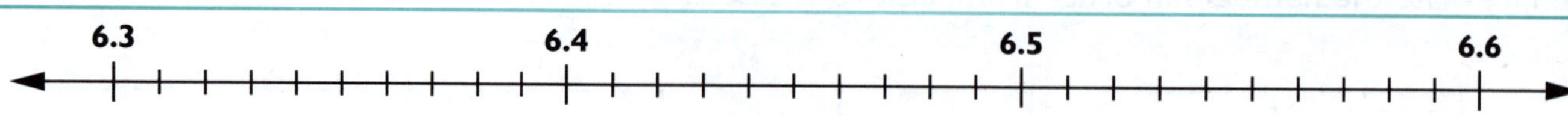

a. 6.34 ______

b. 6.37 ______

c. 6.46 ______

d. 6.48 ______

e. 6.52 ______

f. 6.59 ______

2. Write how far away each number is from the nearest **whole number**.

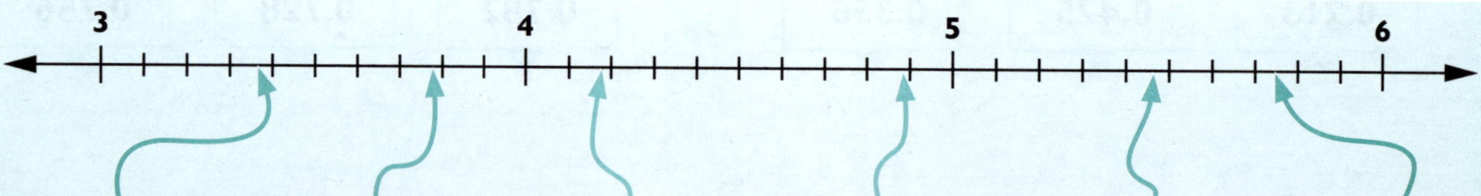

a. 3.37 ______

b. 3.78 ______

c. 4.18 ______

d. 4.89 ______

e. 5.46 ______

f. 5.75 ______

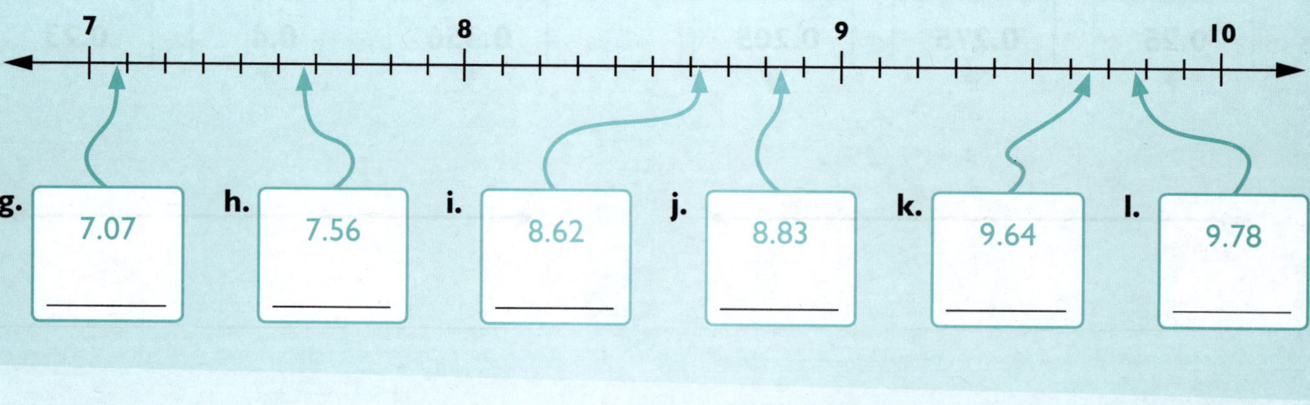

g. 7.07 ______

h. 7.56 ______

i. 8.62 ______

j. 8.83 ______

k. 9.64 ______

l. 9.78 ______

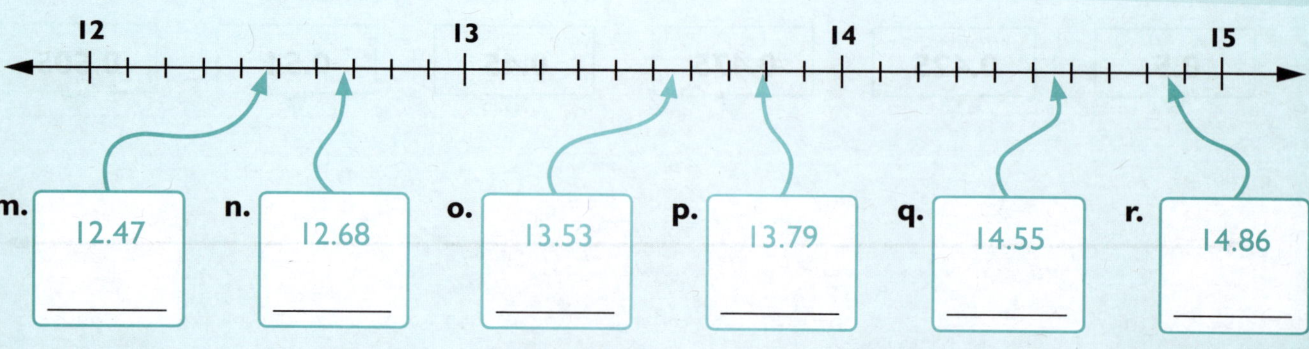

m. 12.47 ______

n. 12.68 ______

o. 13.53 ______

p. 13.79 ______

q. 14.55 ______

r. 14.86 ______

Draw a ✓ on the numbers in Question 2 that are less than 0.2 away from a whole number.

Working with Decimals

Adding Decimals

To add decimal numbers:

- Line up the places taking care that the decimal points are in the same column.
- If the numbers being added are not like decimals, add zeroes to the end of the number to make them like decimals.
- As usual, in addition, start on the right, and add each column in turn.
- Bring the decimal point down in the answer.

Example: 467.5 + 9.78

9.78 has two decimal places but 467.5 has only one.

So, add a zero to make it 467.50, to get like decimals.

	1	1			
4	6	7	.	5	0
+		9	.	7	8
4	7	7	.	2	8

Remember, for a whole number the decimal point lies just to the right of the ones column.

Example: 59 can also be written as 59.0

Subtracting Decimals

To subtract decimal numbers:

- Line up the places taking care that the decimal points are in the same column.
- If the numbers being subtracted are not like decimals, add zeroes to the end of the number to make them like decimals
- Subtract each column, starting with the right column.
- Place the decimal point in the answer directly below the decimal points in the terms.

Example: 827.003 - 739.67

		11	16		9	
	7	~~1~~	6		~~10~~	10
	~~8~~	~~2~~	~~7~~	.	~~0~~	~~0~~	3
–	7	3	9	.	6	7
		8	7	.	3	3	3

Multiplying Decimals

Multiplying decimals is just like multiplying whole numbers.

- Multiply the numbers without the decimal point.
- In the product, place the decimal point so that the number of decimal places is equal to the sum of the decimal places of the factors.

Example: Multiply 23.89 by 98.197.

Solution: Multiply the numbers without the decimal point.

the product will have 5 decimal places because 23.89 has 2 decimal places and 98.197 has 3 decimal places.

```
          2 3 8 9
    ×   9 8 1 9 7
    -------------
        1 6 7 2 3
      2 1 5 0 1 0
      2 3 8 9 0 0
    1 9 1 1 2 0 0 0
  2 1 5 0 1 0 0 0 0
  -----------------
  2 3 4 5 9 2 6 3 3
```

$23.89 \times 98.197 = 2345.92633$

Multiplication of a Decimal by 10, 100, 1000 etc.

When a decimal is multiplied by 10, the decimal point moves to the right by one place.

When a decimal is multiplied by 100, the decimal point moves right by two places, and so on.

Remember, the zeroes at the end of the decimal part have no value.

So, if you need, you can add extra zeroes at the end of the decimal part before moving the decimal point.

Example: 3.67×10

Step 1:
3.67 × 10
1 zero

Step 2:
3 . 6 7
Decimal point shifts one place right

Step 3:
3.67 × 10 = 36.7

Similarly, $3.67 \times 100 = 367$

And $3.67 \times 1000 = 3670$ (add zeroes to 36.7 before shifting the decimal point).

Dividing Decimals

To divide a decimal by a whole number:

- Divide it as you would for whole numbers.
- Place the decimal point in the quotient so that it lines up with the decimal point in the dividend.

Example: 13.44 ÷ 12.

Solution: Divide 13.44 by 12 ignoring the decimal point

- Place the decimal point in the quotient so that it lines up with the decimal point in 13.44

```
      1.12
12 ) 13.44
    −12
      14
     −12
      24
     −24
       0
```

So, 13.44 ÷ 12 = 1.12

```
      1.12
12 ) 13.44
```

Dividing decimals by 10, 100 and 1000

When we divide a decimal by 10,000 or 1000, we move the decimal to the left of the zeroes in the divisor.

Example: 6.78 ÷ 10

Since this is a division problem, we are going to move the decimal to the left.

> Add extra zeroes at the beginning (if required) before moving the decimal because the zeroes before the whole part in a number do not matter.

There is one zero in the divisor 10, so we move the decimal one place to the left.
Add a zero before 6 before moving the decimal point.

Step 1

6.78 ÷ 10 = 0.678

Similarly,

6.78 ÷ 100 = 0.0678

0 6 . 7 8

Step 2

0.6 7 8

To divide a decimal by another decimal

- Count the number of decimal places in the divisor.
- Multiply the dividend and divisor by 10, 100, 1000 depending on the number of decimal places in the divisor. If the divisor has one decimal place, multiply by 10. If the divisor has two decimal places, multiply by 100 and so on.
- Divide.

Example: 2.368 ÷ 0.08

Solution:

The divisor 0.08 has two decimal places, so multiply the dividend and divisor by 100.

Now the divisor is a whole number. Divide normally.

$$\frac{2.368}{0.08} = \frac{2.368 \times 100}{0.08 \times 100}$$

$$= \frac{236.8}{8}$$

```
     29.6
8 ) 236.8
    16
     76
     72
      48
      48
       0
```

Place the decimal point in the quotient directly above the decimal point in 236.8

Remember to shift the decimal point of both numbers the same number of places.

1. Calculate the total mass of these bags at the airport. Record the steps you use.

a.

14.6 kg   13.87 kg

Total mass ____________

b.

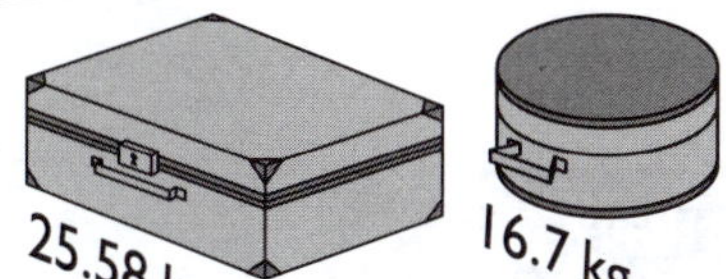

25.58 kg   16.7 kg

Total mass ____________

c.

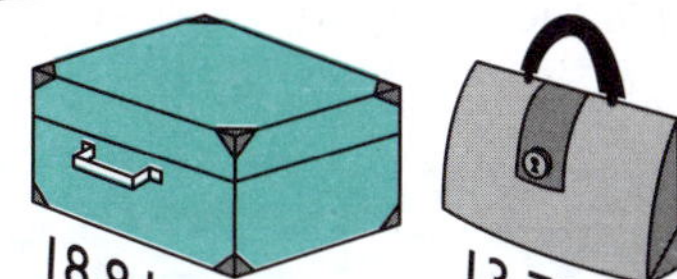

18.8 kg   13.75 kg

Total mass ____________

d.

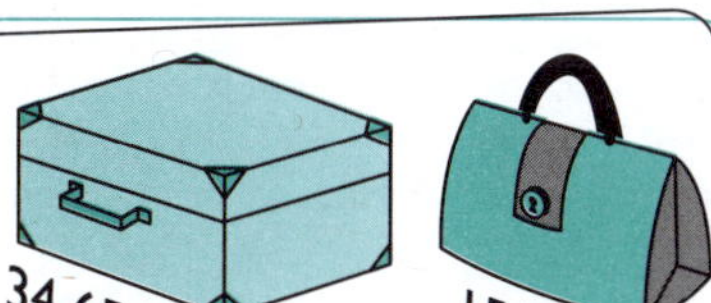

34.65 kg   15.7 kg

Total mass ____________

e.

17.4 kg   21.89 kg

Total mass ____________

f.

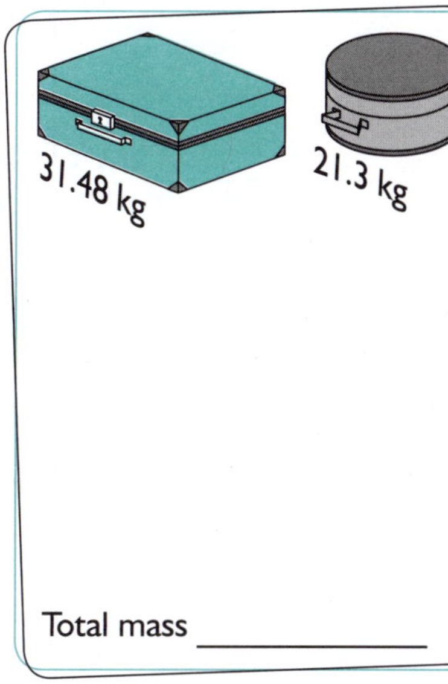

31.48 kg   21.3 kg

Total mass ____________

g.

27.15 kg   14.8 kg

Total mass ____________

h.

19.25 kg   23.9 kg

Total mass ____________

i.

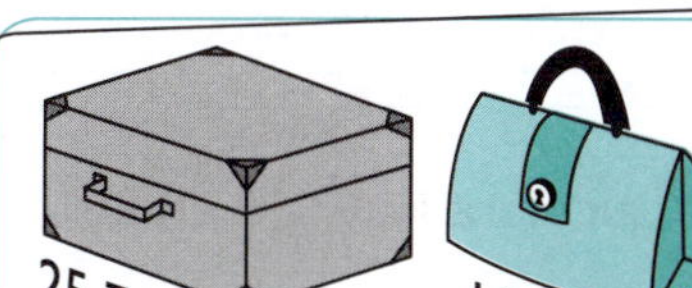

25.7 kg   16.68 kg

Total mass ____________

Place the digits 1 to 6 in the boxes so the answer is close to 30.

□□.□ + □.□□ = ____

Subtracting Tenths

Worksheet 68

1. Calculate how much longer the train journey in Spain is compared to the train journey in

a. Sweden

_______ km

b. Italy

_______ km

c. France

_______ km

d. United Kingdom

_______ km

Fastest Train Journeys

Location	Distance (km)	Average speed (km per hour)
France	203.4	254.3
Germany	93.2	199.7
Italy	261.0	164.9
Japan	192.0	261.8
Spain	470.5	209.1
Sweden	98.0	168.0
UK	303.3	180.2

2. Calculate how much shorter the train journey in Germany is compared to the journey in

a. Italy

_______ km

b. Japan

_______ km

c. UK

_______ km

d. France

_______ km

3. Calculate how much faster the train in Japan travels compared to the trains in

a. Spain

_______ km per hour

b. Sweden

_______ km per hour

c. France

_______ km per hour

d. Italy

_______ km per hour

The fastest record for a train is 515 km per hour. How much faster is this than each average speed above?

Subtracting Tenths and Hundredths

Worksheet 69

TIDE CHART

Day	1st high	2nd high	1st low	2nd low
Monday	4.16 m	3.8 m	0.97 m	0.9 m
Tuesday	3.95 m	3.61 m	0.8 m	0.75 m
Wednesday	3.82 m	3.5 m	0.83 m	0.69 m
Thursday	3.28 m	3.04 m	0.76 m	0.65 m
Friday	2.95 m	2.78 m	0.87 m	0.81 m

Calculate the answers to these mentally.

1. How much higher was the 1st high than the 2nd high on

a. Monday? ________ m
b. Tuesday? ________ m
c. Wednesday? ________ m
d. Thursday? ________ m
e. Friday? ________ m

2. How much lower was the 2nd low than the 1st low on

a. Monday? ________ m
b. Tuesday? ________ m
c. Wednesday? ________ m
d. Thursday? ________ m
e. Friday? ________ m

3. Calculate the difference between the 1st highs on

a. Monday and Tuesday ________ m
b. Tuesday and Wednesday ________ m
c. Wednesday and Thursday ________ m
d. Thursday and Friday ________ m

4. Calculate the difference between the 1st lows on

a. Monday and Tuesday ________ m
b. Tuesday and Wednesday ________ m
c. Wednesday and Thursday ________ m
d. Thursday and Friday ________ m

5. Calculate the difference between the highest high and lowest low on

a. Monday ________ m
b. Tuesday ________ m
c. Wednesday ________ m
d. Thursday ________ m
e. Friday ________ m

What is the difference between each day's highest and lowest tides?

Subtracting Tenths and Hundredths

Worksheet 70

1. Calculate the difference in the mass of these sacks of grain. Record the steps you use.

a. 16.45 kg 8.25 kg

Difference ____________ kg

b. 8.35 kg 5.75 kg

Difference ____________ kg

c. 2.65 kg 8.25 kg

Difference ____________ kg

d. 8.8 kg 6.35 kg

Difference ____________ kg

e. 17.5 kg 8.6 kg

Difference ____________ kg

f. 8.45 kg 12.8 kg

Difference ____________ kg

g. 17.6 kg 3.85 kg

Difference ____________ kg

h. 2.05 kg 8.4 kg

Difference ____________ kg

i. 3.7 kg 12.25 kg

Difference ____________ kg

Draw a *X* on the differences on this page that you think you can figure out without writing any steps.

Game Results

	Current score	Points needed	Personal best
Jacob	257.35		463.15
Harsha	158.60		485.25
Tia	270.45		515.30
Keshav	188.75		396.55
Mina	285.60		471.95
Gaurav	149.45		528.75

1. Figure out the number of points each player needs to reach his or her personal best. Then, complete the chart above.

a. Jacob

b. Harsha

c. Tia

d. Keshav

e. Mina

f. Gaurav

2. Find the difference between these personal bests.

a. Tia and Keshav

Difference = ____________

b. Harsha and Mina

Difference = ____________

c. Mina and Gaurav

Difference = ____________

If 1,000 was the top score, how many more points does Jacob need to reach it?

Adding and Subtracting Decimals—Unequal Places

Worksheet 72

1. Calculate the total mass of the two lead weights.

a. 2.417 kg | 2.68 kg

Total ____________ kg

b. 1.8 kg | 1.956 kg

Total ____________ kg

c. 1.689 kg | 0.52 kg

Total ____________ kg

d. 1.653 kg | 3.8 kg

Total ____________ kg

e. 1.75 kg | 1.312 kg

Total ____________ kg

f. 3.446 kg | 0.28 kg

Total ____________ kg

2. Calculate the difference between these masses.

a. 2.438 kg | 1.26 kg

Difference ____________ kg

b. 3.58 kg | 1.9 kg

Difference ____________ kg

c. 0.95 kg | 2.613 kg

Difference ____________ kg

d. 1.09 kg | 2.561 kg

Difference ____________ kg

e. 1.45 kg | 1.602 kg

Difference ____________ kg

f. 1.258 kg | 3.6 kg

Difference ____________ kg

Draw a ✓ on the calculations you were able to do mentally.

Methods of Multiplying Decimal Fractions

1. **a.** This shaded rectangle shows 13 × 4. Write the total.

b. Shade rectangles to match the other two number sentences. Then write the answers.

13 × 4 = ______

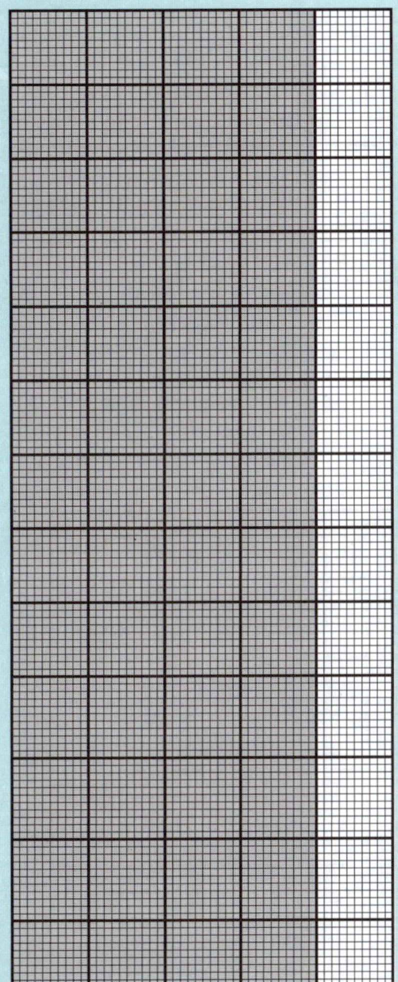

13 × 0.4 = ______

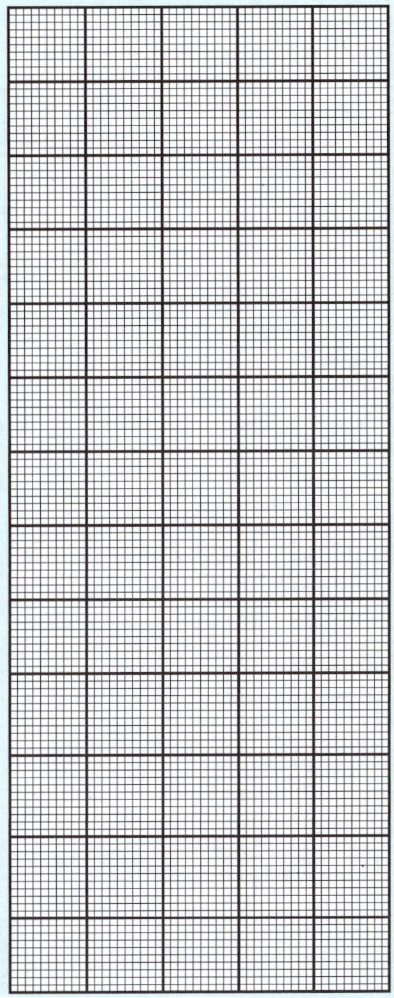

1.3 × 0.4 = ______

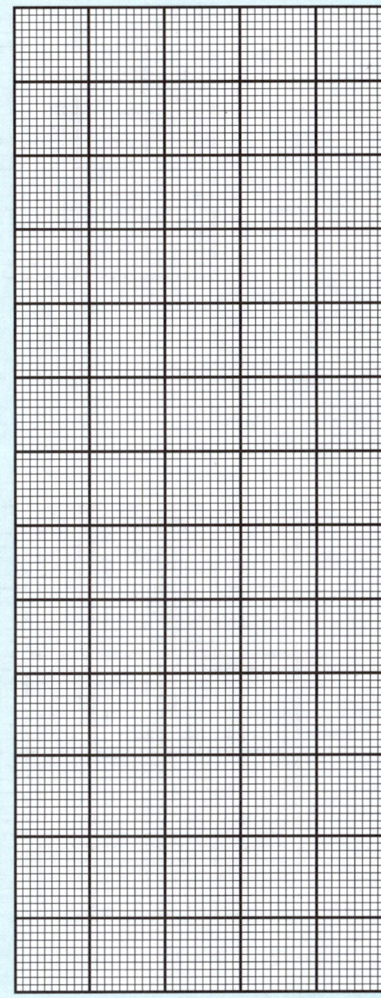

2. Use patterns to help you write the answers.

a. 24 × 4 = ______

24 × 0.4 = ______

2.4 × 0.4 = ______

b. 32 × 6 = ______

32 × 0.6 = ______

3.2 × 0.6 = ______

c. 29 × 8 = ______

29 × 0.8 = ______

2.9 × 0.8 = ______

d. 12 × 12 = ______

12 × 1.2 = ______

1.2 × 1.2 = ______

e. 15 × 8 = ______

15 × 0.8 = ______

1.5 × 0.8 = ______

f. 14 × 5 = ______

14 × 0.5 = ______

1.4 × 0.5 = ______

Write a number sentence to match each of these answers:

a. 24 **b.** 2.4 **c.** 0.24

Using Place Value to Multiply Tenths

1. Follow these steps.

- Colour blue the region that shows the ones. Then write the product.
- Colour red the region that shows the tenths. Then write the product.
- Write the total of the two partial products.

a.

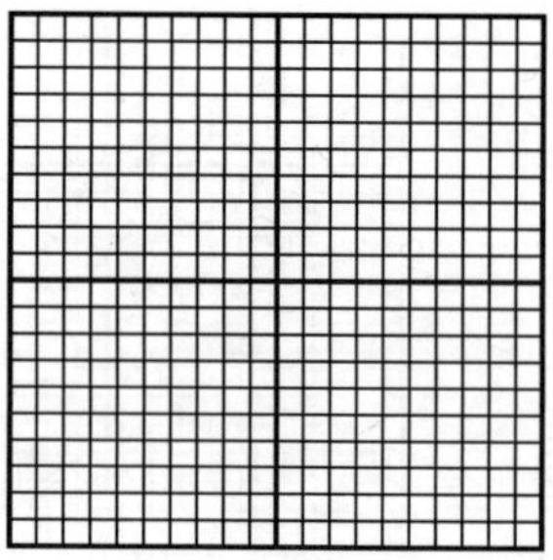

2 × 1 = ☐

2 × 0.7 = ☐

2 × 1.7 = ☐

b.

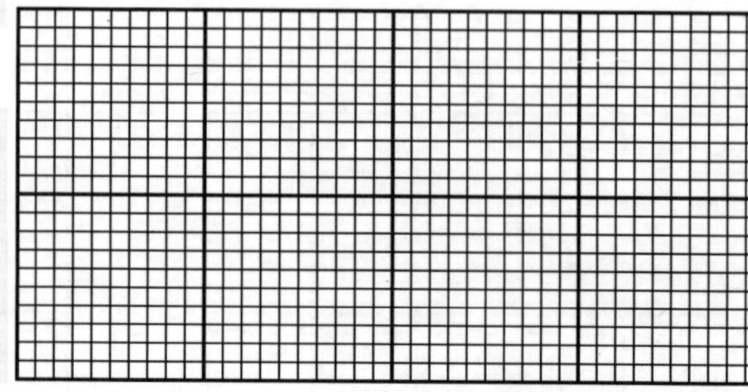

2 × 3 = ☐

2 × 0.8 = ☐

2 × 3.8 = ☐

c.

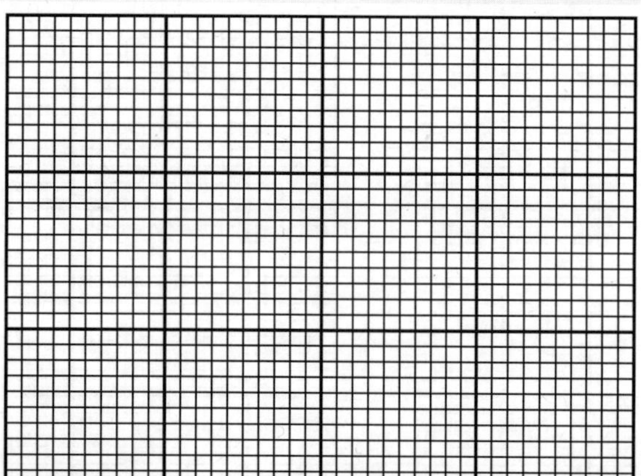

3 × 3 = ☐

3 × 0.6 = ☐

3 × 3.6 = ☐

d.

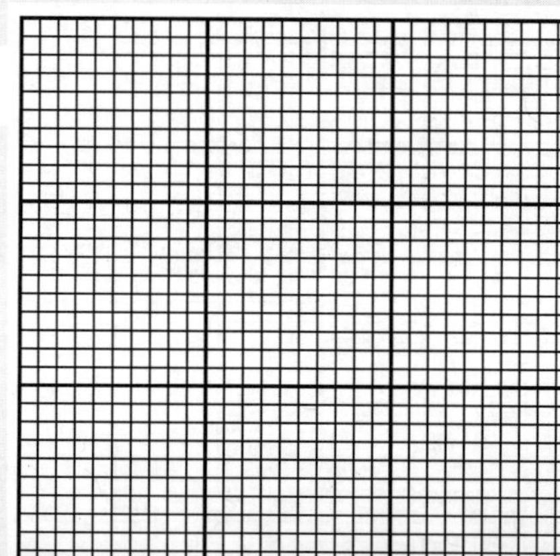

3 × 2 = ☐

3 × 0.4 = ☐

3 × 2.4 = ☐

2. Follow the same steps to complete these.

a.

4 × 6 = ☐

4 × 0.3 = ☐

4 × 6.3 = ☐

b.

8 × 7 = ☐

8 × 0.4 = ☐

8 × 7.4 = ☐

c.

3 × 9 = ☐

3 × 0.6 = ☐

3 × 9.6 = ☐

Imagine your friend was away today. Write the steps you would use to explain how to calculate 3 × 5.7.

Multiplying Tenths and Hundredths

1. Write the missing numbers. Then complete the number sentence.

a. double, double

3.2 → ____ → ____

× ____

____ × 4 = ____

b. double, double

6.4 → ____ → ____

× ____

____ × 4 = ____

c. double, double

4.12 → ____ → ____

× ____

____ × ____ = ____

d. double, double

5.21 → ____ → ____

× ____

____ × ____ = ____

e. double, double

8.25 → ____ → ____

× ____

____ × ____ = ____

f. double, double

2.35 → ____ → ____

× ____

____ × ____ = ____

2. Think 'double double' to complete these number sentences.

a. 6.15 × 4 = ____ **b.** 3.4 × 4 = ____ **c.** 6.3 × 4 = ____

d. 4 × 7.1 = ____ **e.** 4 × 5.5 = ____ **f.** 4 × 8.05 = ____

g. 10.3 × 4 = ____ **h.** 4 × 12.2 = ____ **i.** 15.25 × 4 = ____

Figure out the answers to each of these:

a. 2.4 × 8 = ____ **b. 8 × 1.25 = ____**

Multiplying the Parts

1. Follow these steps to help you figure out 1.25×16.

a. Colour red an area that shows 1×16.

b. Colour yellow an area that shows 0.25×16.

c. Complete this sentence: 1.25×16 **is the same as** ____ $\times 16 +$ ____ $\times 16 =$ ____

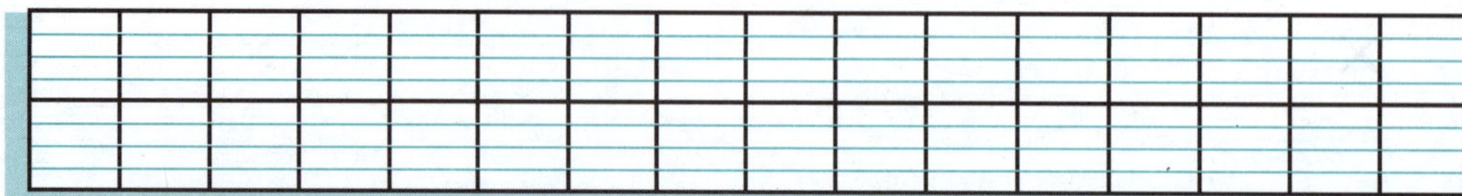

2. Complete these sentences.

a. 1.25×24 **is the same as** ____ $\times 24 +$ ____ $\times 24 =$ ____

b. 3.25×8 **is the same as** ____ $\times 8 +$ ____ $\times 8 =$ ____

c. 1.5×12 **is the same as** ____ $\times 12 +$ ____ $\times 12 =$ ____

d. 2.5×14 **is the same as** ____ $\times 14 +$ ____ $\times 14 =$ ____

e. 2.75×16 **is the same as** ____ $\times 16 +$ ____ $\times 16 =$ ____

3. Use the same thinking to answer these.

a. $1.25 \times 28 =$ ____

b. $2.25 \times 12 =$ ____

c. $1.75 \times 20 =$ ____

d. $1.5 \times 22 =$ ____

e. $3.5 \times 18 =$ ____

f. $2.75 \times 24 =$ ____

4. Complete these.

a. $1.25 \times 32 =$ ____

$1.50 \times 32 =$ ____

$1.75 \times 32 =$ ____

b. $1.25 \times 10 =$ ____

$1.50 \times 10 =$ ____

$1.75 \times 10 =$ ____

c. $1.25 \times 18 =$ ____

$1.50 \times 18 =$ ____

$1.75 \times 18 =$ ____

Write some other two-digit numbers you can multiply by 1.25, 1.5 and 1.75.

Multiplying Numbers Involving Tenths

Worksheet 77

1. Multiply the ones and then the tenths to figure out the **total mass** of each bulk buy. Then complete the number sentence.

a. Buy 8 boxes

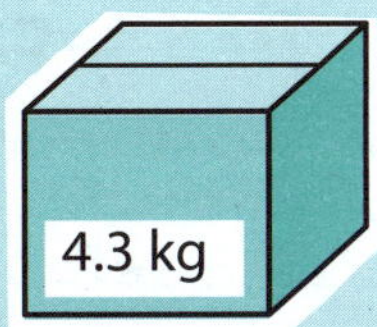

(4 × 8) + (0.3 × 8) = ______

b. Buy 7 bags

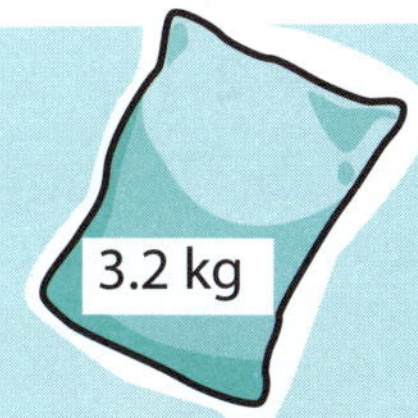

(3 × 7) + (0.2 × 7) = ______

c. Buy 6 bags

(____ × 6) + (____ × 6) = ______

d. Buy 5 boxes

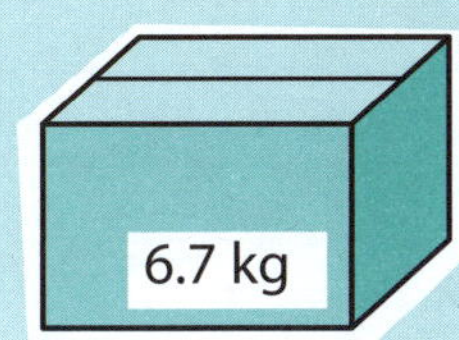

(____ × 5) + (____ × 5) = ______

e. Buy 12 boxes

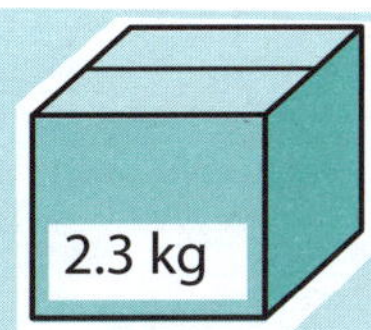

(____ × ____) + (____ × ____) = ______

f. Buy 15 bags

(____ × ____) + (____ × ____) = ______

g. Buy 11 bags

(____ × ____) + (____ × ____) = ______

h. Buy 12 boxes

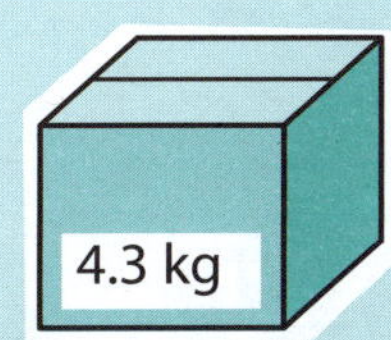

(____ × ____) + (____ × ____) = ______

2. Complete each sentence.

a. 6.4 × 3 (____ × ____) + (____ × ____) = ______ + ______ = ______

b. 3.8 × 3 (____ × ____) + (____ × ____) = ______ + ______ = ______

3. Use the strategy from Question 2 to figure out each of these.

a. 5.6 × 4 = ______ **b.** 2.4 × 15 = ______ **c.** 3.4 × 12 = ______

Write other examples you can solve using the same strategy.

Dividing Decimals

1. Divide the given decimals by the whole numbers below.

a. 7.8 ÷ 2

b. 5.31 ÷ 9

c. 8.33 ÷ 2

d. 2.97 ÷ 7

e. 2.70 ÷ 8

f. 1.78 ÷ 10

g. 873.57 ÷ 40

h. 181.95 ÷ 12

i. 141.7 ÷ 16

Decimal Word Problems

1. Sonia scored 8.007 in gymnastics. Jyoti scored 9.949. How much more than Sonia did Jyoti score?

2. Raman's weekly salary is Rs 1,015.00. How much does he take home each week after deductions are made for income tax of Rs 182.13, state tax Rs 90.74, medicare tax of Rs 310.75, and the retirement plan deduction of Rs 91.50?

3. A director replayed 78 of the 1,000 scenes filmed for a movie. Write a decimal representing the part of the movie the director replayed.

4. Meera purchased fruit worth Rs 30.46 at a store. The cashier gave her Rs 8.46 in change from the Rs 50 that she gave him. How much more money should Meera get from the cashier?

CHAPTER 7

Percentage

Per cent means out of 100. The symbol for per cent is %.

Fractions, decimals and percentages are all different ways of writing the same thing.

20 per cent means 20 out of 100 or $\frac{20}{100}$ or 0.2

Fraction	Decimal	Percentage
$\frac{20}{100}$	0.2	20%

Converting Decimal to Percentage

To convert decimal to percentage, move the decimal point two places to the right.

If required, add extra zeroes after the decimal part before converting it into a percentage.

Example: Express 0.62 as a percentage.

Solution: Moving the decimal point two places to the right,

0.62 = 62%

Converting Percentage to Decimal

To convert a percentage to decimal, move the decimal point two places.

If required, add extra zeroes at the beginning before converting to decimal.

Example: Express 54% as a decimal.

Solution: Remember that the decimal point is after the ones place.

Moving the decimal two places to the left:

54% = 0.54

Conversion of a Percentage to a Fraction

Write the per cent as a fraction by using 100 as the denominator. Reduce or simplify if possible.

Example: Express 75% as a fraction.

Solution:

$$75\ \% = \frac{75}{100}$$

Reducing $\frac{75}{100}$ to the lowest form we get:

$$\frac{\cancel{75}^{\,3}}{\cancel{100}_{\,4}} = \frac{3}{4}$$

$$75\% = \frac{3}{4}$$

Converting a Fraction to a Percentage

Multiply the fraction by 100.

Example: Convert $\frac{2}{5}$ to a percentage.

Solution:

$$\frac{2}{\cancel{5}_{\,1}} \times \cancel{100}^{\,20} = 2 \times 20$$

$$\frac{2}{5} = 40\%$$

Expressing Common Fractions as Percentages

Worksheet 80

1. Write the fraction shown by the arrows on each side of the strip.
The ≈ symbol means 'is approximately equal to'.

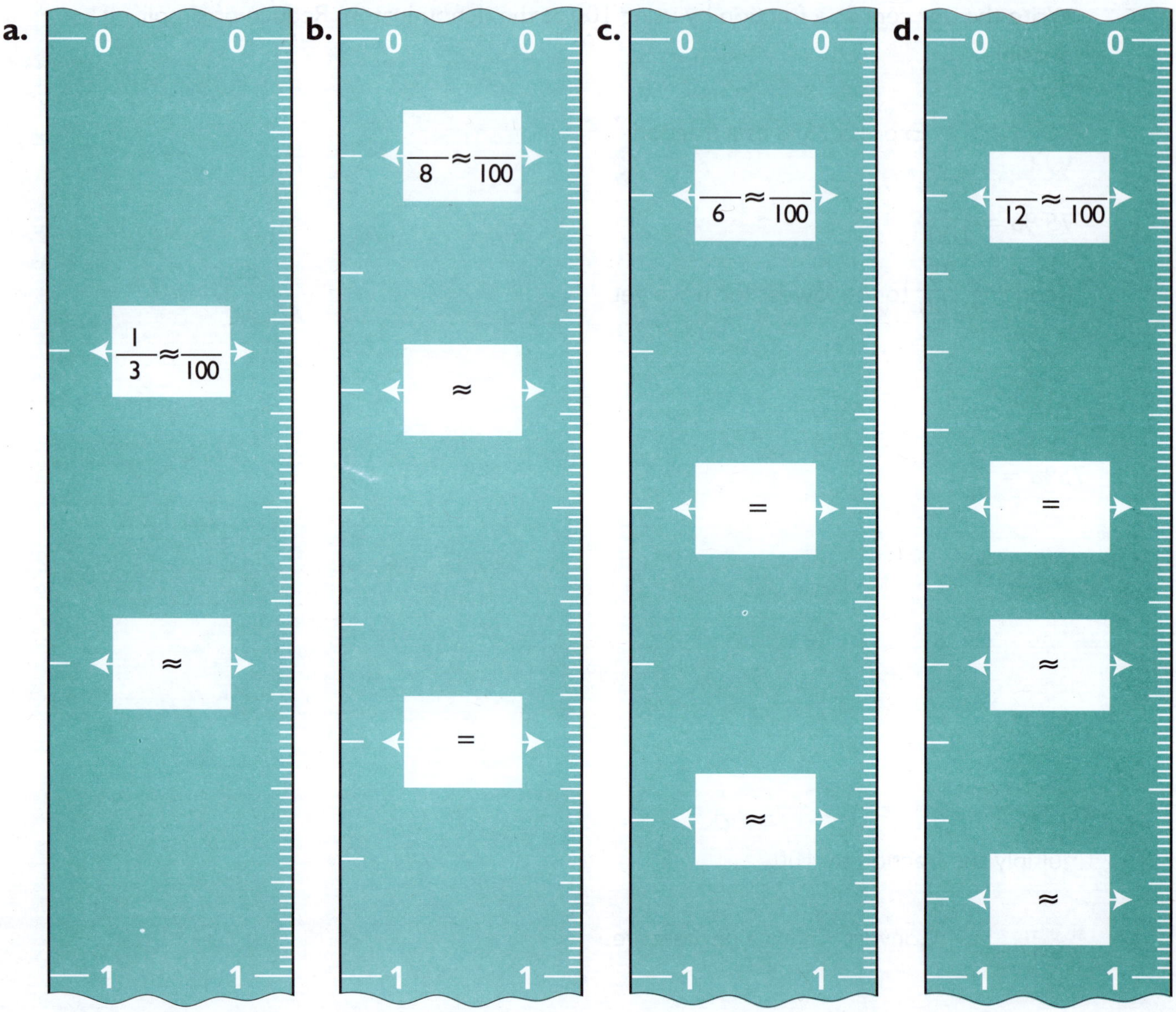

2. Complete each of these.

a. $\frac{2}{3} \approx$ ____ %

b. $\frac{4}{8} =$ ____ %

c. $\frac{7}{8} \approx$ ____ %

d. $\frac{2}{6} \approx$ ____ %

e. $\frac{5}{6} \approx$ ____ %

f. $\frac{3}{12} =$ ____ %

g. $\frac{5}{12} \approx$ ____ %

h. $\frac{9}{12} =$ ____ %

FF Write the fractions on this page that are the same as 0.5.

Relating Fractions and Percentage

1. Each square below is one whole. Shade each fraction. Then write the missing numbers.

a. Shade $\frac{1}{2}$

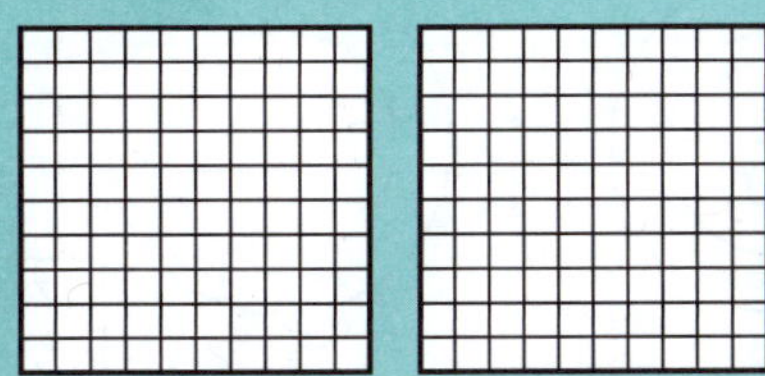

$\frac{\_\_\_}{100}$ __ . _____ _______ %

b. Shade $\frac{3}{5}$

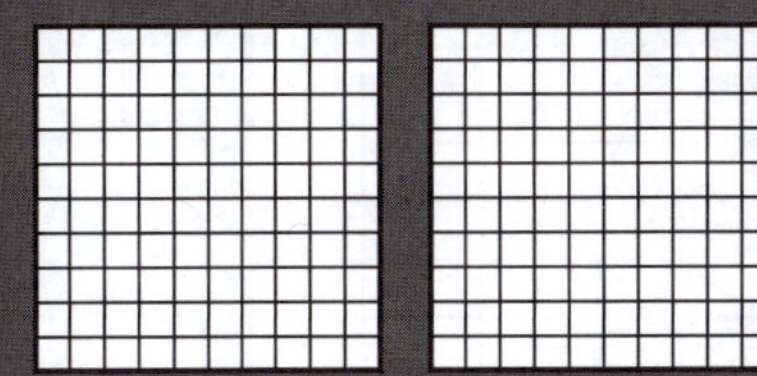

$\frac{\_\_\_}{100}$ __ . _____ _______ %

c. Shade $1\frac{1}{2}$

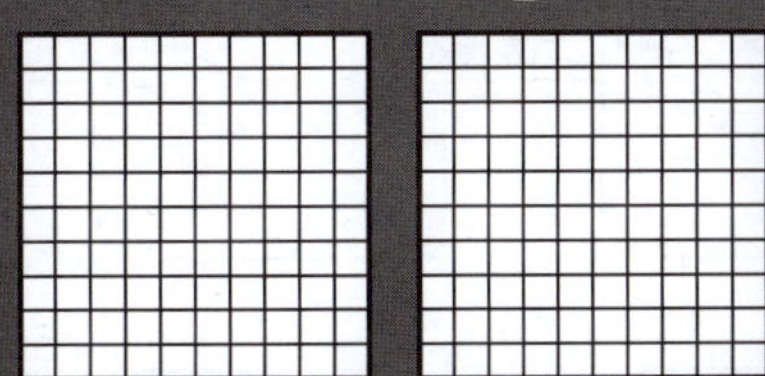

$\frac{\_\_\_}{100}$ __ . _____ _______ %

d. Shade $1\frac{3}{4}$

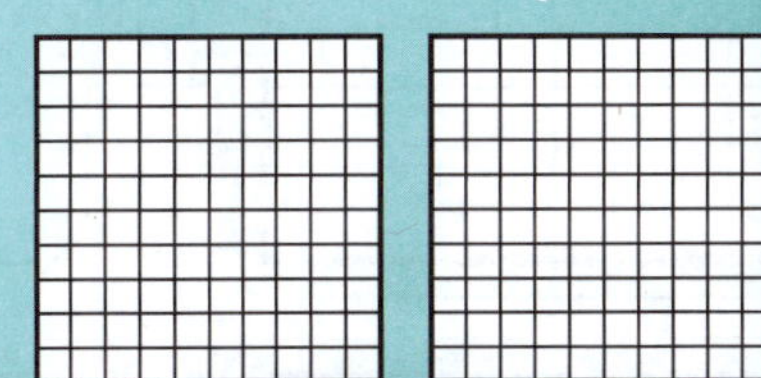

$\frac{\_\_\_}{100}$ __ . _____ _______ %

2. Write the missing parts that match.

a. $\frac{3}{4}$ — $\frac{\_\_\_}{100}$ — 0.___ — ___%

b. $1\frac{1}{5}$ — $\frac{\_\_\_}{100}$ — _____ — ___%

c. $\frac{4}{5}$ — $\frac{\_\_\_}{100}$ — 0.___ — ___%

d. $\frac{4}{20}$ — $\frac{\_\_\_}{100}$ — 0.___ — ___%

e. $2\frac{2}{4}$ — $\frac{\_\_\_}{100}$ — _____ — ___%

f. $1\frac{1}{10}$ — $\frac{\_\_\_}{100}$ — _____ — ___%

3. Write some other sets of matching fractions that are between 1 and 3.

a. ___ — $\frac{\_\_\_}{100}$ — _____ — ___%

b. ___ — $\frac{\_\_\_}{100}$ — _____ — ___%

Relating Percentage to Fractions and Decimals

Worksheet 82

1. Complete the pieces to match.

a. 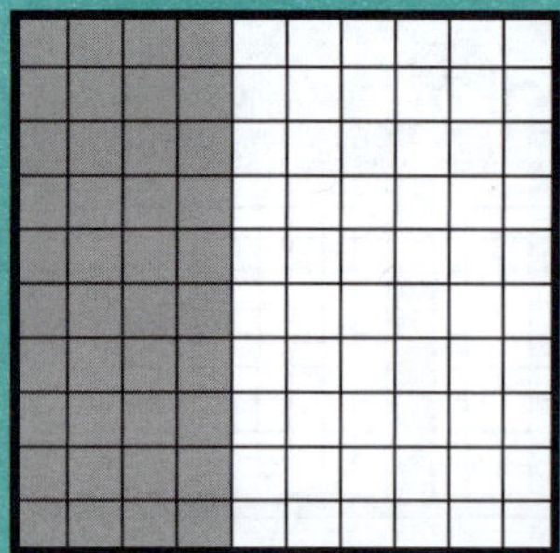

Fraction	Hundredths	Decimal	Percentage
$\frac{4}{10}$	$\frac{\_\_\_}{100}$	0.___	___%

b. 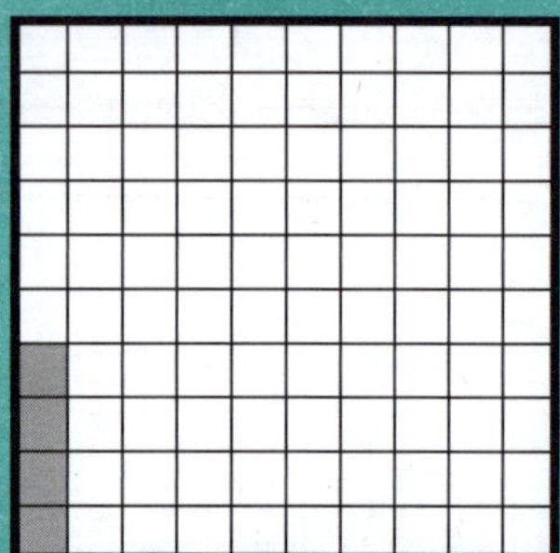

Fraction	Hundredths	Decimal	Percentage
$\frac{\_\_\_}{\_\_\_}$	$\frac{\_\_\_}{100}$	0.___	___%

c. 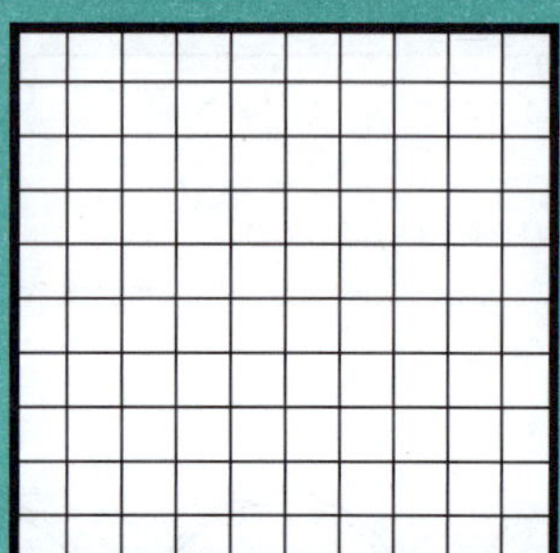

Fraction	Hundredths	Decimal	Percentage
$\frac{6}{25}$	$\frac{\_\_\_}{100}$	0.___	___%

d. 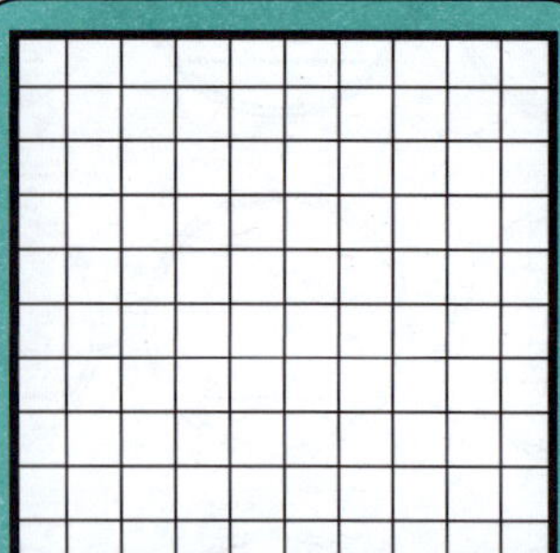

Fraction	Hundredths	Decimal	Percentage
$\frac{4}{20}$	$\frac{\_\_\_}{100}$	0.___	___%

e. 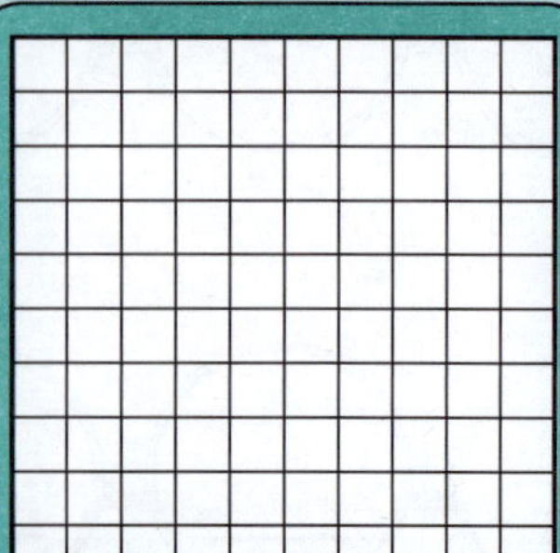

Fraction	Hundredths	Decimal	Percentage
$\frac{3}{5}$	$\frac{\_\_\_}{100}$	0.___	___%

Write three other common fractions that have the same value as $\frac{1}{5}$.

Relating Percentage to Fractions and Decimals

1. Complete these pieces to match.

a.

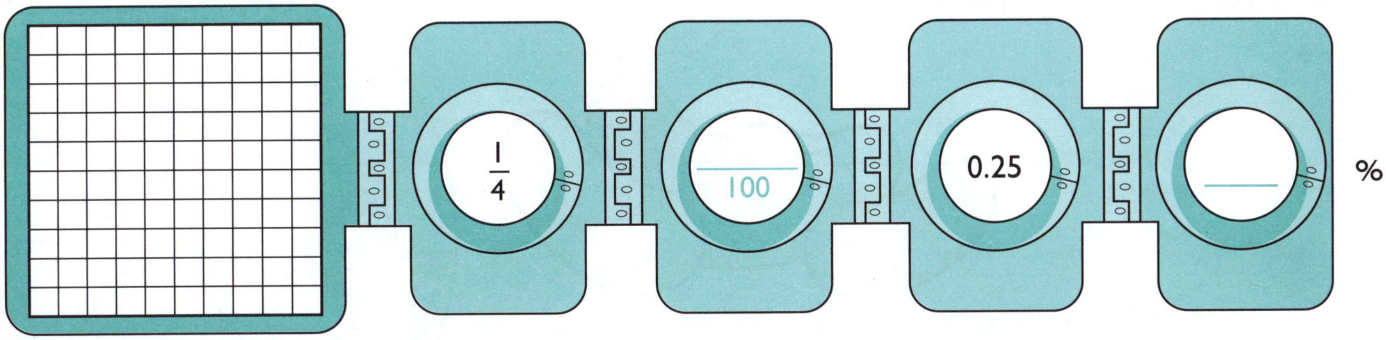

b.

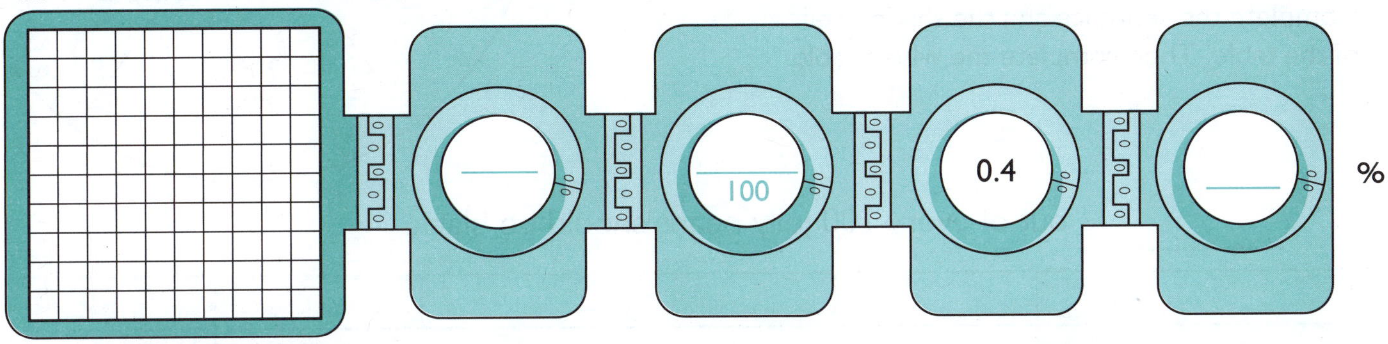

c.

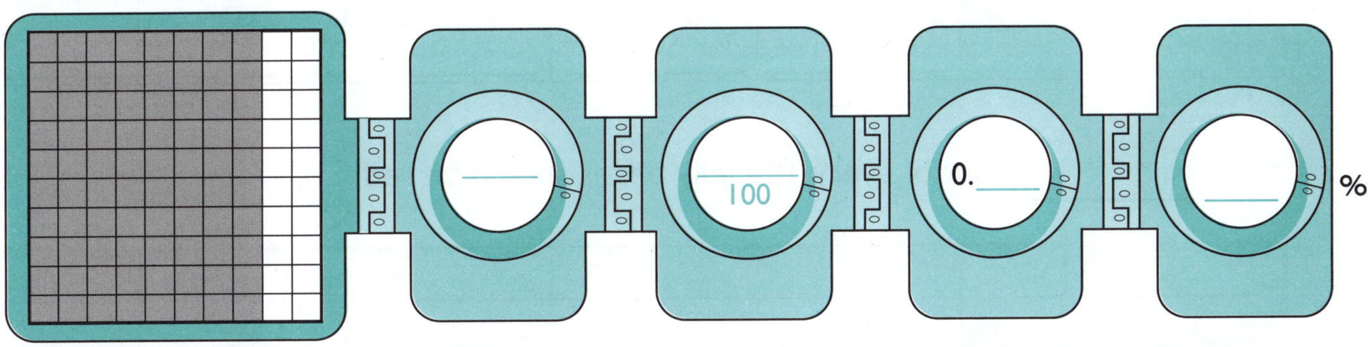

d.

e.

FF Write the decimal fractions in order from least to greatest.

This pie graph shows the percentage of coloured jelly beans in a packet.

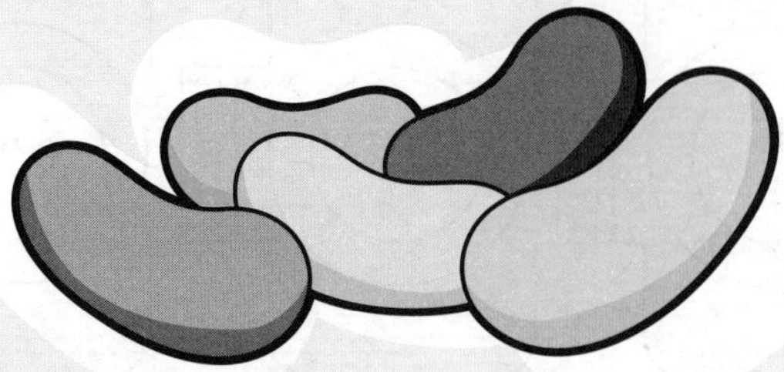

Jelly Bean Colours

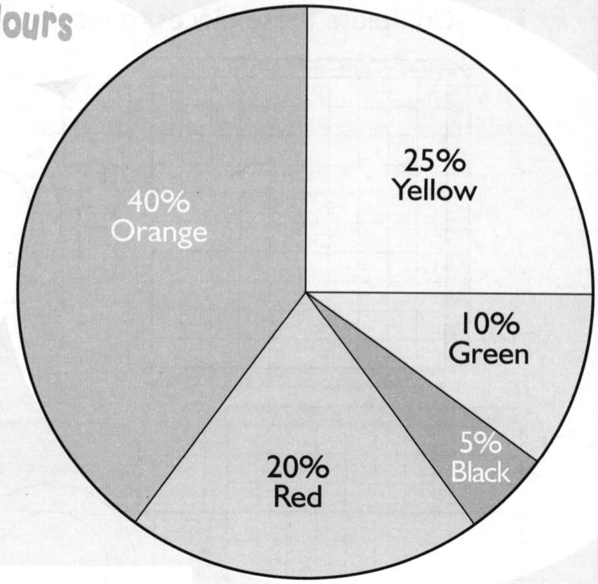

1. Complete the sentence and the shaded cell of the table. Then complete the whole table.

a. ________ out of every 100 jelly beans should be black.

Size of pack	500	200	100	50	25
Number of black jelly beans					

b. ________ out of every 100 jelly beans should be red.

Size of pack	500	200	100	50	25
Number of red jelly beans					

c. ________ out of every 100 jelly beans should be yellow.

Size of pack	500	200	100	50	25
Number of yellow jelly beans					

d. ________ out of every 100 jelly beans should be orange.

Size of pack	500	200	100	50	25
Number of orange jelly beans					

FF **Imagine a packet held 250 jelly beans. Write the number of each colour you would expect to find.**

Working with Percentage

1. There are 200 school days each year. For each question, circle the percentage of the total number of school days.

a. There are 40 days in Term 1. That is

40% 20% 30% 50%

b. There are 50 days in Term 3. That is

20% 50% 25% 30%

c. There are 20 days of swimming classes. That is

20% 40% 10% 15%

2. There are 365 days in total in most years. For each question, circle the percentage of the total number of days in most years.

a. There are 200 school days in a year. That is about

20% 40% 60% 80%

b. There are 104 weekend days in a year. That is about

10% 20% 30% 40%

c. There are 11 public holidays in a year. That is about

1% 3% 5% 9%

3. There are 50 school days in a 10-week term.
What percentage of a term did the following activities take?

a. Year 6 went to camp for 5 days.

b. Class 6 had swimming classes for 10 days.

c. The school prepared for a concert for 25 days.

d. The school had a sports day.

Estimate the percentage of days of a whole year that

a. you are not in school. b. are weekdays.

Favourite Type of Television Programme (Votes)

1. Look at the survey data. Write the total number of votes.

2. What fraction out of 100 voted for

   a. movies?

   b. sports?

   c. soaps?

   d. cartoons?

3. This strip represents 100 votes. Estimate the fraction of 100 votes each program received. Then use different colours to show those fractions on the strip.

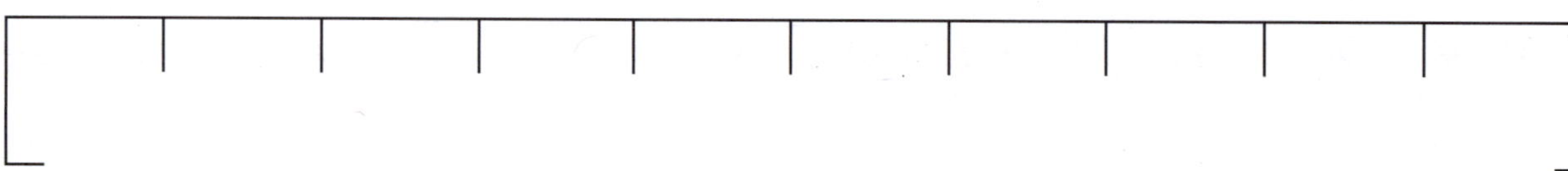

4. Write the percentage of votes received for

   a. movies

   b. sports

   c. soaps

   d. cartoons

5. Which programmes received

   a. **less** than 25% of the votes?

   b. **more** than 25% of the votes?

6. What percentage of people voted for

   a. movies and soaps altogether?

   b. soaps and sports altogether?

   c. sports and cartoons altogether?

7. Write the percentage in Question 4 that is

   a. **equal** to one-fifth

   b. a **little more than** one-third

   c. a **little less than** one-third

Write another way you could represent the data shown on the television above.

Representing Percentage in a Pie Graph

Worksheet 87

100 students from Classes 3, 4, 5 and 6 were surveyed about their favourite type of music. The results are shown below.

CLASS 3	
Pop	25
Hip hop	7
Rock	17
Dance	51

CLASS 4	
Pop	23%
Hip hop	26%
Rock	24%
Dance	27%

CLASS 5	
Pop	$\frac{40}{100}$
Hip hop	$\frac{10}{100}$
Rock	$\frac{26}{100}$
Dance	$\frac{24}{100}$

CLASS 6	
Pop	0.15
Hip hop	0.05
Rock	0.1
Dance	0.7

1. Write each year level above its matching pie graph. Then label each segment of the graph.

a. CLASS ____

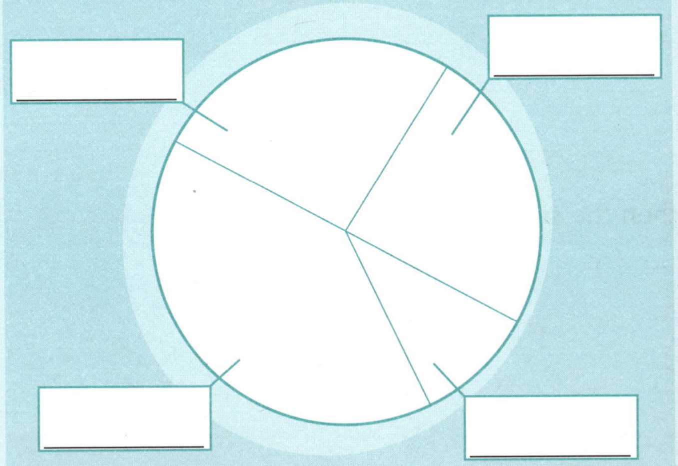

b. CLASS ____

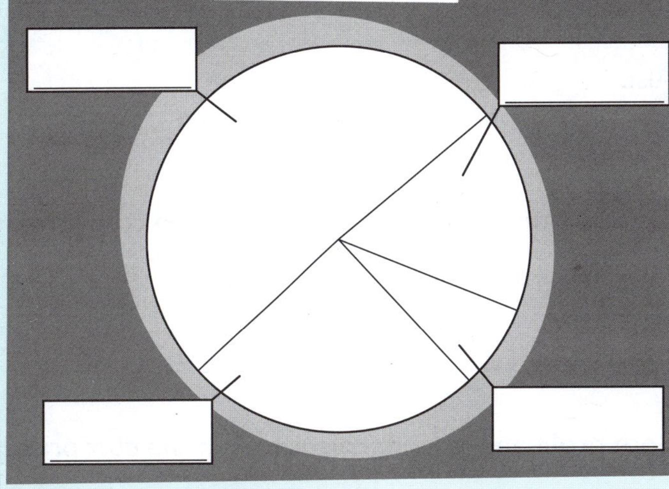

c. CLASS ____

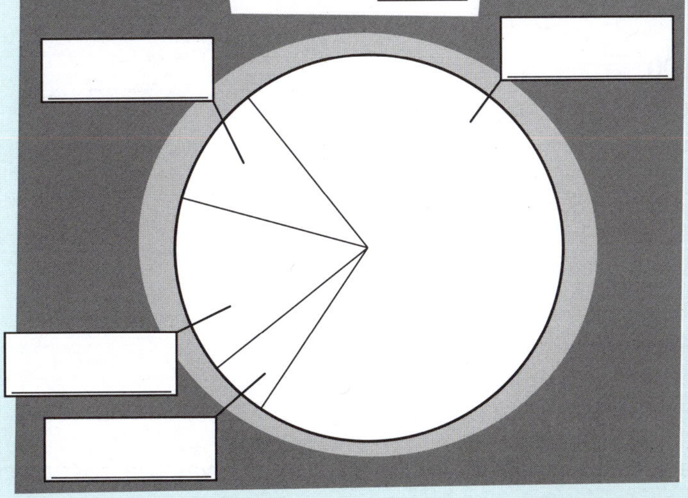

d. CLASS ____

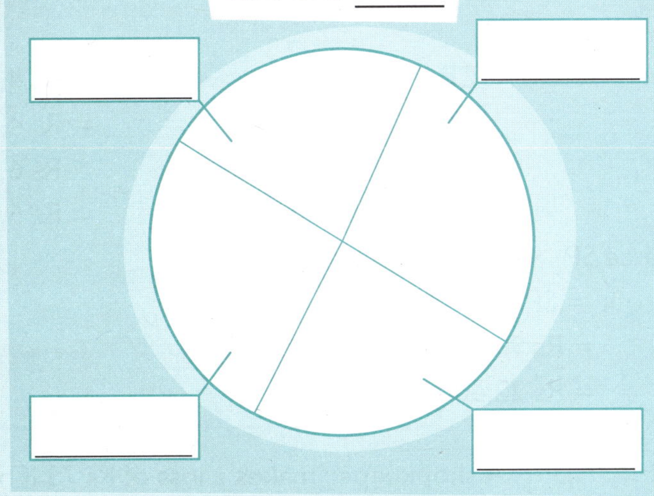

2. Compare the data for dance music. Write the class levels in order from greatest to least.

______ ______ ______ ______

What part of this page did you use to help you answer Question 2?

CHAPTER 8

Profit and Loss

Sachin's mother had bought a cow for Rs 12,000. One day she asked Sachin to go to the market and sell the cow. Sachin sold the cow for Rs 13,580. His mother was very happy with Sachin as she gained Rs 1,580.

In this story
Rs 12,000 is the cost price of the cow.
COST PRICE (CP): The amount of money paid to buy an article is called its cost price.

Rs 13,850 is the selling price of the cow.
SELLING PRICE (SP): The price at which the article is sold is called its selling price.

As the selling price is more than the cost price, a profit has been made.
PROFIT: If the selling price is more than the cost price, then the seller makes a profit.
PROFIT = SELLING PRICE – COST PRICE (SP – CP)
Also
SP = CP + PROFIT and CP = SP – PROFIT

LOSS: If the selling price is less than the cost price, then the seller makes a loss.
LOSS = COST PRICE – SELLING PRICE (CP – SP)
Also
CP = SP + LOSS and SP = CP – LOSS

Both profit and loss are calculated on the cost price.

Example: A shopkeeper bought 15 almirahs for Rs 4,500 each and sold them for Rs 6,000 each. Find his profit or loss.

Solution:

CP of 1 almirah	= Rs 4,500
CP of 15 almirahs	= Rs 4,500 × 15 = Rs 67,500
Selling Price of 1 almirah	= Rs 6,000
SP of 15 almirahs	= Rs 6,000 × 15 = Rs 90,000

Since SP > CP, there is a profit.
Profit = SP – CP
= Rs 90,000 – Rs 67,500
= Rs 22,500

Example: A shopkeeper makes a loss of Rs 75 if he sells a calculator for Rs 225. What was the cost price for each calculator?

Solution: As the shopkeeper has made a loss, the CP will be more than the SP.
CP = SP + LOSS
CP = Rs 225 + Rs 75
CP = Rs 300

1. Find the SP of the following.

a. CP = Rs 140, loss = Rs 59

b. CP = Rs 542, loss = Rs 127

c. CP = Rs 49.50, loss = Rs 35.65

d. CP = Rs 279, loss = Rs 4.95

e. CP = Rs 1086, loss = Rs 132

1. Find the profit or loss in each of the following.

a. CP = Rs 657, SP = Rs 432

b. CP = Rs 60.50, SP = Rs 132.60

c. CP = Rs 1009, SP = Rs 1278

d. CP = Rs 864, SP = Rs 955

e. CP = Rs 129.65, SP = Rs 75.90

Profit and Loss Problems

1. My father bought a watch for Rs 10,786. He used it for three months and sold it for a loss of Rs 7,453. How much did he sell the watch for?

2. Mrs Saini sold a pair of gold bangles for Rs 22,450. She made a profit of Rs 6,525. What is the cost price of the bangles?

3. The farmer bought a horse for Rs 7,680. He sold the horse for Rs 7,500. Find his profit or loss.

4. I sold a video game for Rs 2,350 and made a profit of Rs 875. How much had I bought the video game for?

- A **line** is a collection of points along a straight path that goes on and on in opposite directions. It has no end points.

Any two points on the line can be used to name it. We write the name of a line passing through two different points A and B as 'line AB' or as $\overleftrightarrow{AB}$.

- A line segment is a part of a line. It has two end points.

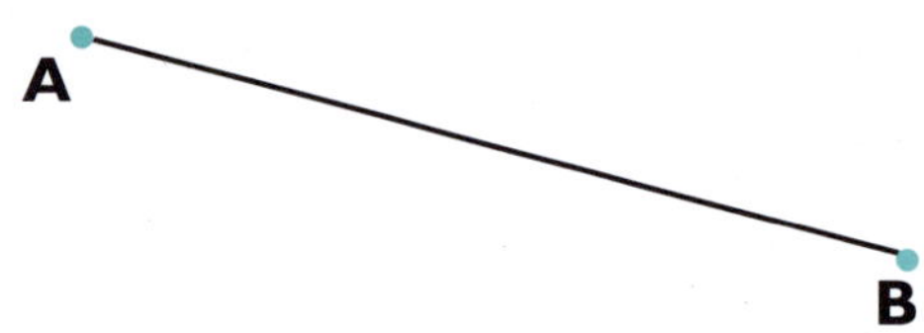

We write the name of a line segment with endpoints A and B as 'line segment AB' or as $\overline{AB}$.

- A ray is a part of a line. It has a beginning but no end point.

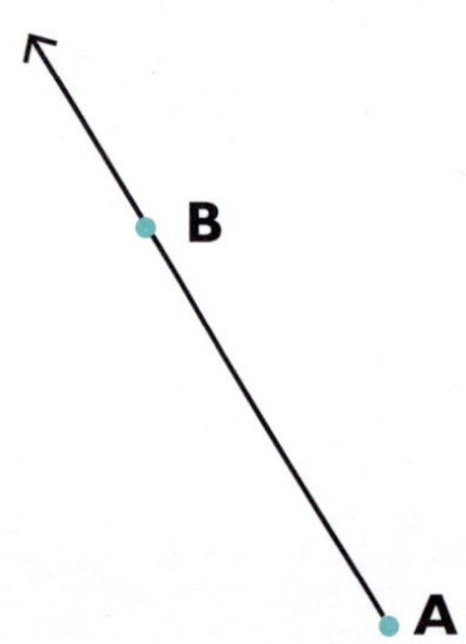

We write the name of a ray with end point A and passing through a point B as 'ray AB' or as $\overrightarrow{AB}$.

Angles

An angle is a figure formed when two rays share a common end point.
The point where the rays intersect is called the vertex of the angle.
The two rays are called the sides or the arms of the angle.

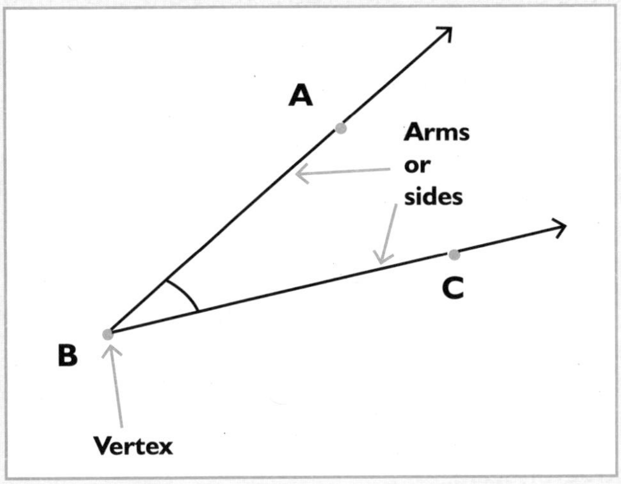

The figure shows an angle made by two rays, AB and BC.
B is the vertex of the angle.
The angle is called ∠ABC or ∠CBA or simply ∠B (the vertex letter is always written in the middle).

Measuring Angles

A protractor is used to measure angles. Angles are measured in degrees. The symbol for degree is °.

To Measure an Angle Using a Protractor

Place a protractor over the angle, with the centre of the protractor over the angle's vertex.
The bottom of the protractor is placed on one side of the angle.
Follow the scale round and read the number where the other side crosses the scale. (Always read the scale starting from zero.)

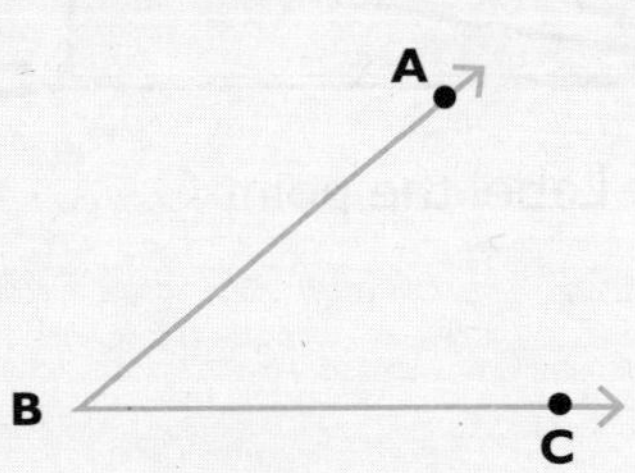

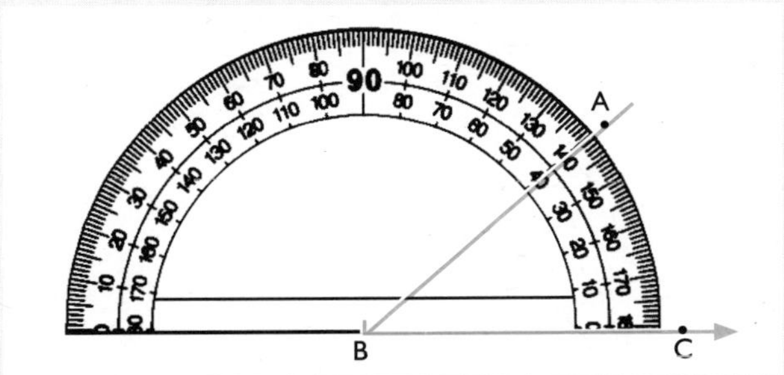

∠ABC measures 40°

Drawing Angles

Drawing Angles

To draw an angle with a protractor:

1. Draw a ray (an arm of the angle).
2. Place a dot at one end of the arm. This dot represents the vertex of the angle.
3. Place the centre of the protractor at the vertex dot and the baseline of the protractor along the arm of the angle.
4. Find the required angle on the scale and then mark a small dot at the edge of the protractor.
5. Join the small dot to the vertex with a ruler to form the second arm of the angle.
6. Label the angle.

Example: Draw an angle of 75°.

Solution:

Draw a ray BA using a ruler.

Place the centre of the protractor at B.
Side BA of the angle should line up with the base of the protractor scale.
Follow the scale round and find 75° on the scale.

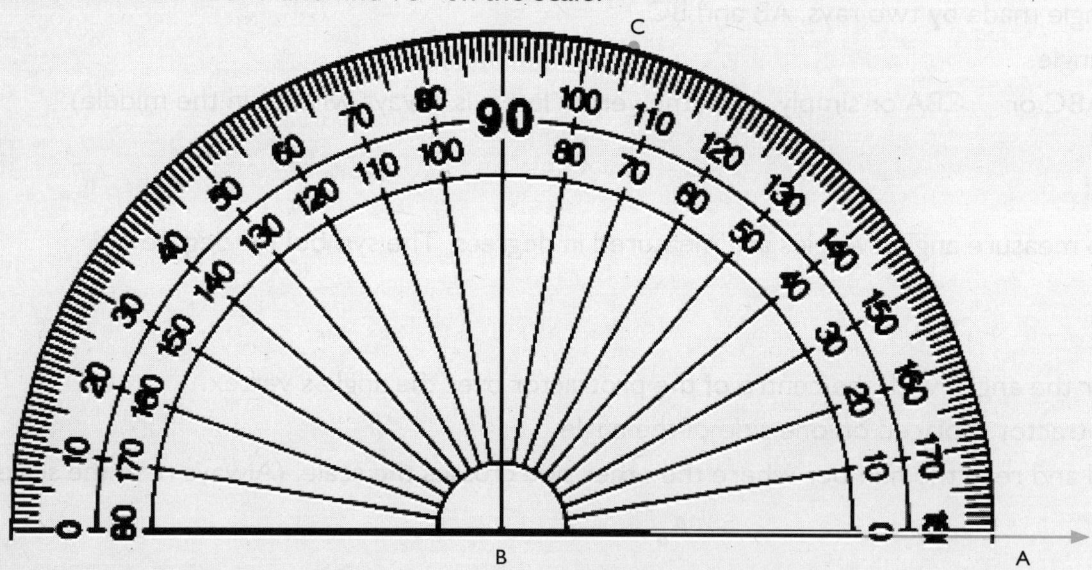

Mark a small dot at the edge of the protractor. Label the point C.
Join the vertex B to the point C.

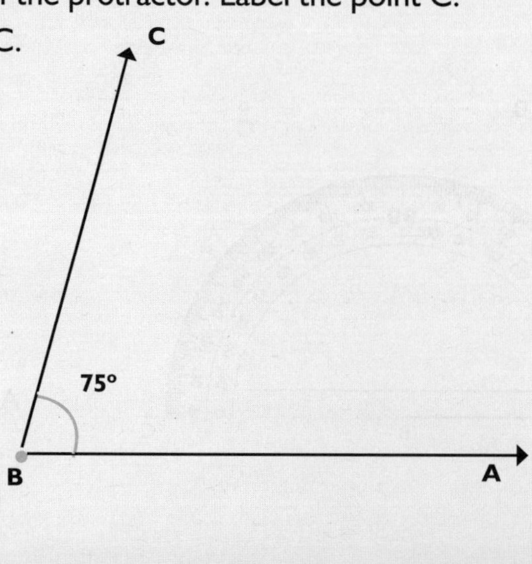

∠ABC measures 75°.

Types of Angles

Acute angle: An angle measuring between 0 and 90 degrees is an acute angle.

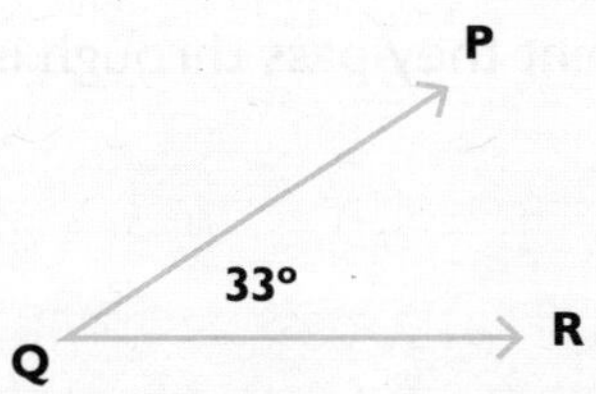

Right angle: An angle measuring 90 degrees is a right angle.

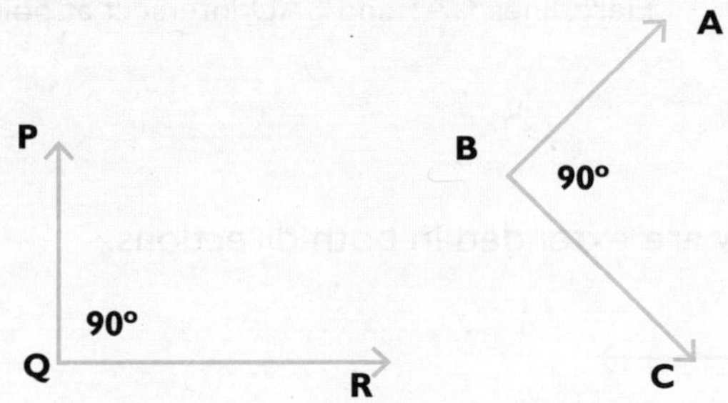

Obtuse angle: An angle measuring between 90 degrees and 180 degrees is an obtuse angle.

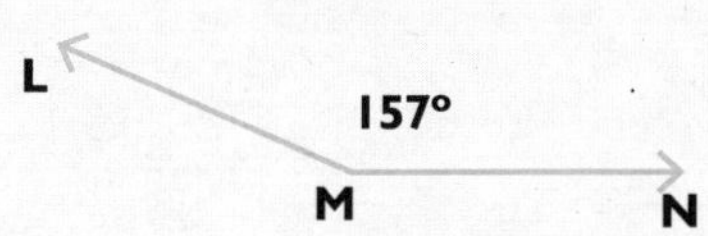

Straight angle: An angle measuring 180 degrees is called a straight angle.

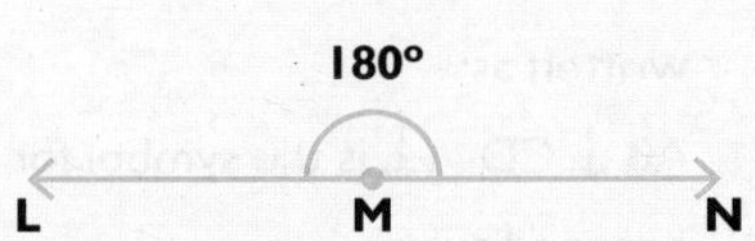

Reflex angle: An angle measuring more than 180 degrees is a reflex angle.

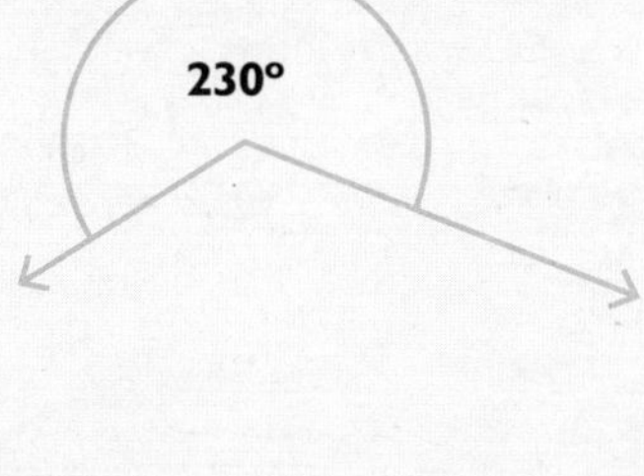

Intersecting, Parallel and Perpendicular Lines

Two or more lines or line segments may intersect (cross) each other or may be parallel.

Intersecting lines cross each other or pass through a point. The point they pass through is called the point of intersection.

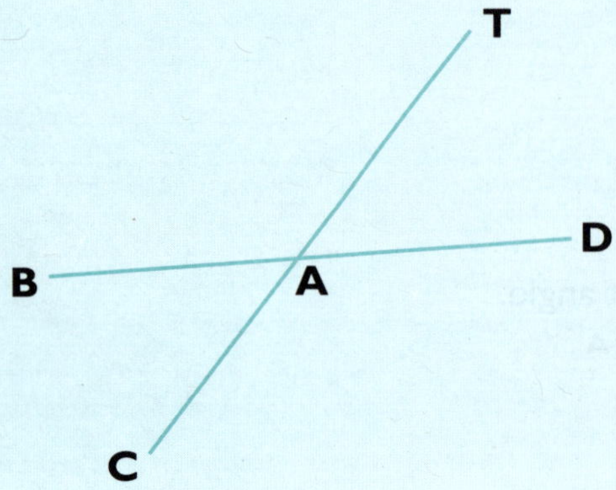

Here, lines CAT and BAD intersect at point A.

Parallel lines never meet, no matter how far they are extended in both directions.

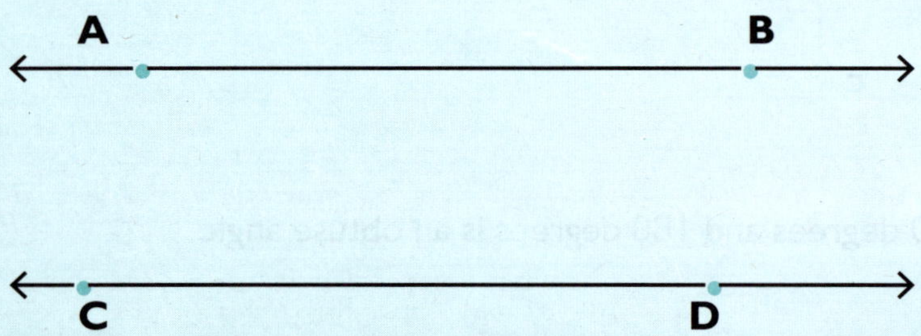

Line AB is parallel to line CD.
This is written as AB // CD
(// is the symbol for parallel).

Perpendicular lines intersect and form four right angles.

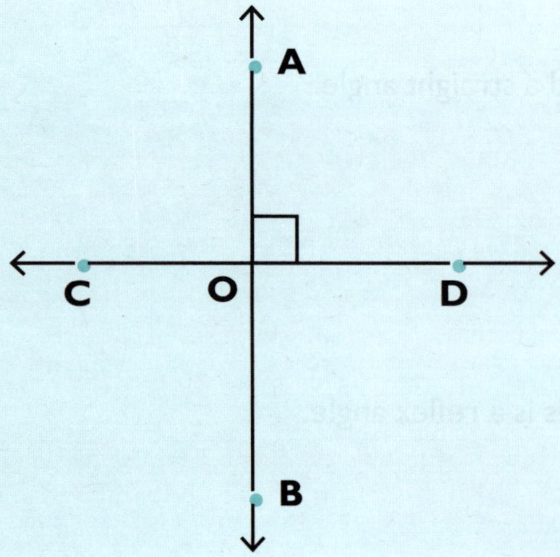

Here, lines AB and CD intersect at O and form four right angles.

Line AB is perpendicular to line CD which is written as:

AB ⊥ CD (⊥ is the symbol for perpendicular).

We can sometime use an angle tester to measure each of the internal angles.

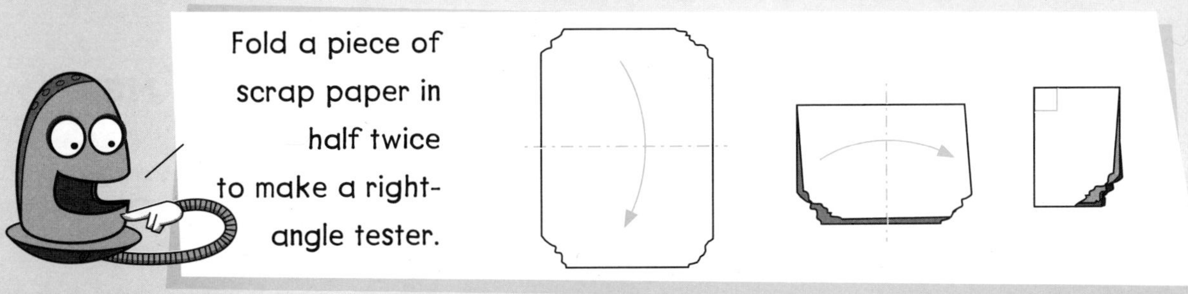

1. Use a protractor to measure the following internal angles.

a.

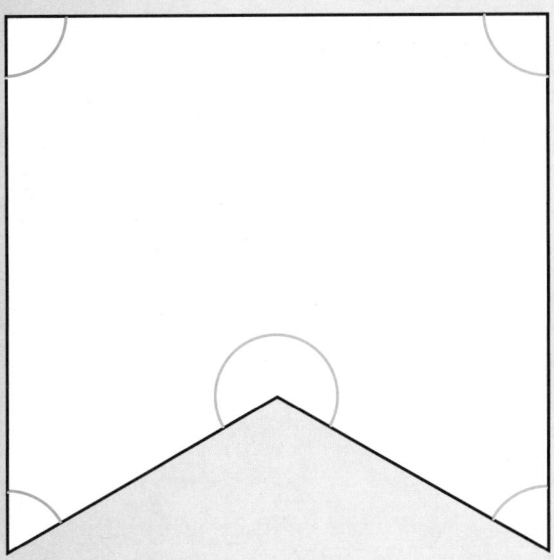

b.

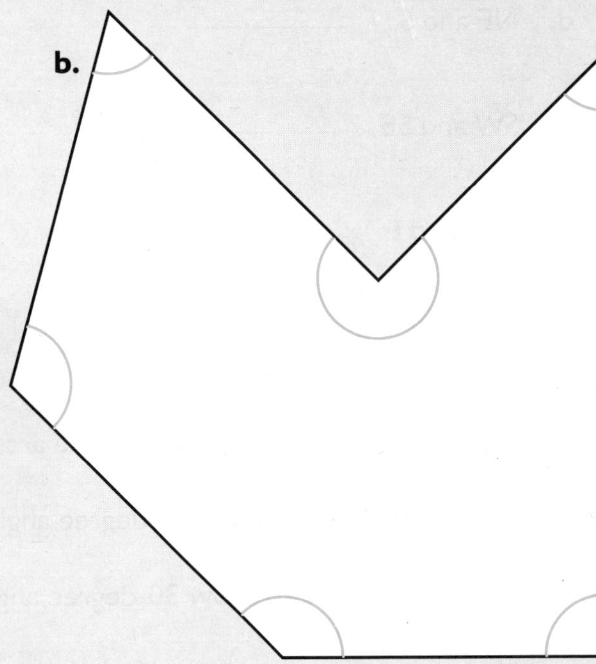

c.

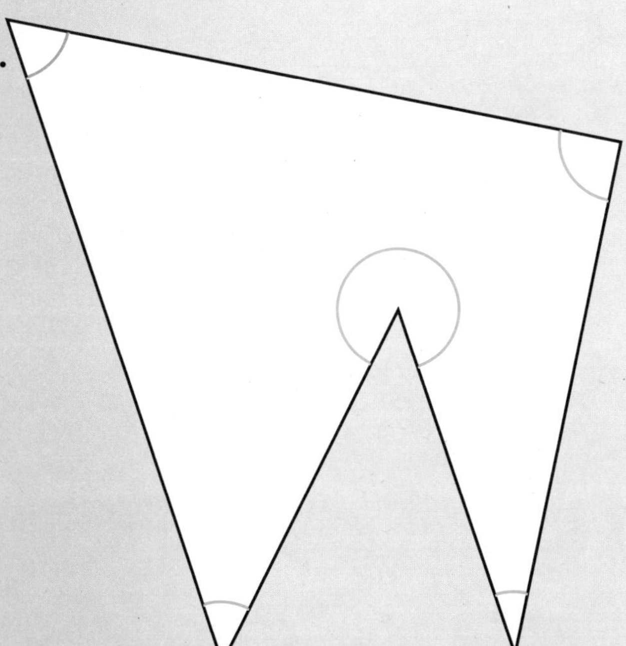

d.

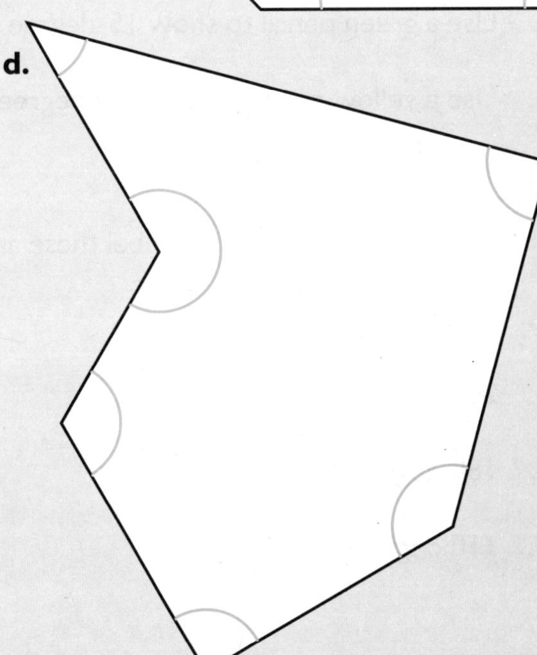

Use a tester to draw a polygon with five or six sides.

Using a Protractor

Worksheet 92

1. Use a protractor to measure the angle between

a. N and E ____________

b. W and S ____________

c. E and W ____________

d. NE and S ____________

e. SW and SE ____________

f. NW and E ____________

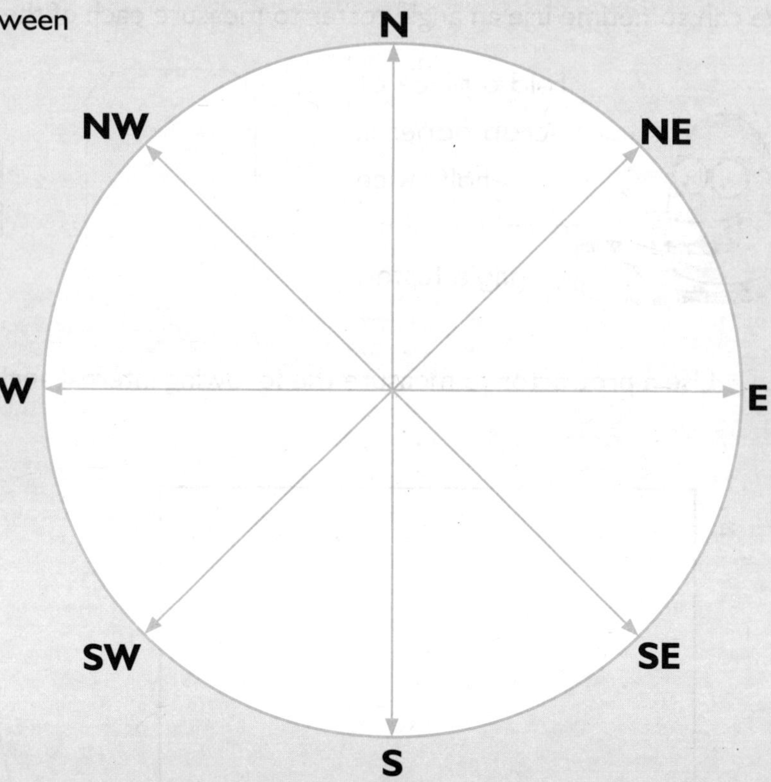

2. Use a protractor to help you draw these arcs.

a. Use a red pencil to show 45-degree angles.

b. Use a blue pencil to show 30-degree angles.

c. Use a green pencil to show 15-degree angles.

d. Use a yellow pencil to show 90-degree angles.

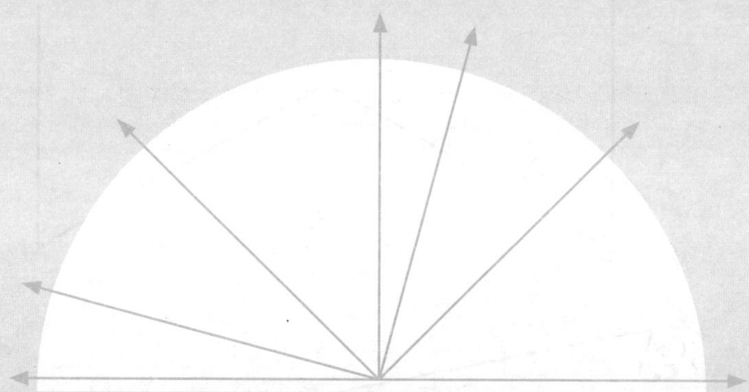

3. Use a protractor to draw and label these angles.

a. 135 degrees

b. 20 degrees

c. 160 degrees

d. 110 degrees

1. Use a right-angle tester to help you colour the angles.

a. Use red to mark the angles that are greater than a right angle.

b. Use green to mark the angles that are equal to a right angle.

c. Use blue to mark the angles that are less than a right angle.

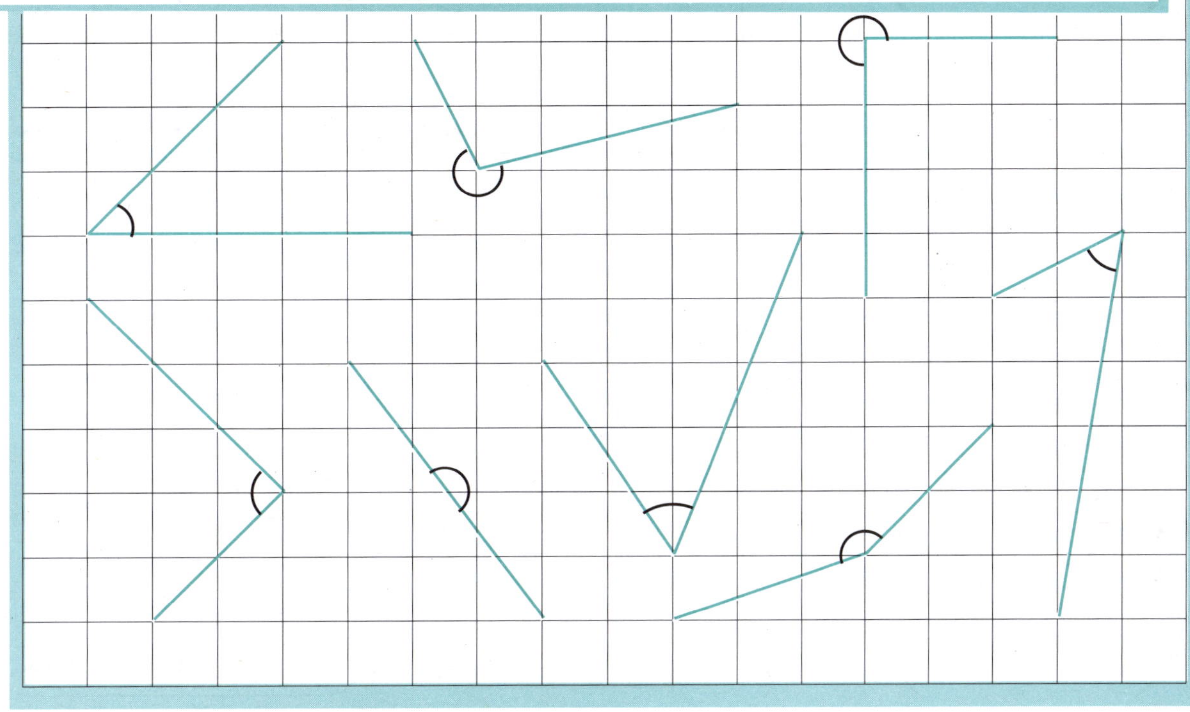

2. Use a right-angle tester to help you

a. draw one angle that is less than a right angle.

b. draw one angle that is equal to a right angle.

c. draw one angle that is greater than a right angle.

Draw a 2D shape that has all angles inside the shape less than a right angle.

1. Estimate the amount of turn each needle has made from 'E'. Write your answer in degrees.

a.

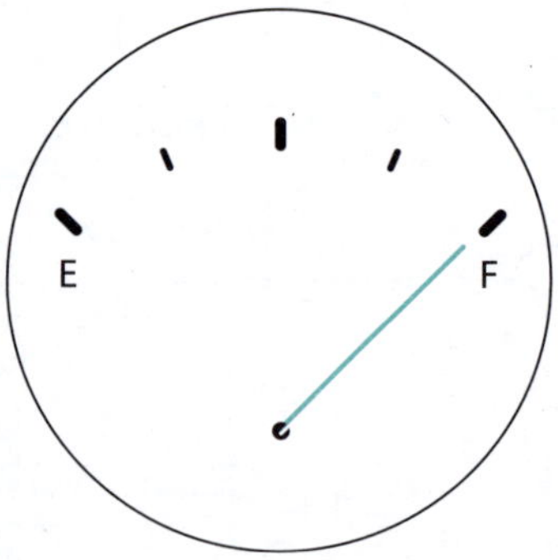

b.

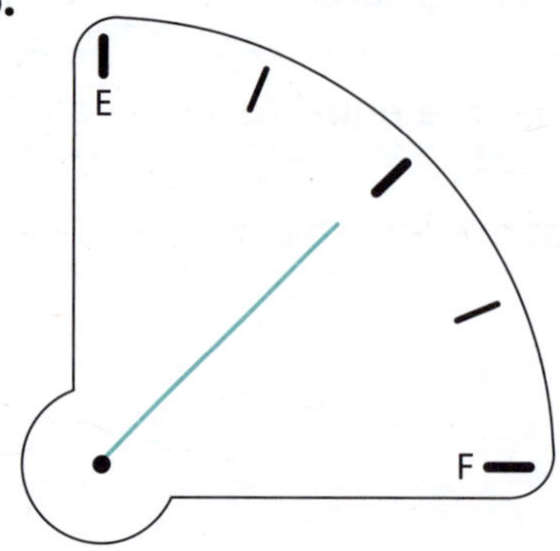

c.

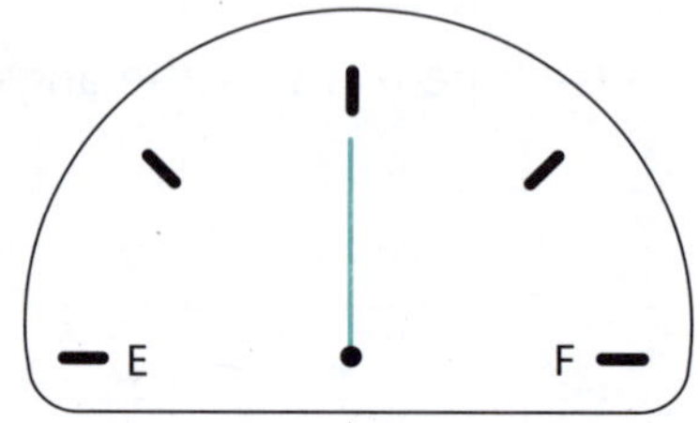

d.

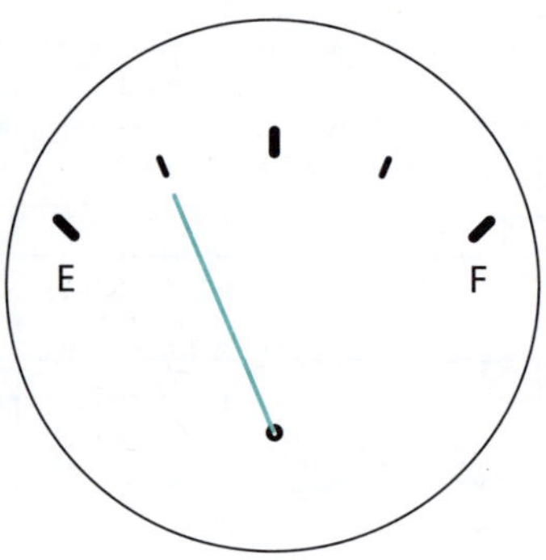

e.

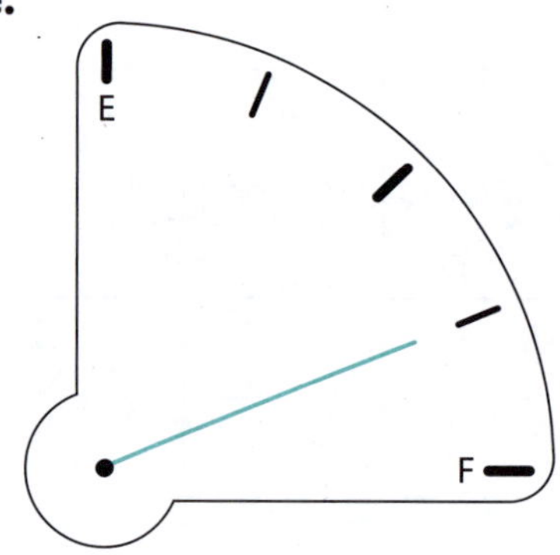

f.

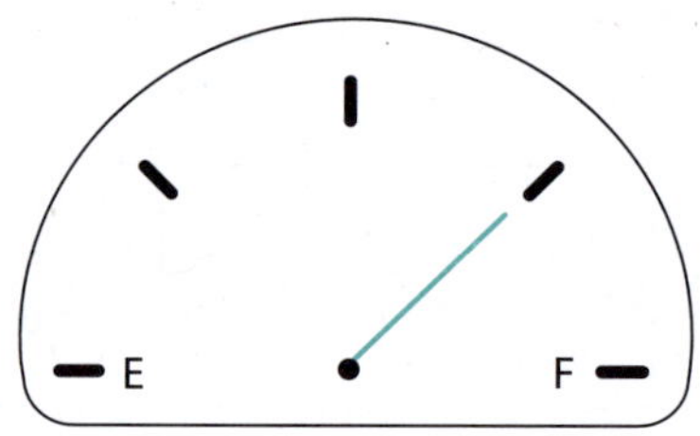

2. Draw the new position of the needle to show the amount of turn from 'E'.

a.

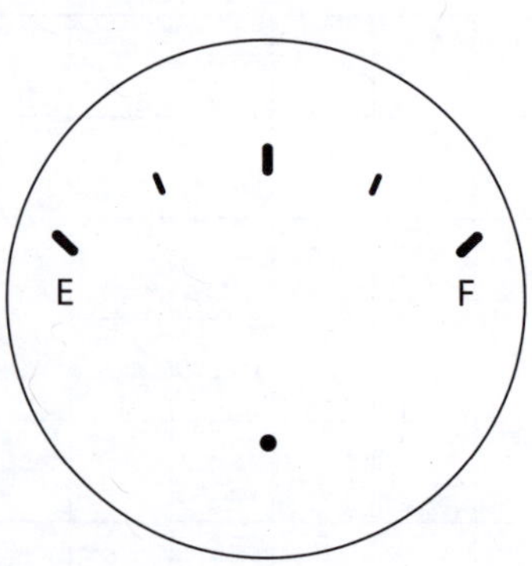

45°

b.

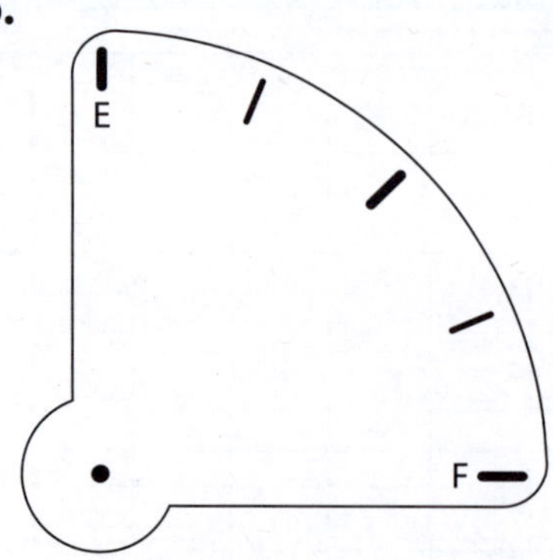

90°

c.

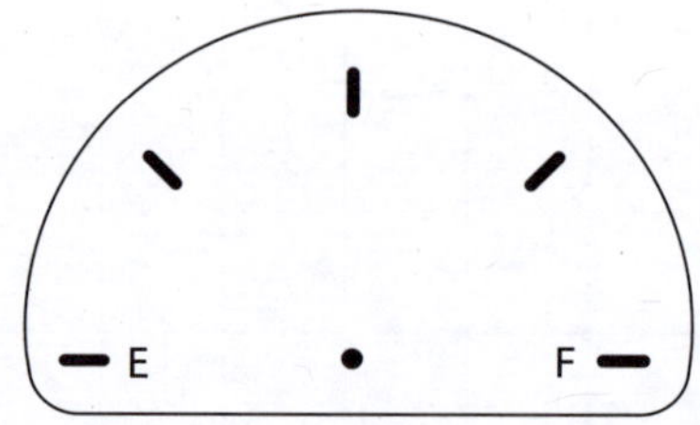

30°

Use a protractor to measure each angle in Question 1 exactly. Write the answers in brackets beside the estimates you wrote.

Calculating Angles

Worksheet 95

1. Look at the square on the right.

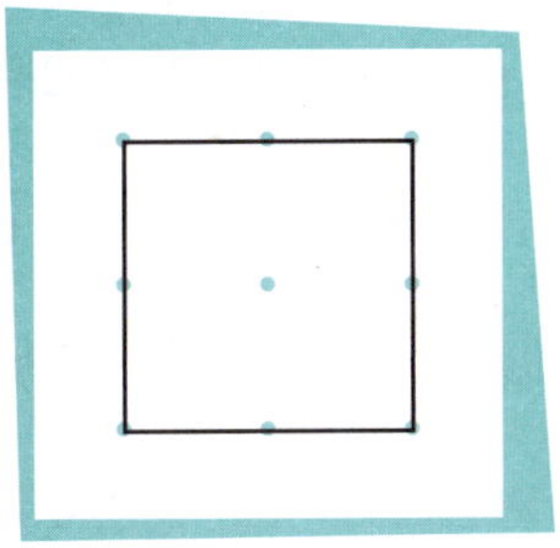

a. What is each internal angle equal to? ____________ degrees

b. What would half of each angle be? ____________ degrees

c. Draw diagonal lines to show each angle divided in half.

2. Look at the picture below. Calculate the angles without using a protractor.

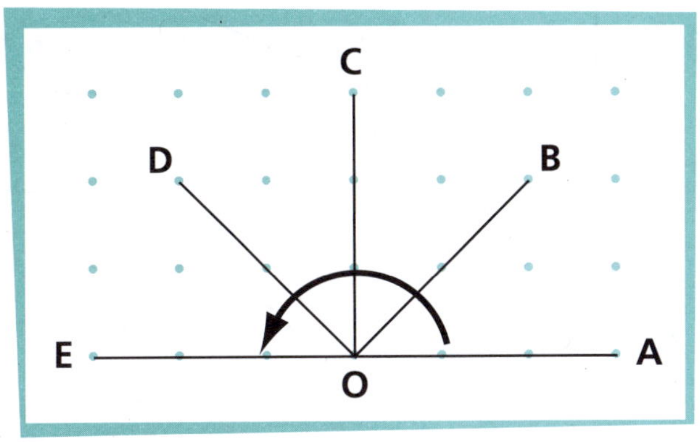

a. Angle **AOC** 90°

b. Angle **AOB** ____________

c. Angle **AOD** ____________

d. Angle **AOE** ____________

e. Angle **BOD** ____________

3. The sum of all angles around a point is 360 degrees. Look at the picture to the right. Follow the arrow and calculate the angles without using a protractor.

a. Angle **AOG** 270°

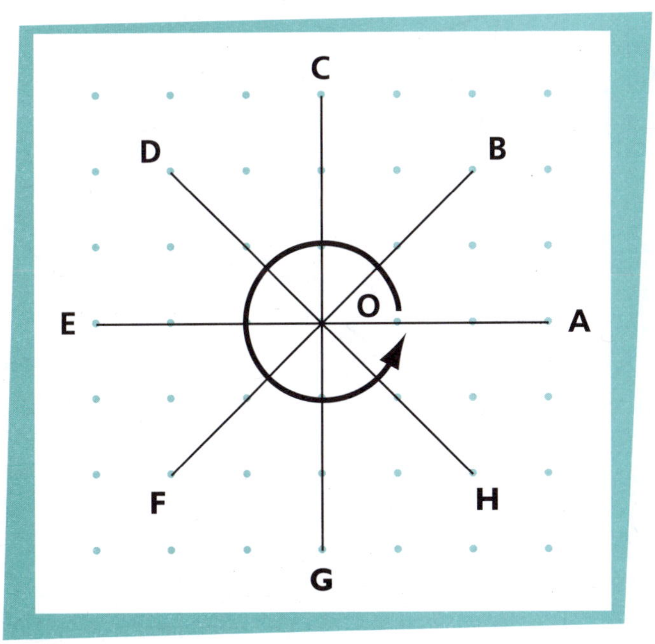

b. Angle **AOF** ____________

c. Angle **AOH** ____________

d. Angle **GOC** ____________

e. Angle **EOH** ____________

f. Angle **BOH** ____________

g. Angle **COG** ____________

h. Angle **FOG** ____________

i. Angle **BOE** ____________

Imagine four angles arranged to make a full turn around a common vertex. If one is 160° and another is 45°, what could the other two angles be?

1. Look at the angles inside each shape below.

a. Draw a ✓ on the angles that are **more than** a right angle.

b. Draw a ✗ on the angles that are **less than** a right angle.

Use a right-angle tester to help you.

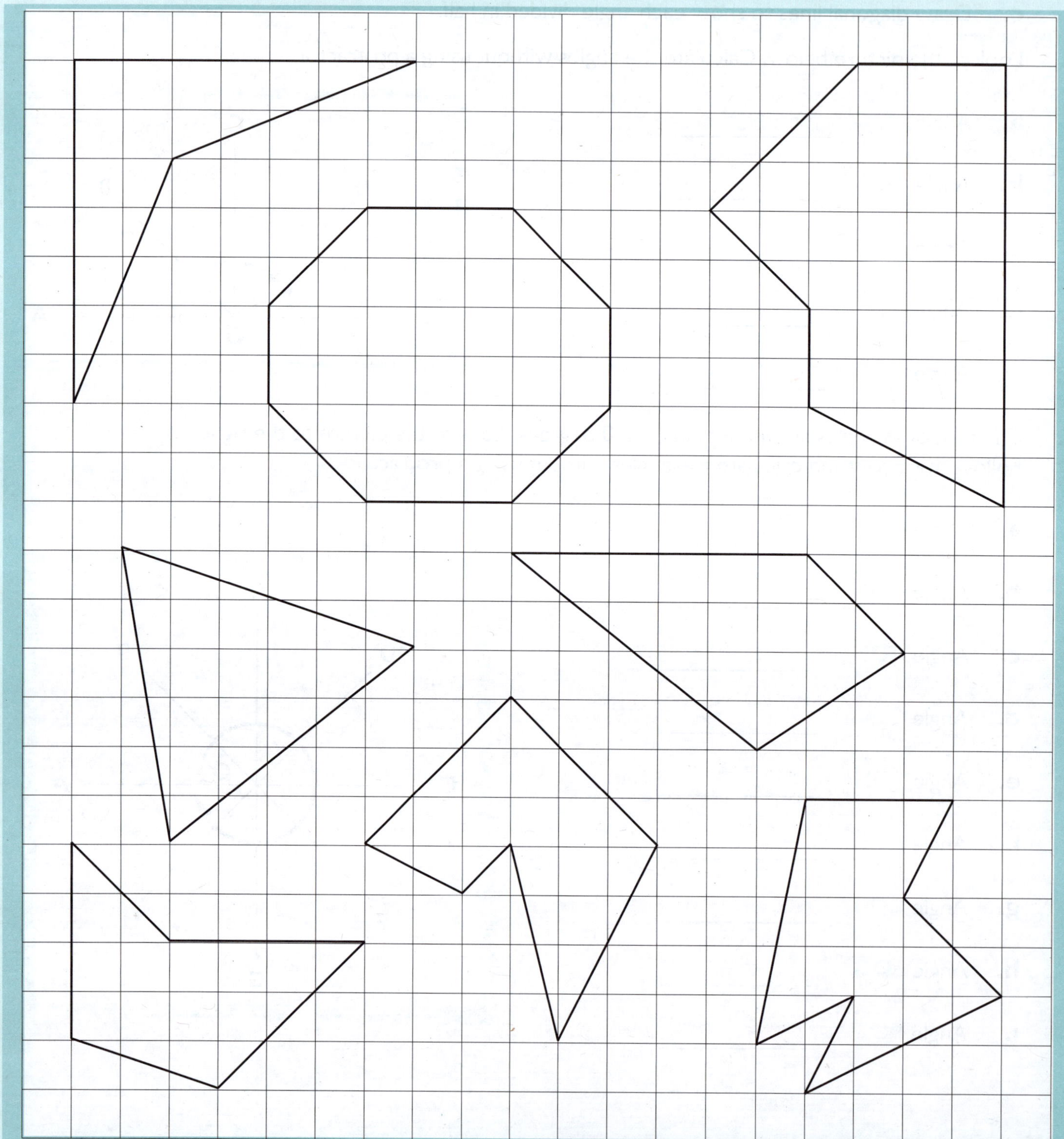

Try to draw a 2D shape that has exactly three right angles inside the shape. Write what you notice.

Working with Perpendicular Lines

1. Use different colours to mark pairs of lines that are perpendicular to each other.

a. **b.** **c.** **d.** **e.**

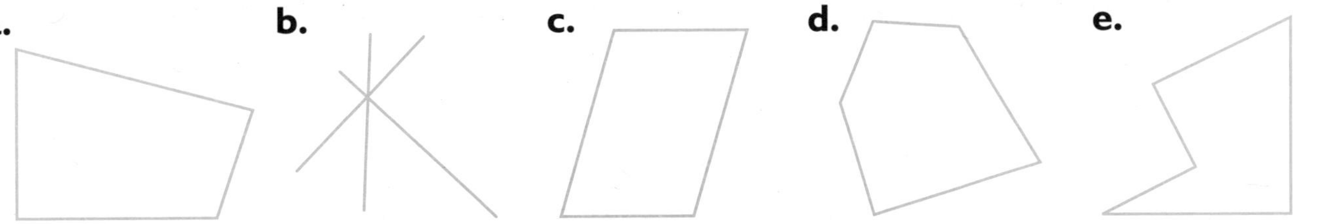

2. Circle points where perpendicular lines meet. Then write the number of points you have circled. The first one has been done for you.

a. **b.** **c.** **d.** **e.**

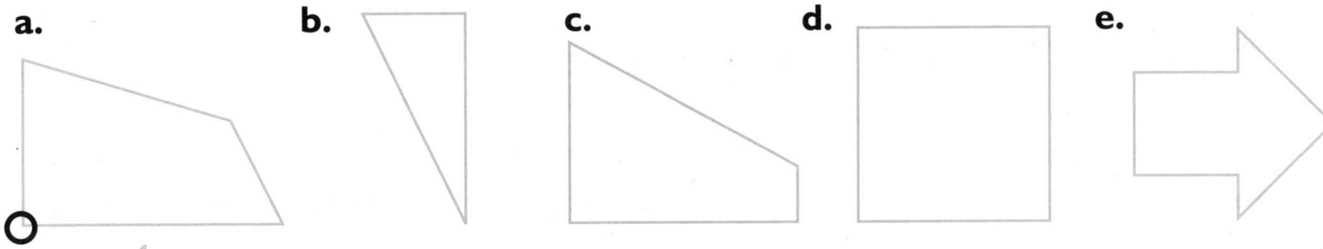

a. 1 ______ b. ______ c. ______ d. ______ e. ______

3. Use a right-angle tester to help you draw a polygon that has

a. 5 sides and only 1 pair of perpendicular lines

b. 6 sides and 2 pairs of perpendicular lines

A **polygon** is a closed shape made up of line segments.

The **triangle** is the simplest polygon. It is made up of three line segments and three angles.

Look at the triangle ABC

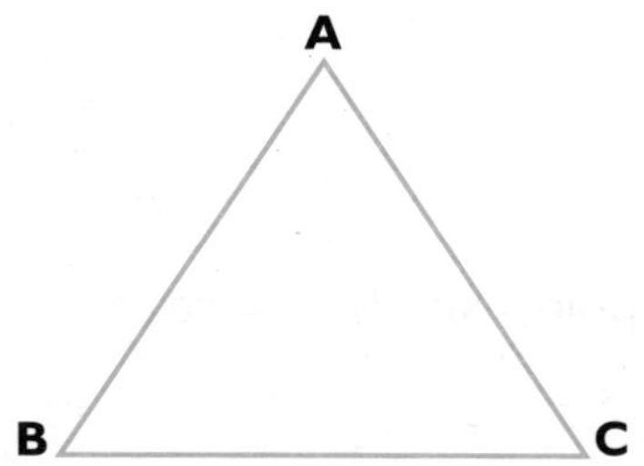

- The symbol used for triangle is △
- The triangle is made up of three line segments, AC, CB and AB
- It has three angles: ∠ABC, ∠BAC and ∠ACB
- It has three **vertices**: A, B and C.

Types of Triangles According to the Sides

A triangle can be an equilateral triangle, an isosceles triangle or scalene triangle depending on the length of its sides.

An equilateral triangle is a triangle with three equal sides.
It also has three equal angles, each measuring 60°.

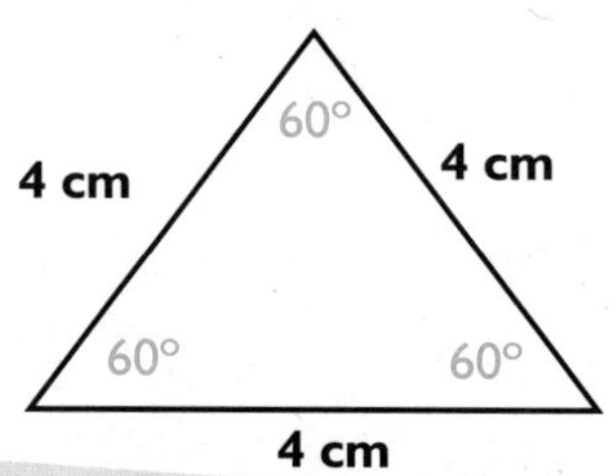

An isosceles triangle has two equal sides and two equal angles. An equilateral triangle is a special isosceles triangle in which all three sides and all the angles are equal.

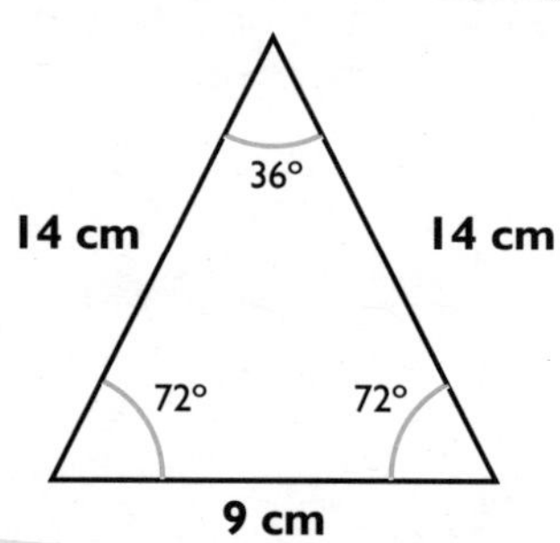

FF **Write why a triangle cannot have two pairs of perpendicular lines.**

A scalene triangle has no equal sides and no equal angles.

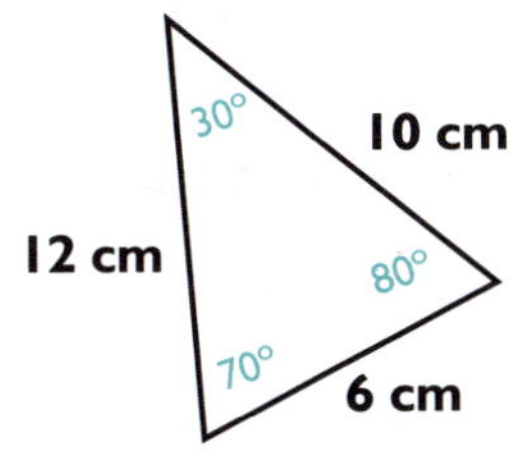

Types of Triangles According to their Angles

Acute-angled triangle: All the angles of such a triangle are less than 90°.

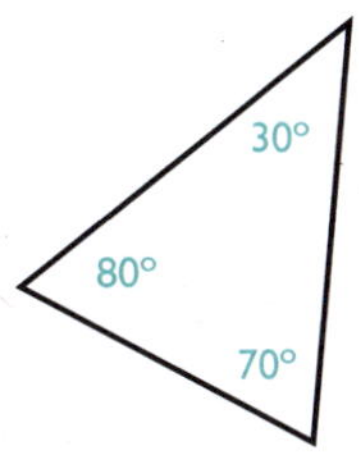

Right-angled triangle: One of the angles of such a triangle is equal to 90°.

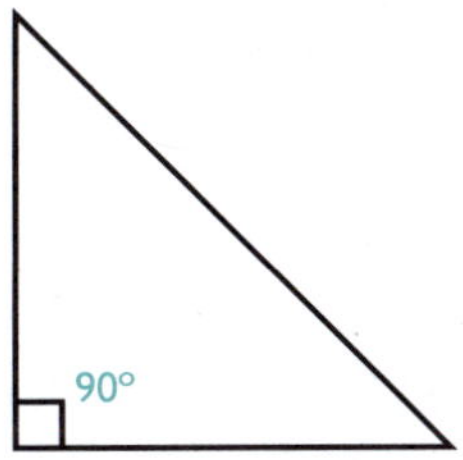

Obtuse-angled triangle: One of the angles of such a triangle is more than 90°.

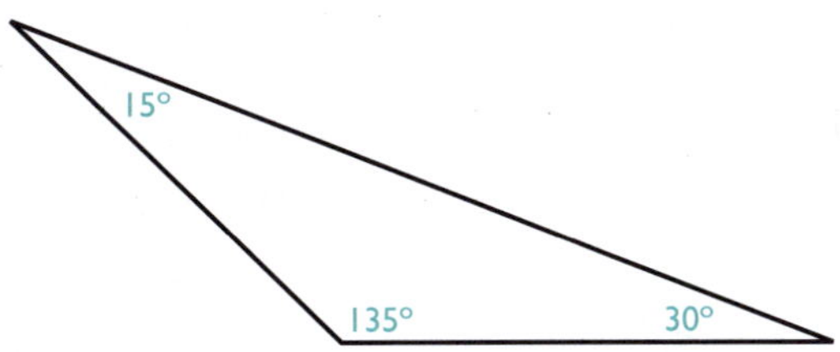

Sometimes, triangles can have two names such as an acute, isosceles triangle. Such a triangle has two sides equal but all the angles are less than 90°.

Sum of angles in a triangle

The sum of the three angles of a triangle is always 180°, whatever the type or size of the triangle.

If you know the measure of any two angles of a triangle, you can find the measure of the third.

Example: Find ∠EDF

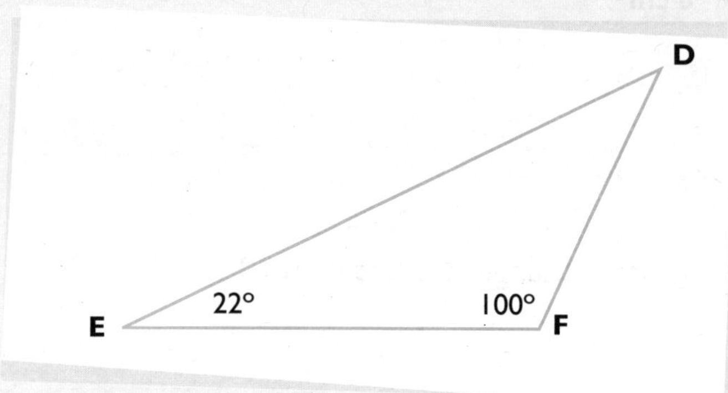

Solution:

∠DEF = 22° and ∠DFE = 100°

The sum of the angles of a triangle is 180°

Therefore , ∠DEF + ∠DFE + ∠EDF = 180°

22° + 100° + ∠EDF = 180°

∠EDF = 180° – 122°

∠EDF = 58°

Identifying Angles Inside Triangles

1. Use a right-angle tester to help you identify the triangles below.

a. Place a red ✓ inside the triangles that have one right angle.

b. Place a blue ✓ inside the triangles that have all angles less than a right angle.

c. Place a green ✓ inside the triangles that have one angle greater than a right angle.

2. Use a right-angle tester to help you draw and label different triangles to match a, b and c in Question 1.

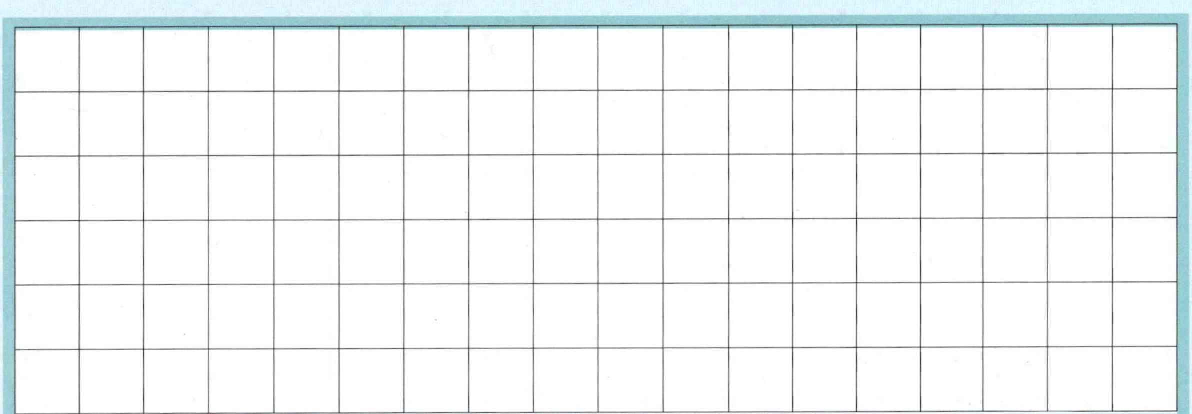

Try to draw a triangle with two angles greater than a right angle. Write what you notice.

Examining Types of Triangles

1. Look at the triangles below. For each triangle, make sides that are the same length the same colour.

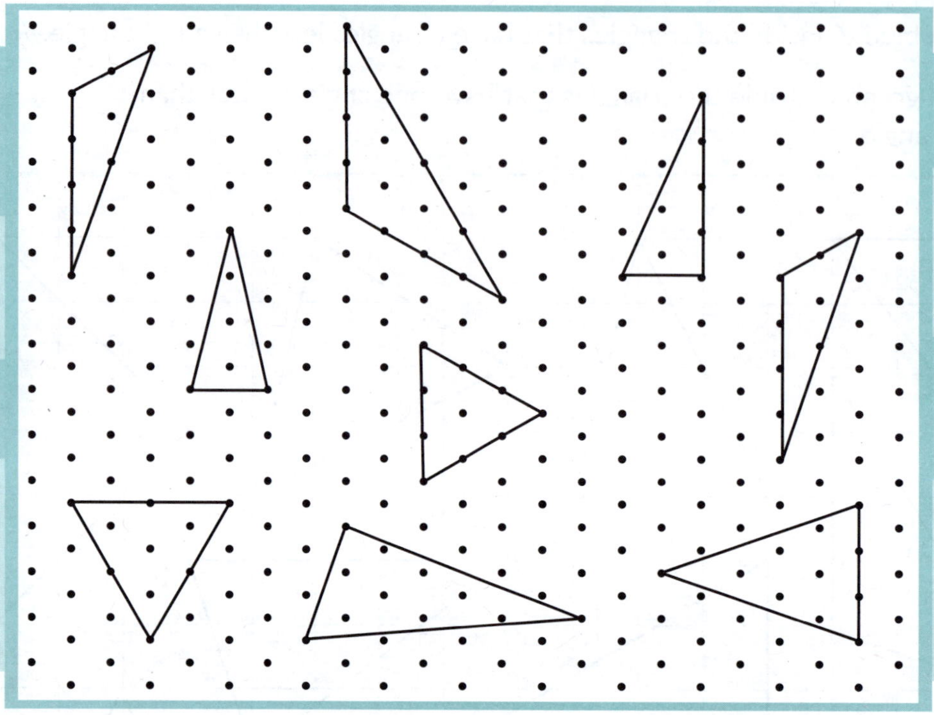

2. On the dotted paper below, draw two equilateral triangles, two isosceles triangles and two scalene triangles. Make each triangle different and label each one.

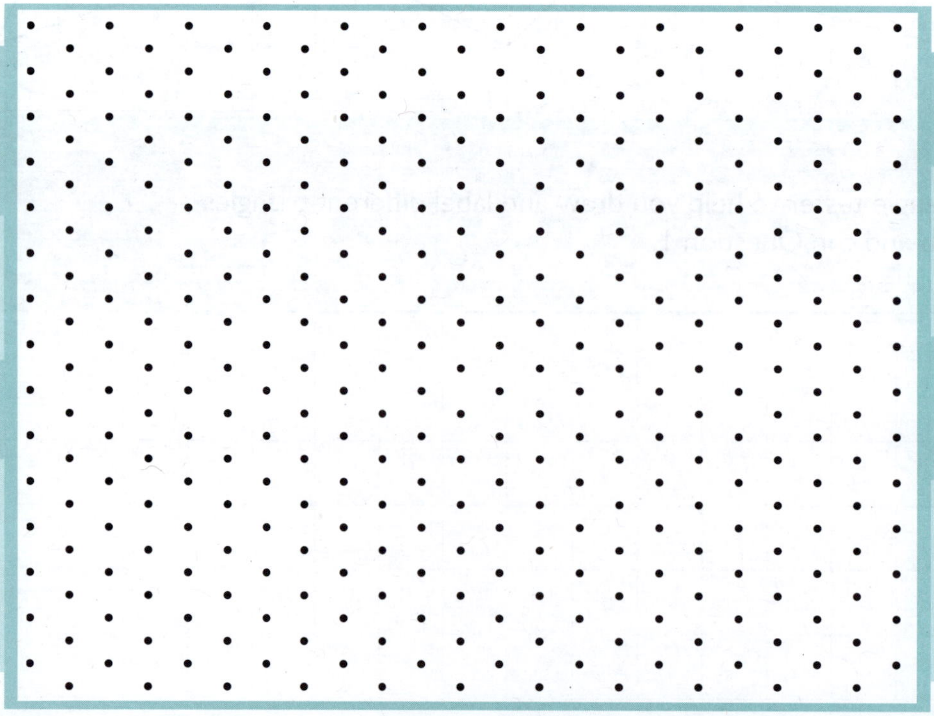

Use a ruler to draw two angle arms that are each 10 cm long. Draw a third line to create a triangle. Measure and write each interior angle in degrees.

Comparing Sides of Triangles

1. Look at the triangles below.

a. Place a red ✓ inside the triangles with exactly two sides of equal length.

b. Place a blue ✓ inside the triangles with all sides of equal length.

c. Place a green ✓ inside the triangles with all sides of different lengths.

2. Look at the quadrilateral on the right.

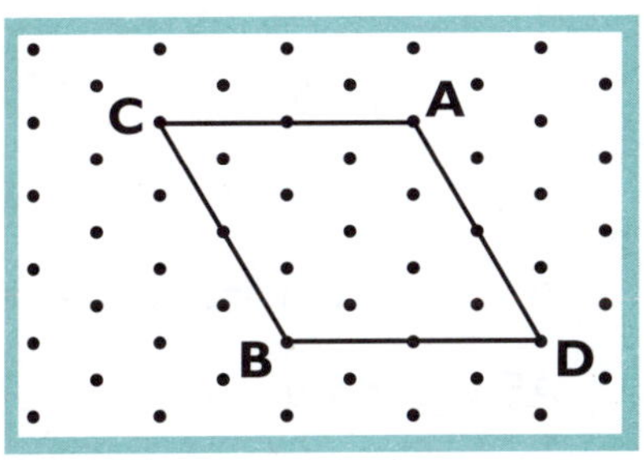

a. Draw a line from point A to point B.

Write what you notice about the triangles.

b. Draw a line from point C to point D. Write what you notice about the triangles.

Use a ruler and a right-angle tester to draw a triangle with one right triangle and two sides the same length.

Circles

A circle is a special shape. It is the collection of points that are all the same distance from a fixed point. The fixed point is called the centre of the circle. A circle is named by its centre point.

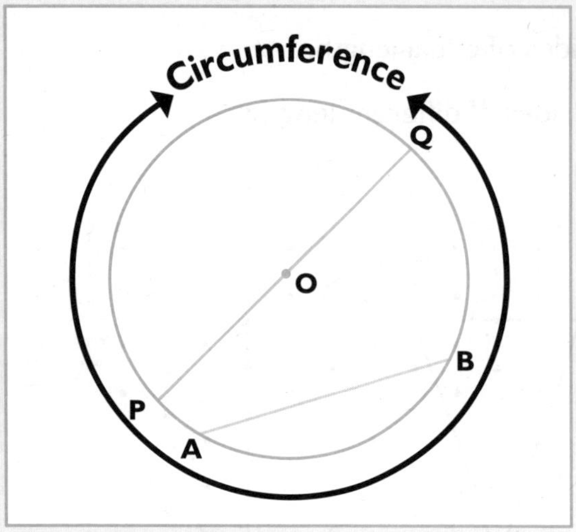

The collection of points is the circle.

O is the **centre** of the circle.

OQ and OP are the **radius** of the circle. They pass through the centre O.

There can be innumerable radii in a circle.

A line segment which has its end points on the circle and passes through the centre is called the **diameter.** PQ is the diameter of the circle.

The diameter divides the circle into two equal halves.

The diameter of a circle is twice its radius.

Or

The radius of a circle is half its diameter.

A **chord** is a line segment which has its end points on the circle.

AB is a chord.

The diameter is the longest chord in the circle.

The distance around the circle is called its **circumference**.

How to Draw a Circle with a Given Radius

Circles are drawn with a special instrument called a compass.

The distance between the tip of the compass and the tip of the pencil is the radius of the circle.

Example: Draw a circle O with radius 5 cm.

Solution:

- Mark a point O on paper.

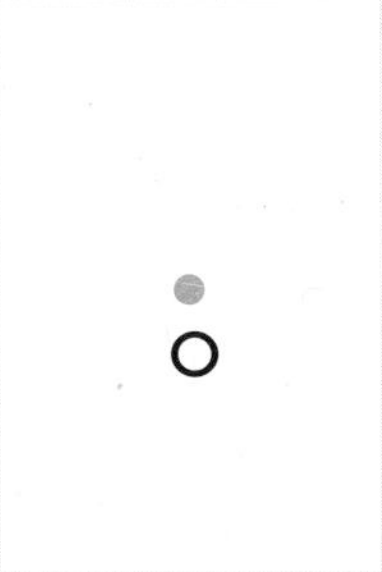

- Open the compass so that the point and pencil are 5 cm apart.
  (Use a ruler to measure the distance between the tip of the compass and pencil tip.)

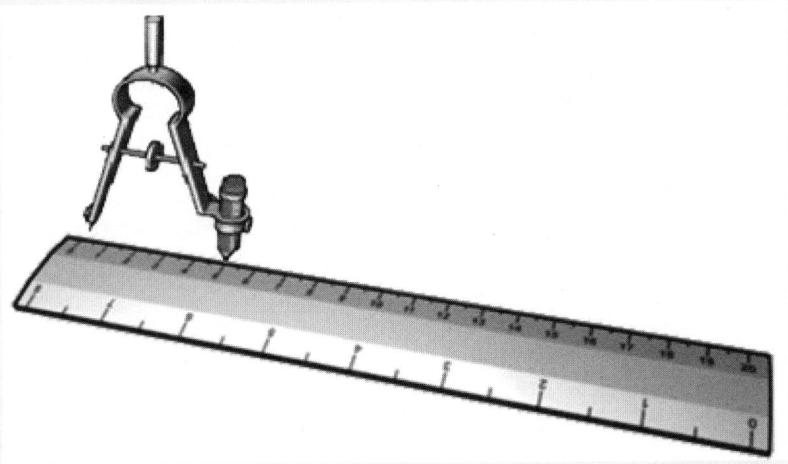

- Place the compass tip at O.

- Holding the compass at the same point, move the pencil tip around.

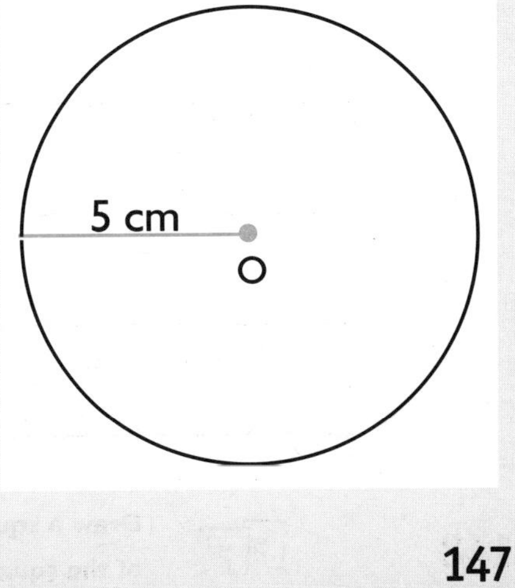

Identifying Parts of a Circle

Worksheet 101

1. Examine these circles. Colour the radii blue.

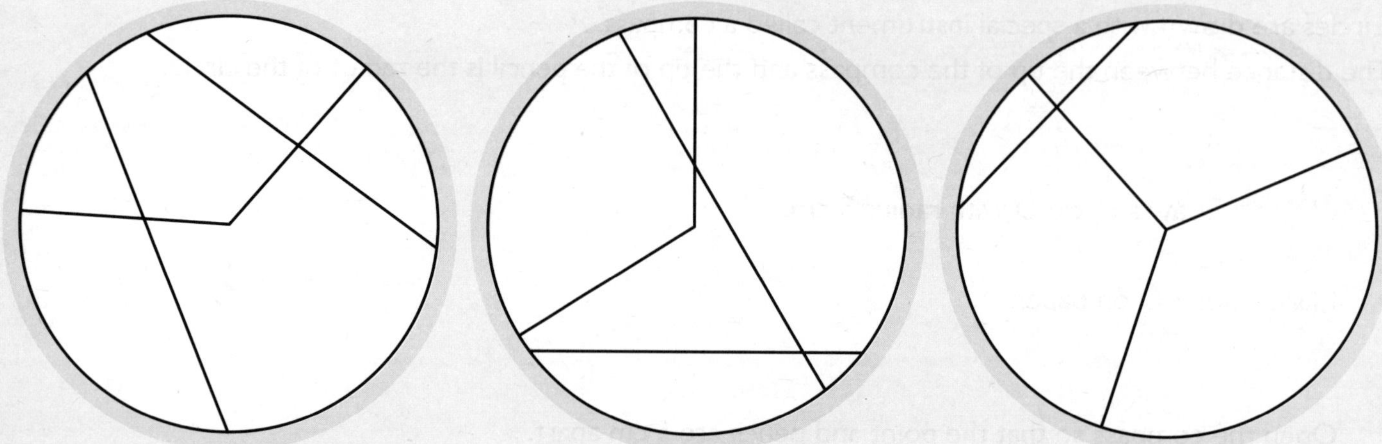

2. Draw a circle and label these parts:

a. the circumference

b. a radius

c. a diameter

d. the centre

3. This circle has three diameters shown.

a. Colour a pair of arcs that you know are the same length.

b. Write what you notice about a pair of arcs that are the same length.

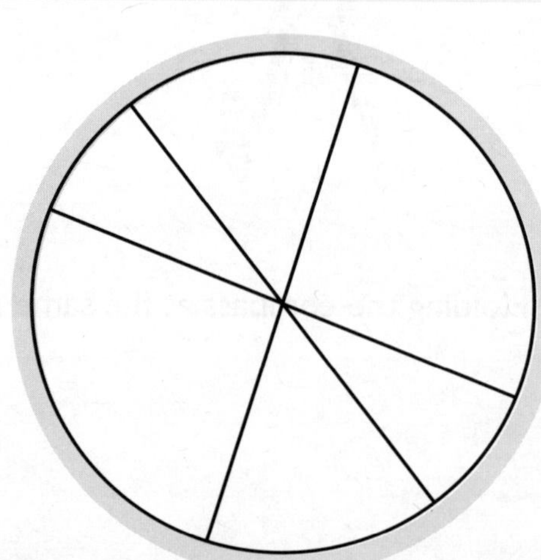

Draw a square. Then draw a circle that touches each corner of the square.

1. Name the part of the circle. Write diameter, chord, centre, or radius.

a.

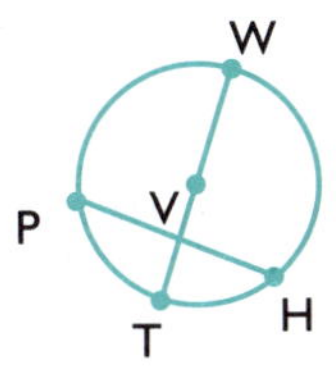

HP

____

b.

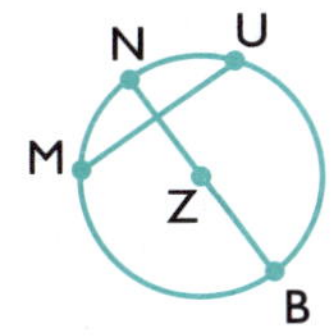

ZN

____

c.

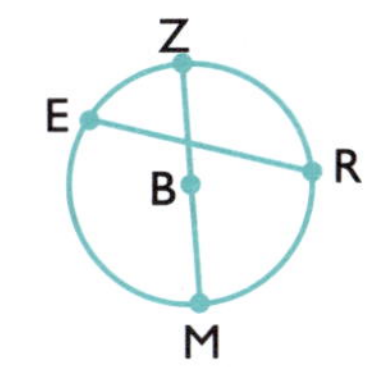

MZ

____

d.

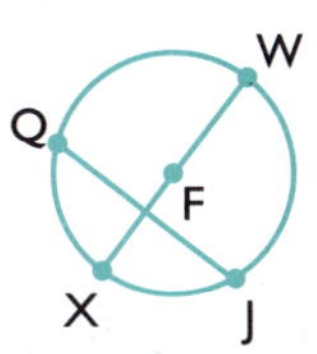

F

____

e.

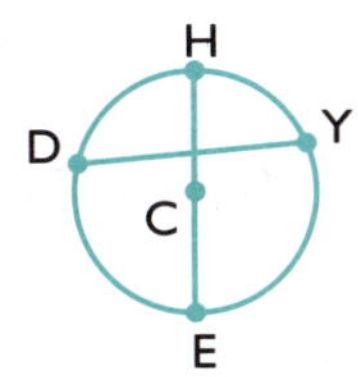

EH

____

f.

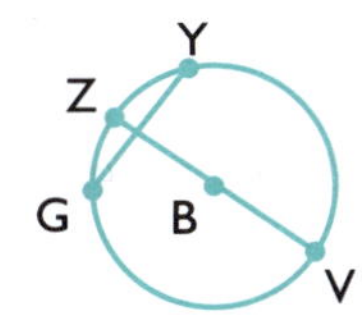

YG

____

2. What is the diameter of a circle with radius:

a.	8 cm		**b.**	10 m		**c.**	35 cm	
d.	2.4 cm		**e.**	6 mm		**f.**	8.2 cm	

3. What is the radius of a circle with diameter:

a.	22 cm		**b.**	270 m		**c.**	16 mm	
d.	14.8 cm		**e.**	34 mm		**f.**	110 cm	

4. Draw the following.

a. Construct a circle with centre S and radius 4 cm.

b. Construct a circle with centre P and diameter 12 cm.

c. Construct a circle with diameter 7 cm. What is its radius?

d. Construct a circle with centre A and radius 4.5 cm.

Measurement

CHAPTER 10

Length

Length is the measurement of something from one end to the other.

The base unit of length is metre (m). The other units are:

kilometre	hectometre	decametre	metre	decimetre	centimetre	millimetre
km	hm	dam	m	dm	cm	mm
1000 m	100 m	10 m		$\frac{1}{10}$ m	$\frac{1}{100}$ m	$\frac{1}{1000}$ m

Mass

The base unit for measuring mass is gram (g). The other units are:

kilogram	hectogram	decagram	gram	decigram	centigram	milligram
kg	hg	dag	g	dg	cg	mg
1000 g	100 g	10 g		$\frac{1}{10}$ g	$\frac{1}{100}$ g	$\frac{1}{1000}$ g

Capacity

Capacity is the amount a container can hold.

The basic unit is litre (l). The other units are:

kilolitre	hectolitre	decalitre	litre	decilitre	centilitre	millilitre
kl	hl	dal	l	dl	cl	ml
1000 l	100 l	10 l		$\frac{1}{10}$ l	$\frac{1}{100}$ l	$\frac{1}{1000}$ l

Converting Units of Measurement

To convert from one unit to another, look at the conversion ladder given below:

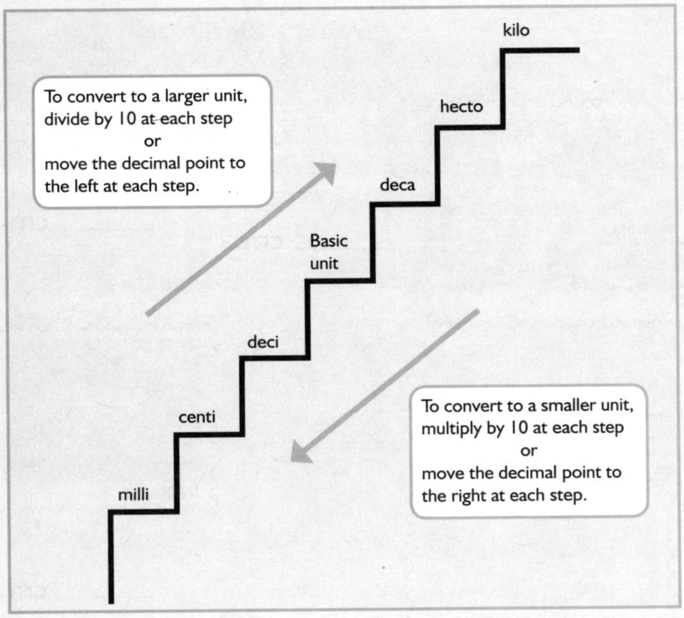

Example: Convert

a. 45 ml into litre.

b. 3.6 km into dm.

Solution:

a. We are converting a smaller unit (ml) to a larger unit (l), so we will divide.
To convert from ml to l, we move 3 steps. Therefore, we will divide by 1,000 (10 for each step) or move the decimal point 3 places to the left.

$$45 \text{ ml} = 45/1{,}000 \text{ litre}$$
$$= 0.045 \text{ litre}$$

b. We are converting a larger unit (km) to a smaller unit (dm), so we will multiply by 10 at each step. We move 4 steps to reach dm from km.
Therefore, we will multiply by 10,000 or move the decimal point 4 places to the right.

$$3.6 \text{ km} = 3.6 \times 10{,}000 \text{ dm}$$
$$= 36{,}000 \text{ dm}$$

1. Measure and label the dimensions of these stamps in centimetres.

a.
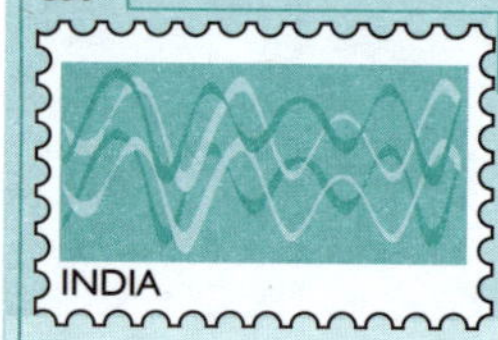

_______ cm
_______ cm

b.

_______ cm
_______ cm

c.

_______ cm
_______ cm

d.

_______ cm
_______ cm

e.

_______ cm
_______ cm

f.

_______ cm
_______ cm

2. Measure and label the dimensions of these stamps in millimetres.

a.
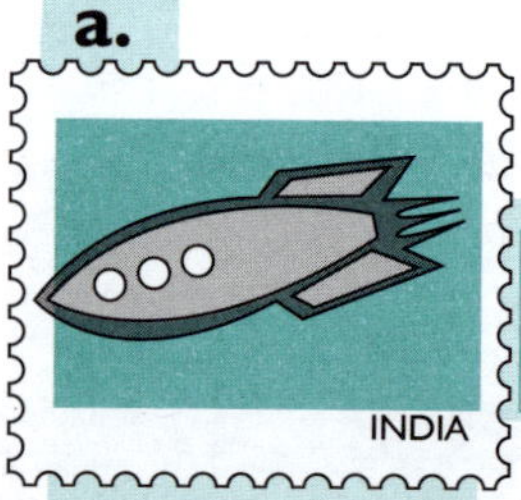

_______ mm
_______ mm

b.

_______ mm
_______ mm

c.
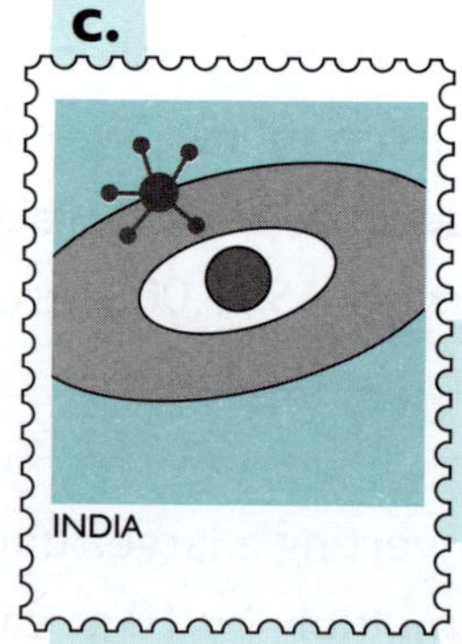

_______ mm
_______ mm

d.

_______ mm
_______ mm

e.
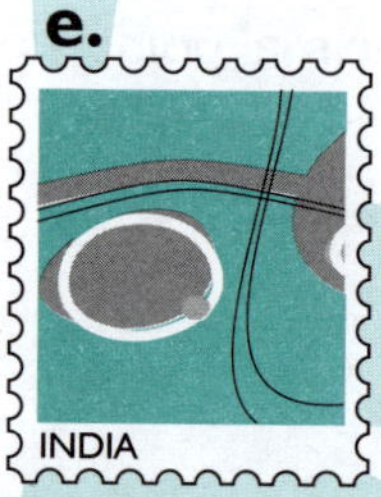

_______ mm
_______ mm

f.
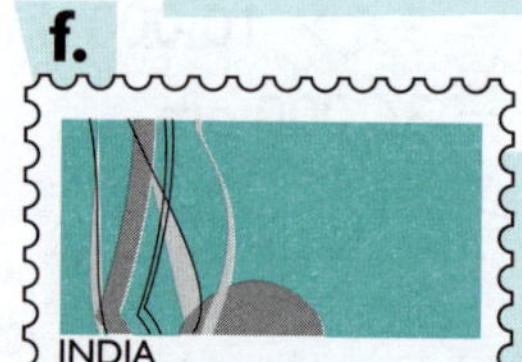

_______ mm
_______ mm

Using a different coloured pencil, write your answers for Question 1 in millimetres.

Relating Metres to Millimetres

1. Complete.

a. 6 m **is the same as** ______ mm

b. 9 m **is the same as** ______ mm

c. 4 m **is the same as** ______ mm

d. 11 m **is the same as** ______ mm

e. 15 m **is the same as** ______ mm

f. $7\frac{1}{2}$ m **is the same as** ______ mm

2. Write each dimension in metres.

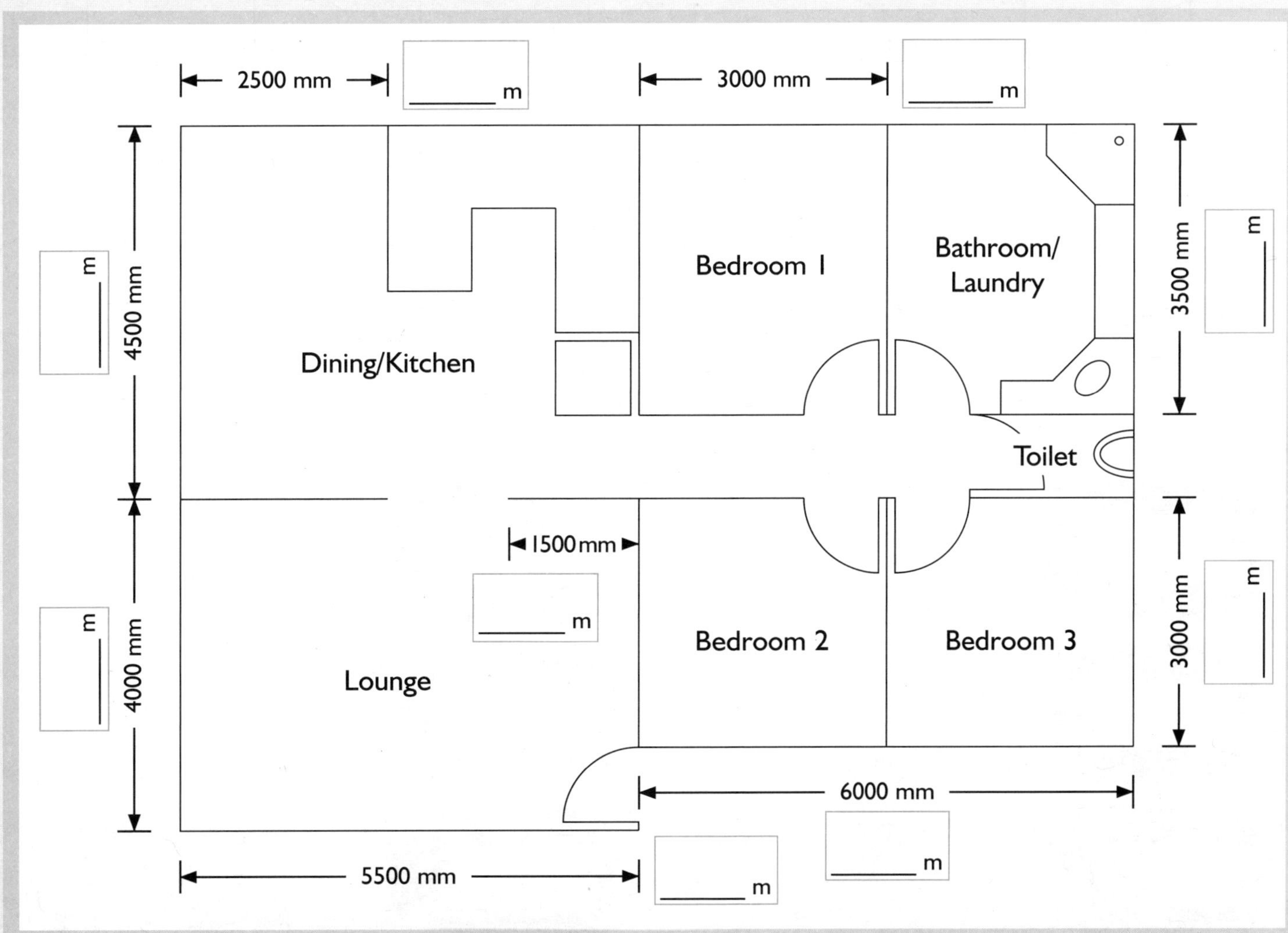

FF Write the maximum length and width of the house in metres.

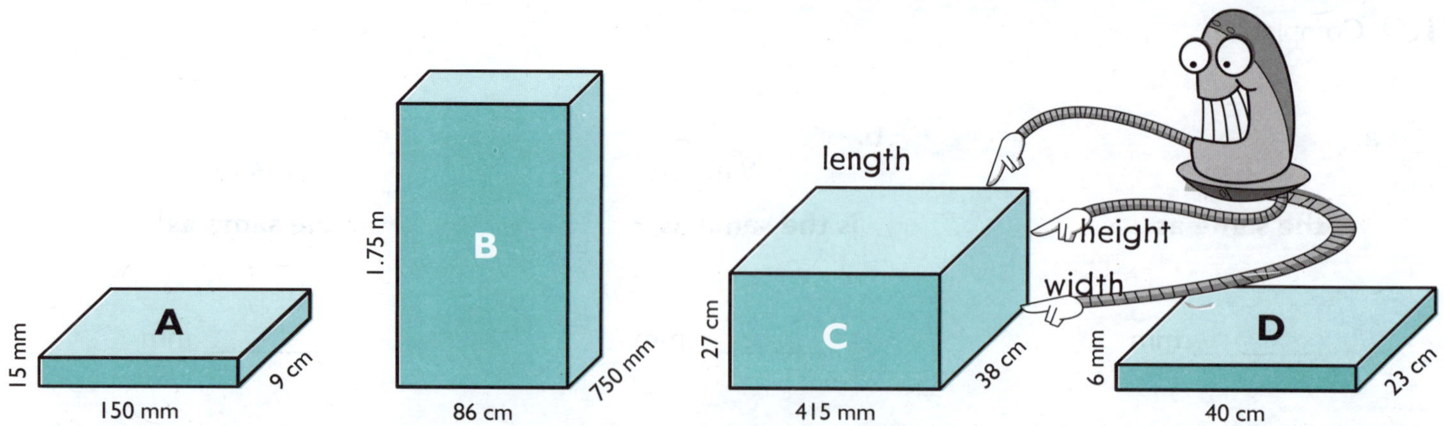

1. Complete the tables to show the dimensions of each package.

Box A	Length	Width	Height
	mm	mm	mm
	cm	cm	cm
	m	m	m

Box B	Length	Width	Height
	mm	mm	mm
	cm	cm	cm
	m	m	m

Box C	Length	Width	Height
	mm	mm	mm
	cm	cm	cm
	m	m	m

Box D	Length	Width	Height
	mm	mm	mm
	cm	cm	cm
	m	m	m

2. Write numbers to show equal lengths.

a. 215 mm | ____ cm | ____ m

b. ____ mm | 65 cm | ____ m

c. ____ mm | ____ cm | 3.75 m

d. ____ mm | ____ cm | 5 m

e. ____ mm | 5 cm | ____ m

f. 5 mm | ____ cm | ____ m

Figure out the shortest length of ribbon that is needed to wrap once around Box D. Allow 10 cm for the knot.

Converting Units of Length

1. Complete each chart.

a.

1 km	=	______	m
	=	______	cm
	=	______	mm

b.

2.5 km	=	______	m
	=	______	cm
	=	______	mm

c.

4.75 km	=	______	m
	=	______	cm
	=	______	mm

d.

0.25 km	=	______	m
	=	______	cm
	=	______	mm

2. Write the missing numbers.

a.

______ km	=	1,500	m
	=	______	cm
	=	______	mm

b.

______ km	=	______	m
	=	750,000	cm
	=	______	mm

c.

______ km	=	______	m
	=	230,000	cm
	=	______	mm

d.

______ km	=	______	m
	=	______	cm
	=	230,000	mm

e.

______ km	=	230,000	m
	=	______	cm
	=	______	mm

f.

______ km	=	______	m
	=	______	cm
	=	9,900,900	mm

g.

______ km	=	1	m
	=	______	cm
	=	______	mm

h.

______ km	=	1.5	m
	=	______	cm
	=	______	mm

FF Sydney Tower is 309 metres tall. Write this height in kilometres and in millimetres.

Adding Mixed Units of Length

Worksheet 107

Kavita, Rita, Deepak and Chintu measured three lengths of string.

	Kavita	Rita	Deepak	Chintu
A	3 m	4 m	2.5 m	4 m
B	140 cm	69 cm	187 cm	12 cm
C	186 mm	211 mm	103 mm	635 mm
Total	? ______	? ______	? ______	? ______

1. What do the students need to do before they can calculate the total length?

____

2. Figure out the total length of each student's string.
Write your answers in metres, centimetres and then millimetres.

Kavita	Rita	Deepak	Chintu
______ m	______ m	______ m	______ m
______ cm	______ cm	______ cm	______ cm
______ mm	______ mm	______ mm	______ mm

3. Who had the maximum length of string? ______________

4. Who had the shortest length of string? ______________

5. The total length of whose string was closest to

a. $4\frac{1}{2}$ metres? ______________ **b.** $4\frac{3}{4}$ metres? ______________

Draw a ✓ on the student totals that you could figure out mentally.

Solving Problems Involving Length

Here are three ways of using a ribbon to decorate a gift.

1. If you allow 20 cm for the bow, how much ribbon will you need for each method?

a. Method A ______ cm **b.** Method B ______ cm **c.** Method C ______ cm

2. Figure out how much ribbon is needed to decorate each of these in the three different methods. Allow 20 cm for the bow.

a.

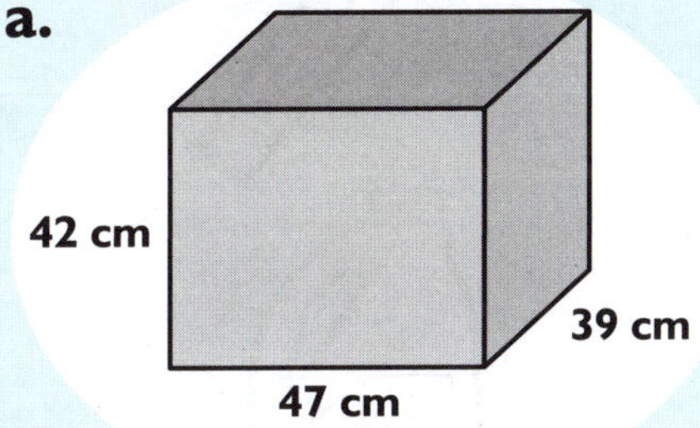

Method A ____________

Method B ____________

Method C ____________

b.

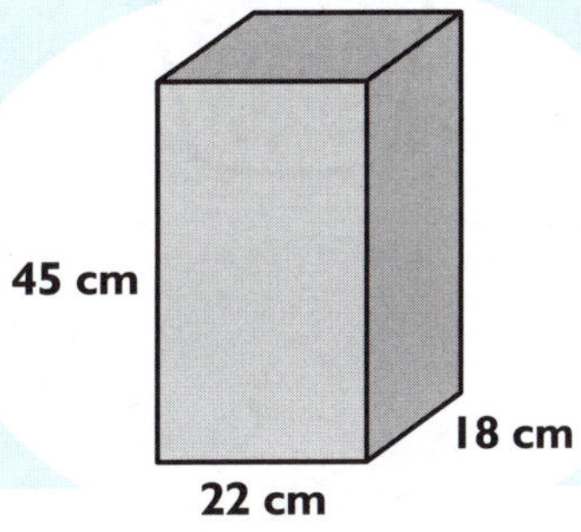

Method A ____________

Method B ____________

Method C ____________

c.

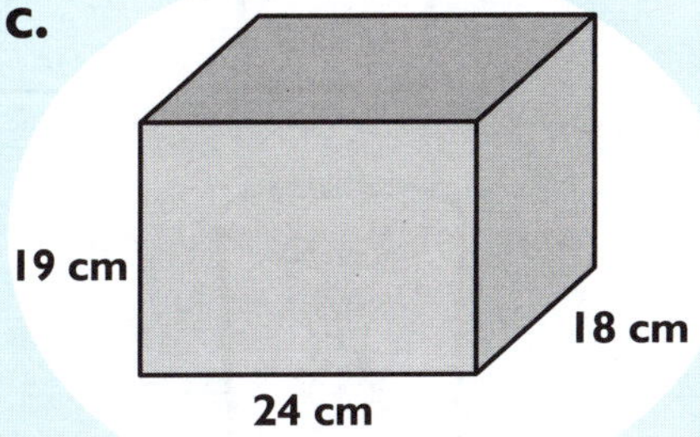

Method A ____________

Method B ____________

Method C ____________

3. How much ribbon is needed to decorate these? Allow 20 cm for each bow.

a.

____

b.

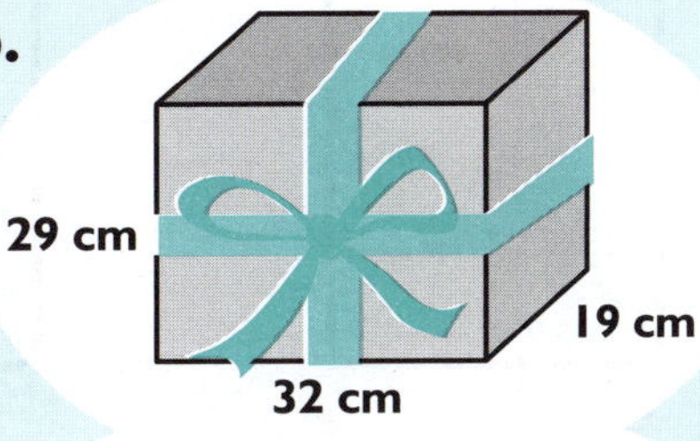

____

c.

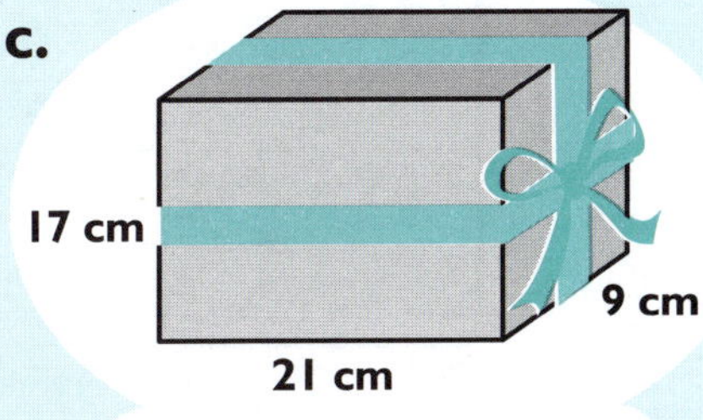

____

Imagine you have 1 m of ribbon. Allow 20 cm for the bow. Write the dimensions of the biggest box you can wrap using Method A.

Revising Millilitres—Fractions of a Litre

1. Write these as a decimal fraction of a litre.

a. 100 millilitres ______ l **b.** 10 millilitres ______ l **c.** 1 millilitre ______ l

2. Write each capacity as a decimal fraction of 1 litre.

a.

______ l

b.
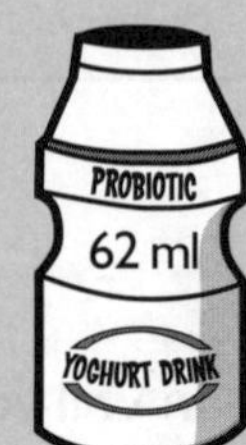

______ l

c.

______ l

d.

______ l

e.

______ l

f.
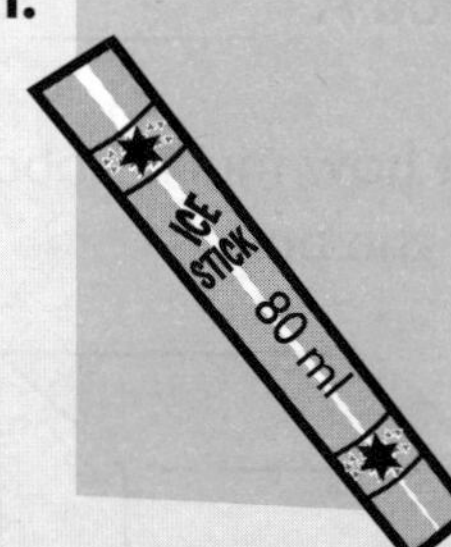

______ l

g.

______ l

h.

______ l

i.

______ l

3. Read the scale. Then write the capacity as a decimal fraction of 1 litre.

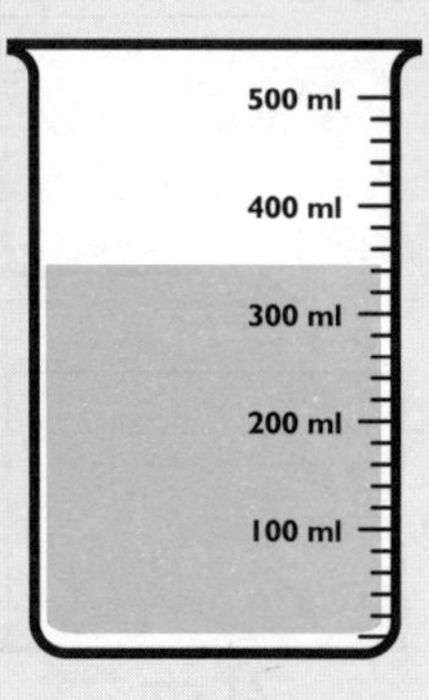

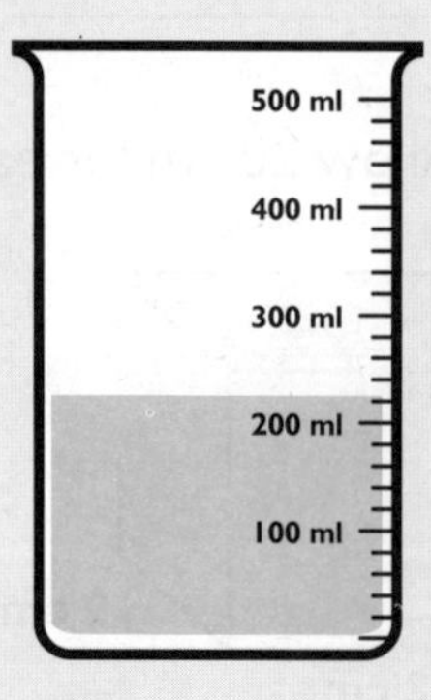

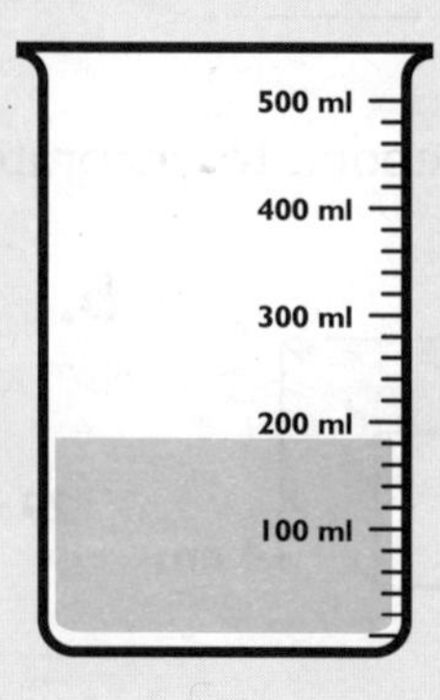

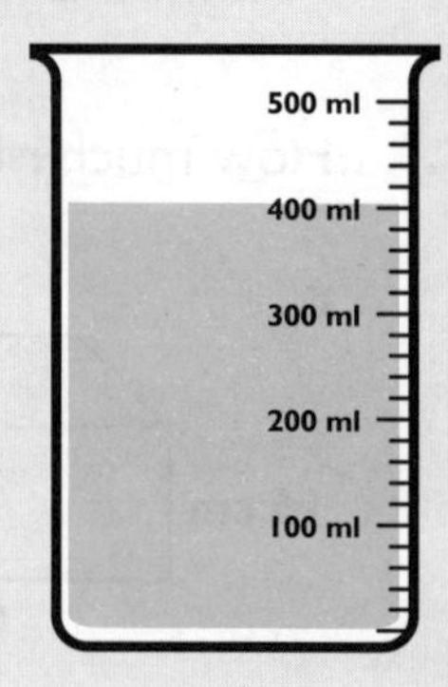

a. ______ l **b.** ______ l **c.** ______ l **d.** ______ l

Use the orange juice and pineapple juice to figure out some combinations that are close to three litres of fruit juice.

Reading Scales and Making Conversions

Draw a ✓ on the three masses that match the amount shown on the scale.

a.

$1\frac{1}{2}$ kg	$1\frac{1}{4}$ kg
1250 g	1.25 kg

b.

4 g	4.0 kg
4 kg	4000 g

c.

0.5 kg	$\frac{1}{2}$ kg
50 g	500 g

d.

$2\frac{1}{2}$ kg	2500 g
4500 g	2.5 kg

e.

750 g	$\frac{3}{4}$ kg
34 kg	0.75 kg

f.

3.5 g	3.500 kg
3.5 kg	3 kg 500 g

g.

0.1 kg	$\frac{1}{4}$ kg
0.25 kg	250 g

h.

2.25 kg	250 kg
$2\frac{1}{4}$ kg	2 kg 250 g

i.

$1\frac{3}{4}$ kg	1.75 kg
1750 g	175 kg

Rewrite these in order from the least to the greatest:
1.5 kg 150 g 1.15 kg 1 kg 15 g

Volume is defined as the amount of space within an object.
Volume is measured in cubic units such as cubic centimetre or cm^3, cubic metre or m^3, etc.
One cubic unit is the volume of a cube with each side or edge equal to 1 unit.

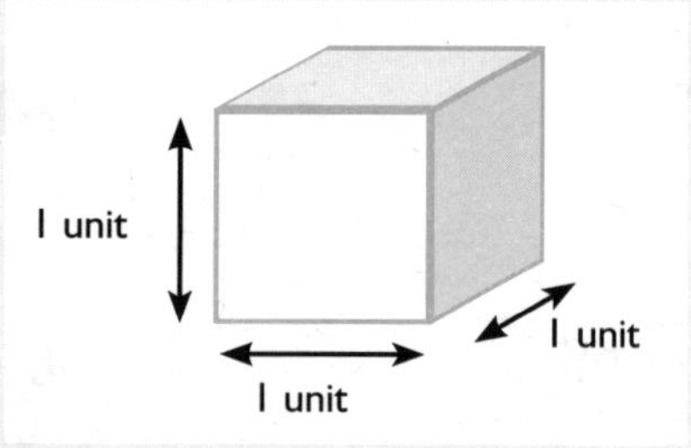

A cuboid is a solid with six rectangular faces.
A cube is a solid with six square faces. Its length, breadth and height are equal.

Look at the cuboid below:

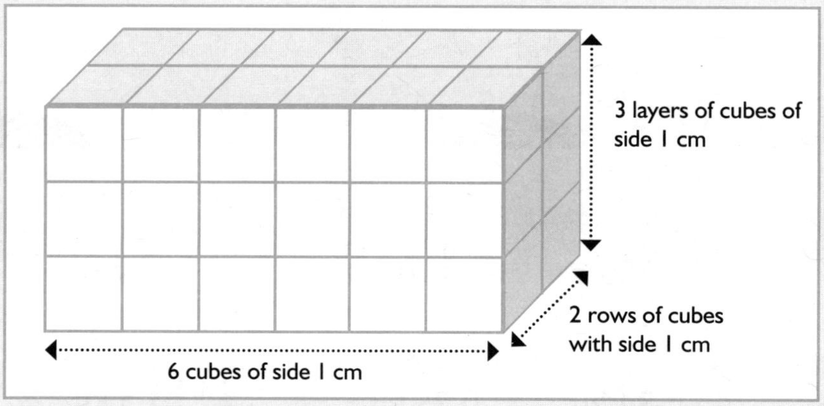

There are 36 cm cubes that are joined to make this cube. Therefore, we say that the volume of this cuboid is 36 cubic cm or 36 cm^3.

Look at the figure above once again.
Length = 6 cm
Width = 2 cm
Height = 3 cm

If we multiply the length, width and height, we get:
$6 \text{ cm} \times 2 \text{ cm} \times 3 \text{ cm} = 36 \text{ cm}^3$
Therefore,
volume of a cuboid = length × width × height

Volume of a Cube

Since all the edges of a cube are equal,

volume of a cube = side × side × side

Example 1: What is the volume of a Rubik's cube with side 3 cm?

Solution:

Volume of a cube= side × side × side

Volume = 3 cm × 3 cm × 3 cm

= 27 cm^3

Example 2: An Olympic-size swimming pool has a length of 50 m, width of 25 m and depth of 2 m. How much water is required to fill it?

Solution: Volume of a cuboid = length × width × height

Water required = 50 m × 25 m × 2 m

= 2,500 m^3

Working with Cubic Centimetres

1. This small container is **filled** with water.

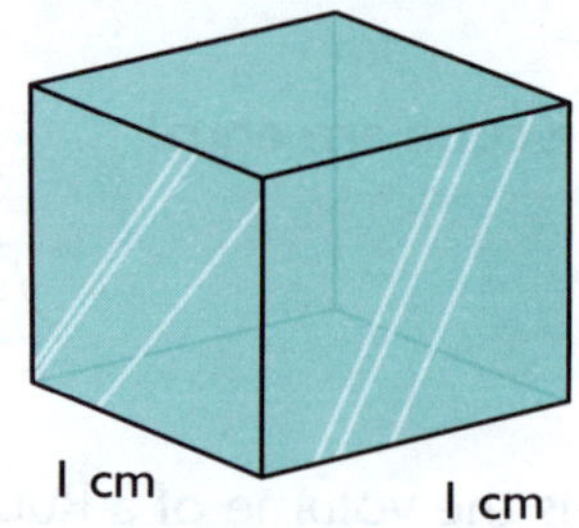

One cubic centimetre of water is equivalent to:

Volume
______ cm^3

2. a. Use the dimensions to calculate the volume of each container.

	Dimensions (cm)			Volume (cm^3)
	Width	Height	Length	
Container A	3	4	6	
Container B	4	5	6	
Container C	4	4	4	
Container D	5	8	10	
Container E	10	10	10	

b. Write what you noticed about Container E.

______

c. Figure out the dimensions of other containers that have the same volume as Container E.

	Containers of water			
	A	B	C	D
Width				
Height				
Length				

1. Work out the number of cubes in each prism. Then complete the table.

A

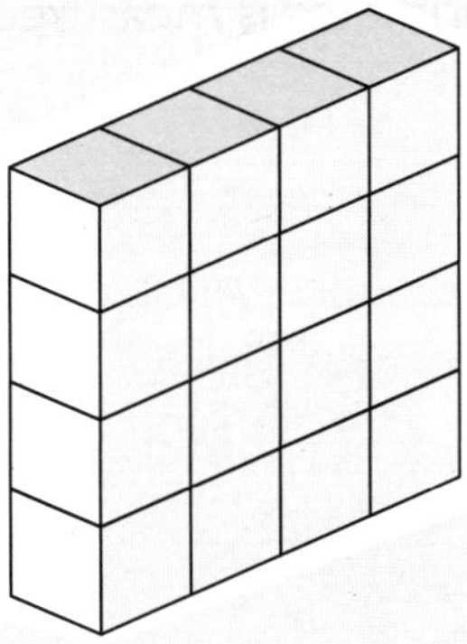

B

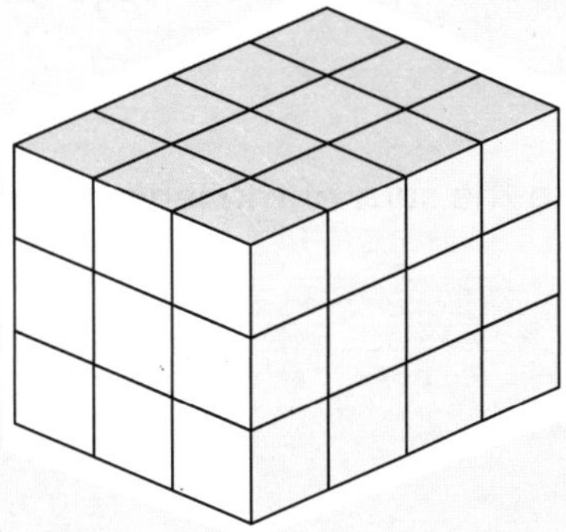

C

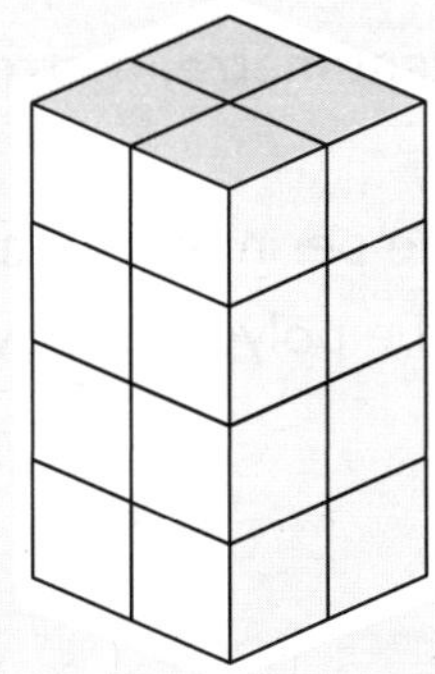

Prism	Number of cubes in one layer	Number of layers	Total number of cubes
A			
B			
C			

2. Work out the number of cubes in each prism. You can draw lines on the prisms to help. Then complete the table.

A

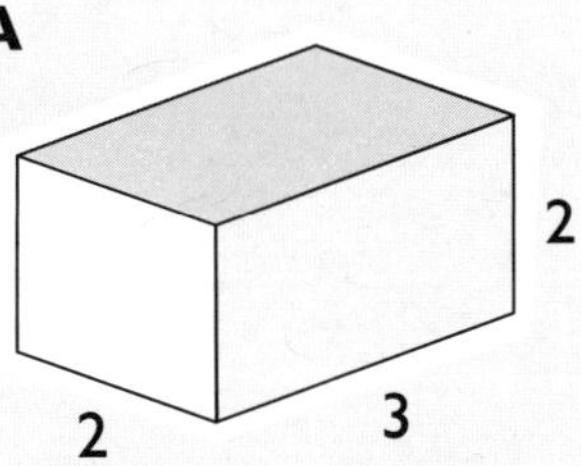

B

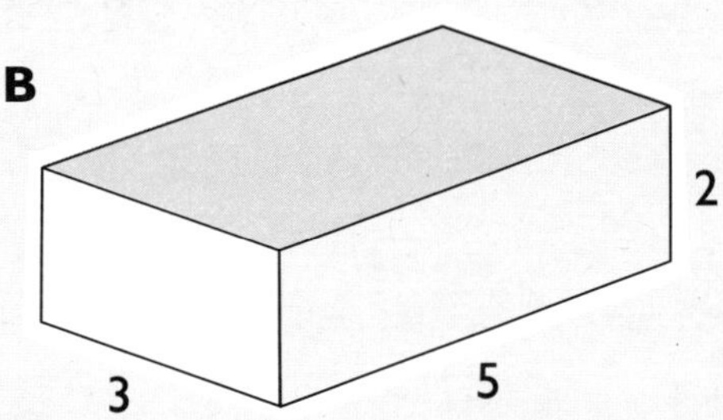

C

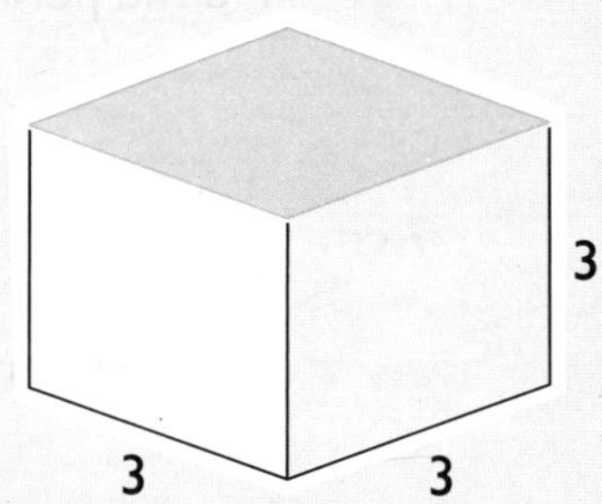

Prism	Number of cubes in one layer	Number of layers	Total number of cubes
A			
B			
C			

Build a prism that has 32 cubes. Then write the dimensions.

Perimeter

The perimeter of an object is the distance of the outside 'edge' of the object. Perimeter is measured in units such as centimetre, metre, kilometre.

To find the perimeter of a polygon, take the sum of the length of each side.
Look at the polygon below.

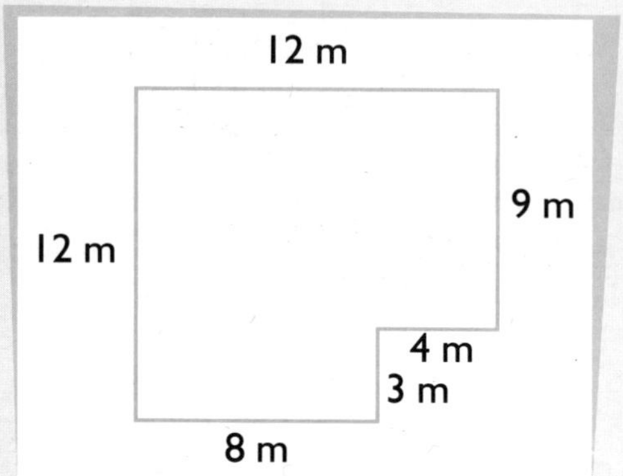

The perimeter of the polygon = 12 m + 12 m + 9 m + 4 m + 3 m + 8 m

Perimeter = 48 m

Perimeter of a triangle

Perimeter of a triangle = sum of the length of its sides.

Example: Find the perimeter of a triangle with sides measuring 12 cm, 9 cm and 7 cm.

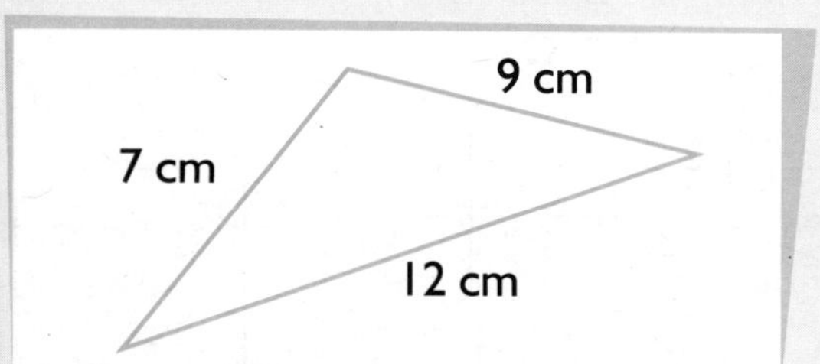

Solution:

Perimeter = 12 cm + 9 cm + 7 cm = 28 cm

Perimeter of a Rectangle

Perimeter = sum of all the sides.
As the opposite sides of a rectangle are equal,
Perimeter of a rectangle = length + breadth + length +breadth.
Perimeter of a rectangle = 2 × length + 2 × breadth.
Perimeter of a rectangle = 2 × (length + breadth).

Example: A rectangle has a length of 45 m and a breadth of 35 m. Find the perimeter.

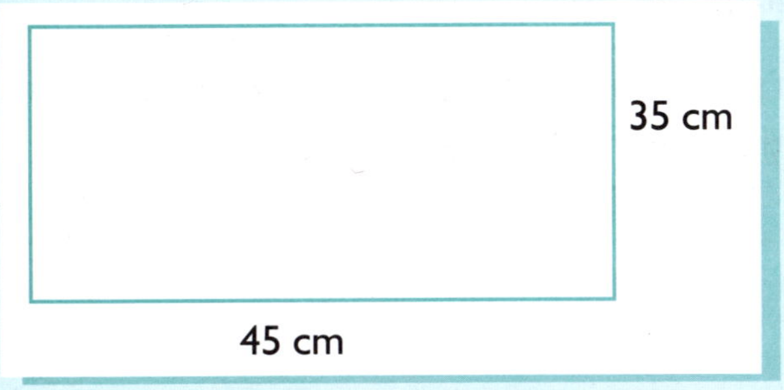

Solution:

Perimeter of a rectangle = 2 × (length + breadth)

Perimeter = 2 × (45 + 35)

= 2 × 80

= 160 m

Perimeter of a Square

As all sides of a square are equal:

Perimeter of a square = side + side + side + side.

Perimeter of a square = 4 × side.

Example: Find the perimeter of a square each side of which measures 6 cm.

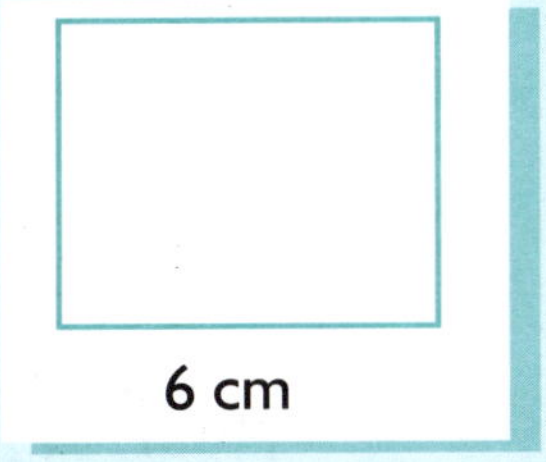

Solution:

Perimeter = 4 × 6 cm

= 24 cm

Area

Area is the size of an enclosed or marked region. It is the amount of surface in a closed figure.

The shaded portion of the figures shows their area.

The area of a shape tells how many square units are needed to cover the shape. Area can be measured in units such as square centimetres (cm^2), square metres (m^2), etc.

You can find the area by drawing a shape on graph paper, and counting the squares inside the shape.

Example: Find the area of the figure drawn on the centimetre squared paper.

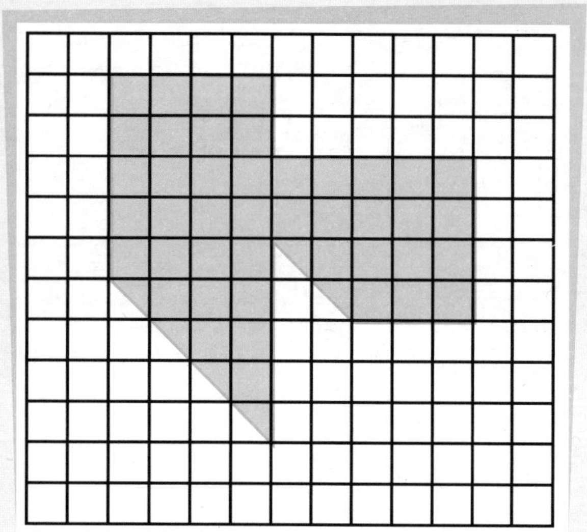

There are 43 complete square and 6 half squares. Two half squares make 1 complete square.
Therefore, the area of the figure is 46 cm^2.
This method of finding the area is inconvenient if the figure is large or there are too many squares to count.
We can use simple formulae to calculate the area.

Area of a Rectangle

Look at the rectangle with length 5 cm and breadth 3 cm.
We need 15 cm squares to cover the surface.
Thus, the area of the rectangle is = 15 cm^2
=5 cm × 3 cm

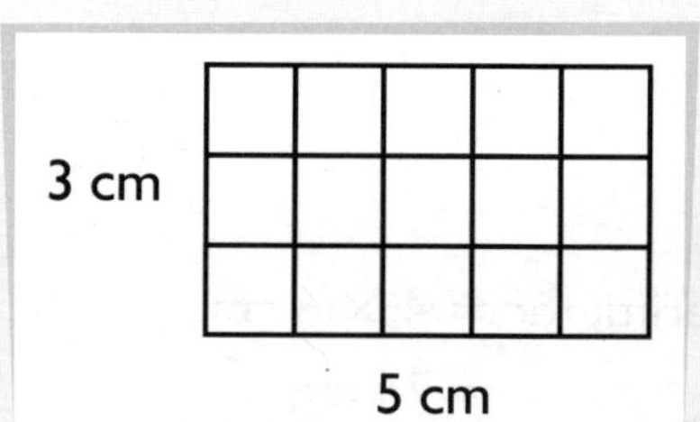

Area of a rectangle = length × breadth

Area of a Square

A square is special kind of rectangle. Its length and breadth are equal. Therefore,

Area of a square = side × side

Example: A square-shaped garden has a side of 6 m. What is its area?

Solution : Area of a square = side × side
Area of the garden = 6 m × 6 m
= 36 m^2

1. Figure out the perimeters of these shapes.

a.

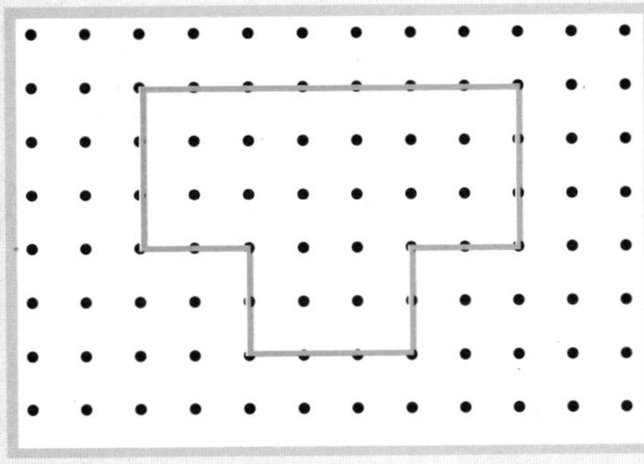

Perimeter = ______ units

b.

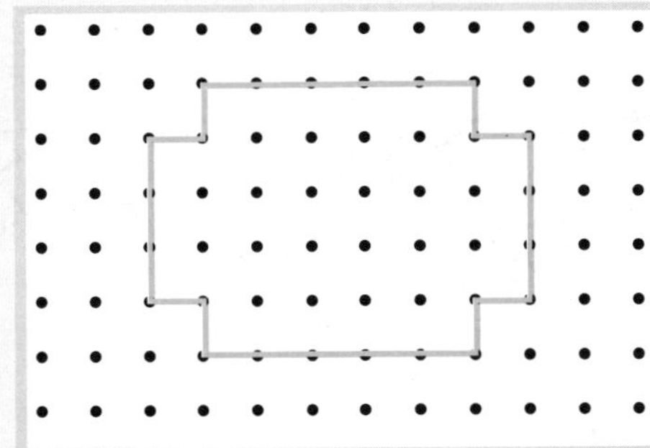

Perimeter = ______ units

c.

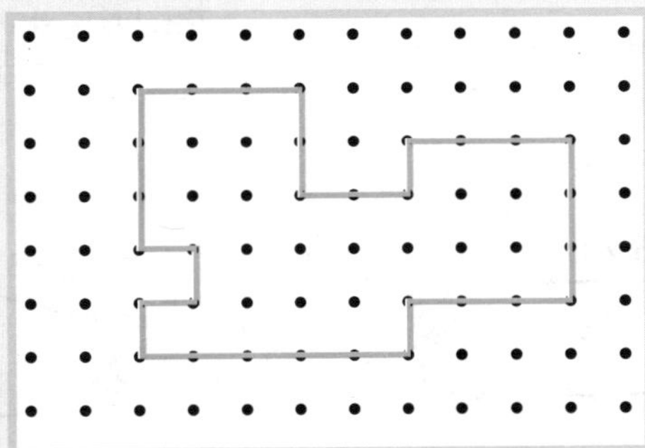

Perimeter = ______ units

d.

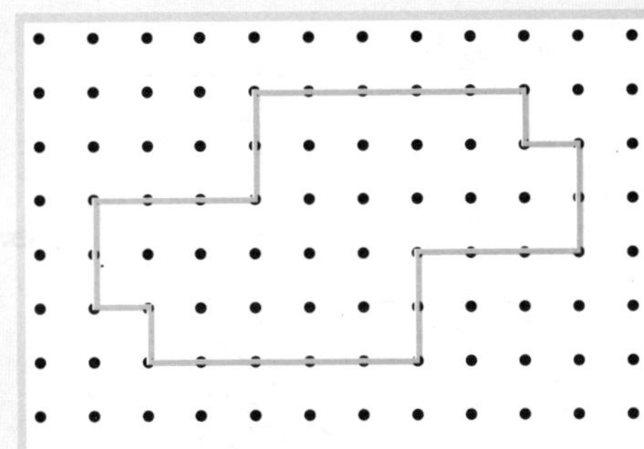

Perimeter = ______ units

2. Figure out and write the perimeter of the rectangle.
Then calculate the perimeters of the other two shapes.

a.

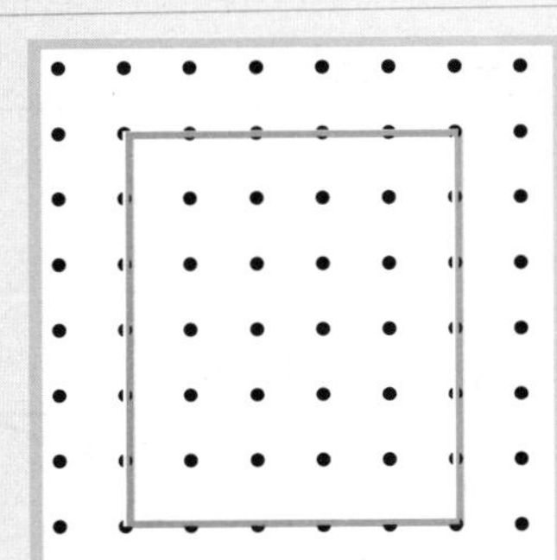

Perimeter = ______ units

b.

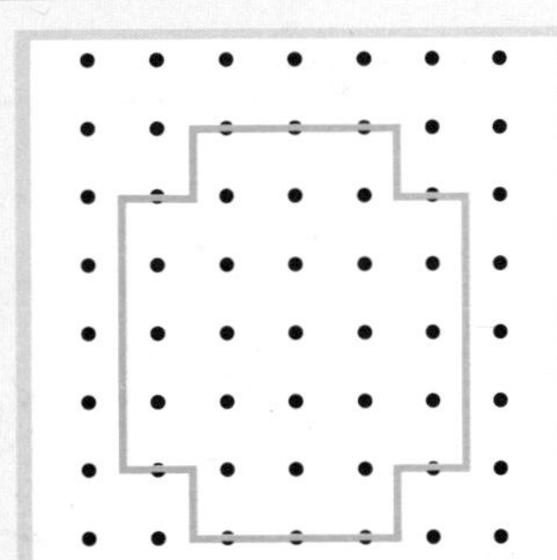

Perimeter = ______ units

c.

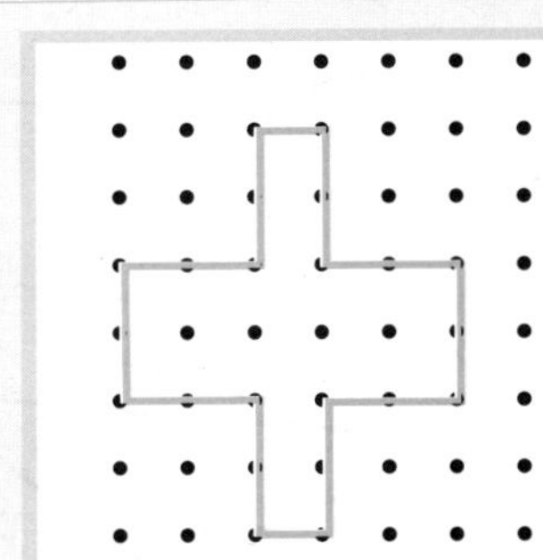

Perimeter = ______ units

What did you notice? ____

____

____

Use your ruler. Draw and label the dimensions of three different shapes that have a perimeter equal to 20 centimetres.

1. Calculate the total perimeter of each garden. Record the steps you use.

a.

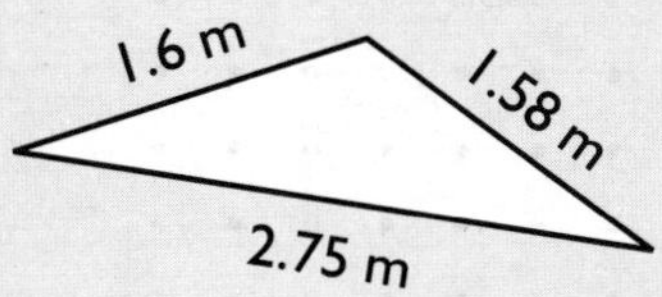

Total length ____________

b.

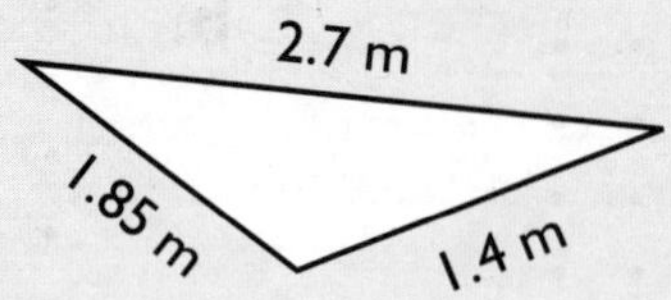

Total length ____________

c.

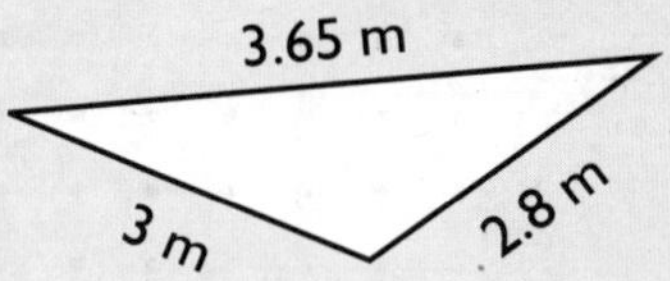

Total length ____________

d.

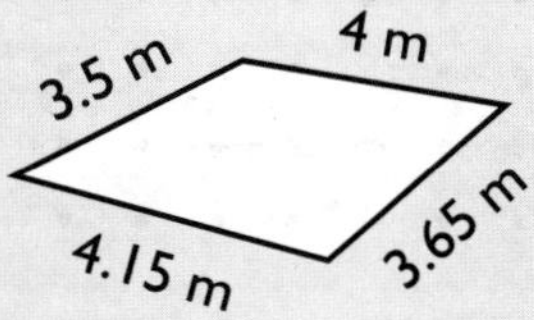

Total length ____________

e.

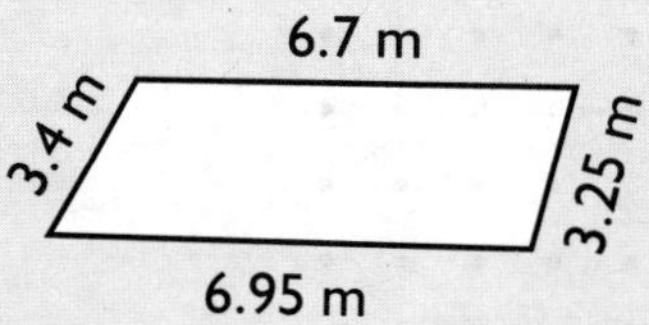

Total length ____________

f.

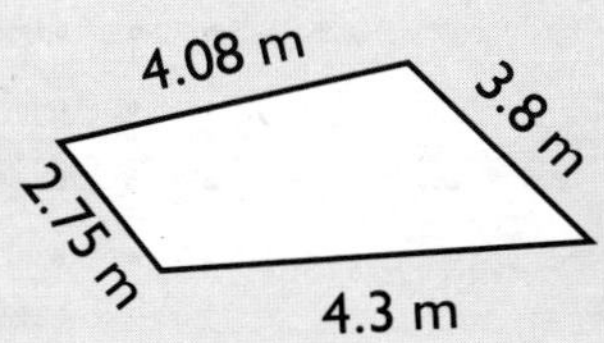

Total length ____________

g.

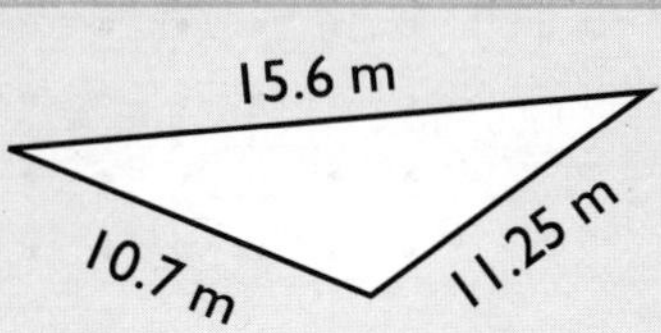

Total length ____________

h.

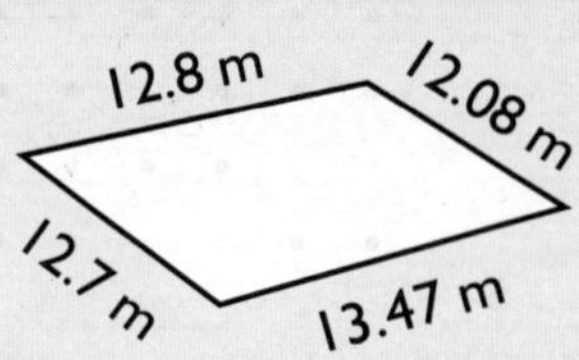

Total length ____________

i.

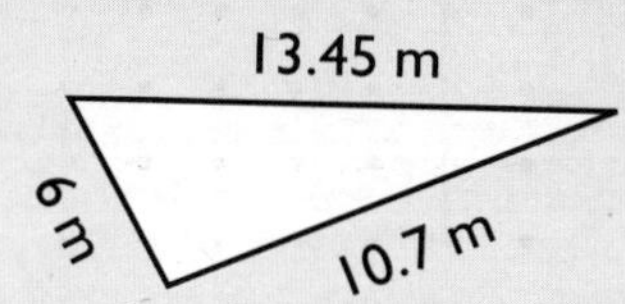

Total length ____________

FF **Draw and label a quadrilateral that has a perimeter of 10 metres. All sides should be of different lengths.**

Measuring Perimeter

1. Calculate the perimeter of each triangle in your head.
Use pairs of numbers you can add together easily.

a.

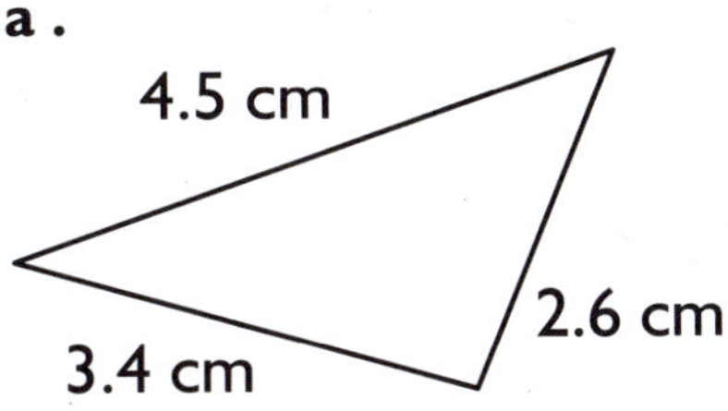

Perimeter ______ cm

b.

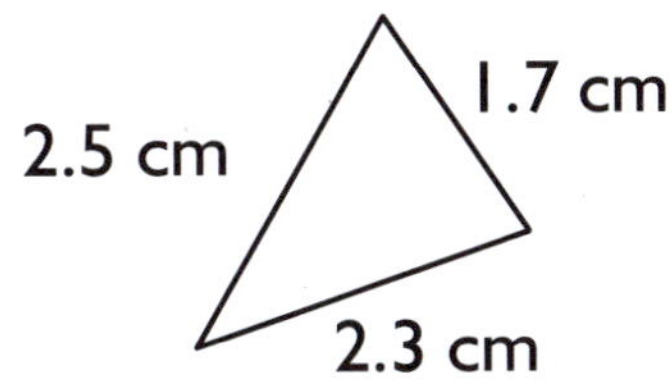

Perimeter ______ cm

c.

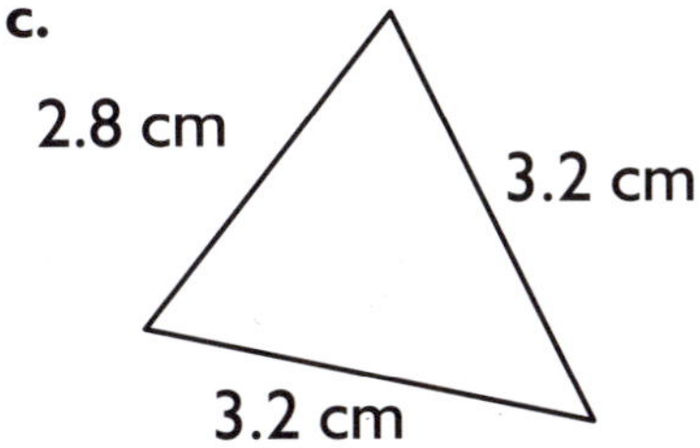

Perimeter ______ cm

d.

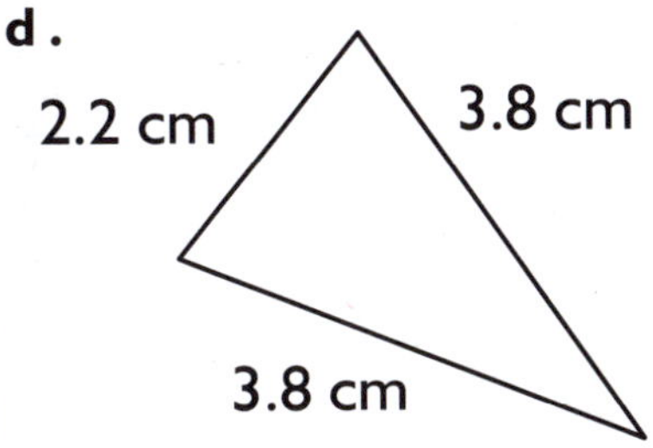

Perimeter ______ cm

e.

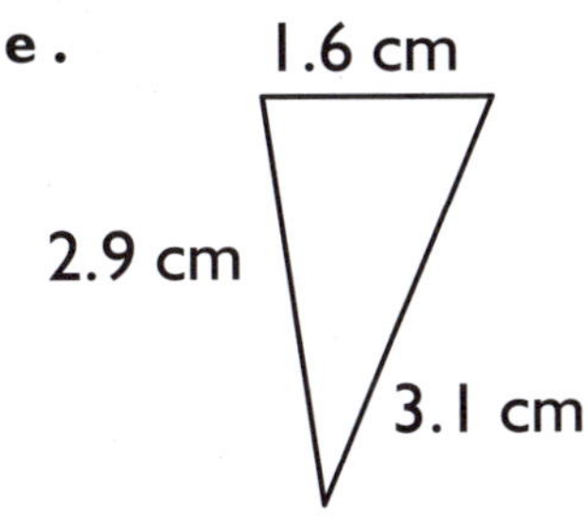

Perimeter ______ cm

f.

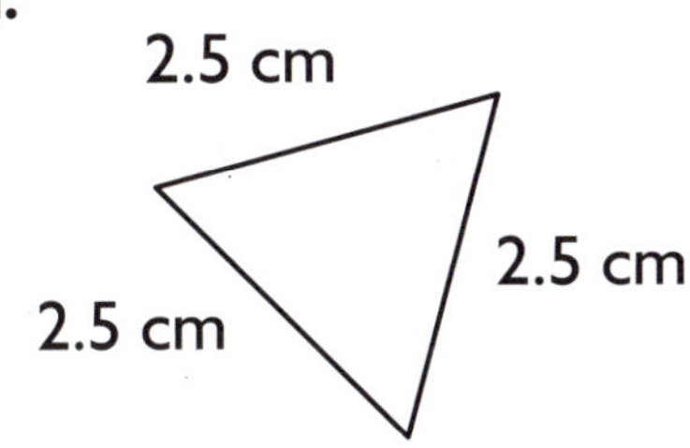

Perimeter ______ cm

2. Use the same method to calculate the total distance that each student walked.

	Day 1	Day 2	Day 3	Day 4	Total
Hemali	2.3 km	2.6 km	2.7 km	2.4 km	______ km
Sonali	3.5 km	2.8 km	3.2 km	4.3 km	______ km
Yudi	3.1 km	3.3 km	3.4 km	3.5 km	______ km
Chitra	2.8 km	2.9 km	3.7 km	3.1 km	______ km

3. Draw ⌒ to connect numbers you would add together first.
Then write the answer.

a. $3.6 + 2.5 + 1.4 + 3.5 =$ ________

b. $5.1 + 4.8 + 3.9 + 2.2 =$ ________

c. $5.3 + 2.6 + 4.4 + 2.7 =$ ________

d. $2.8 + 3.3 + 1.7 + 4.2 =$ ________

1. Mentally calculate the perimeter of each quadrilateral. Look for pairs of numbers that add easily together.

a.

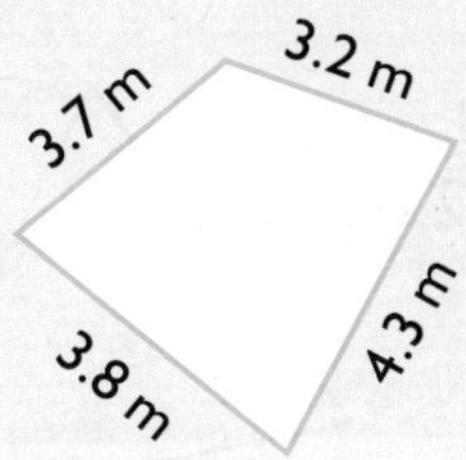

Perimeter = ______

b.

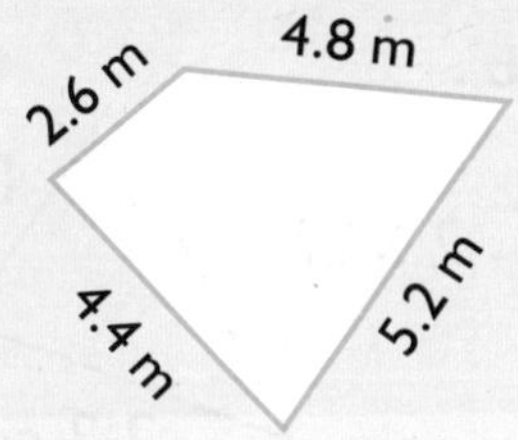

Perimeter = ______

c.

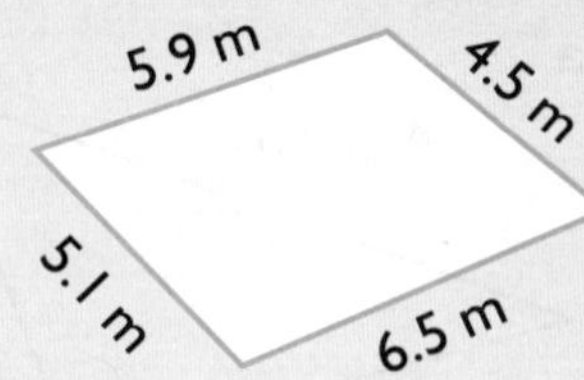

Perimeter = ______

d.

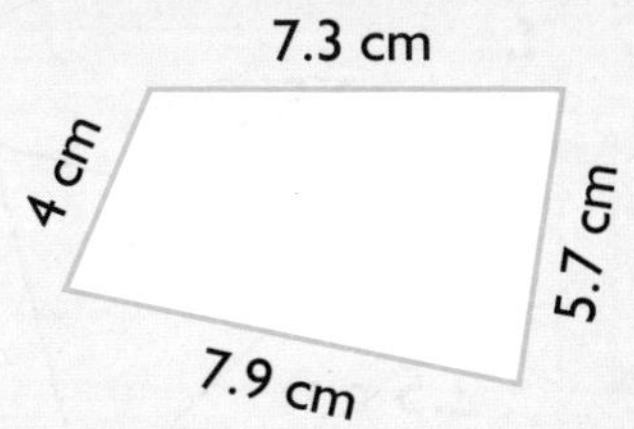

Perimeter = ______

e.

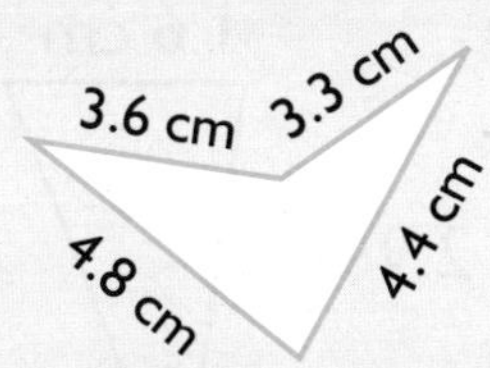

Perimeter = ______

f.

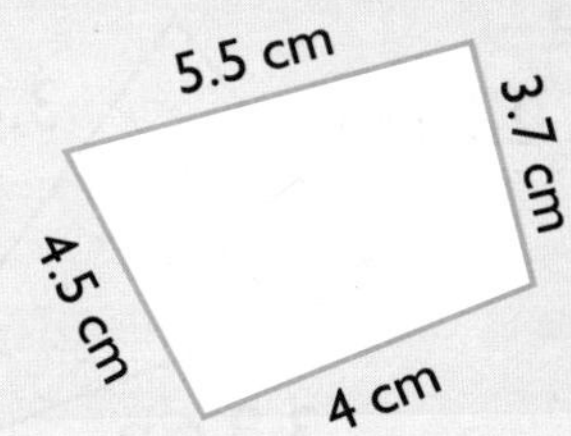

Perimeter = ______

2. Use the same method you used in Question 1 to calculate the total rainfall for each week.

Total Rainfall for February

					Total
Week 1	3.7 mm	4.5 mm	12.3 mm	11.5 mm	______ mm
Week 2	5.9 mm	15.6 mm	3.1 mm	5.4 mm	______ mm
Week 3	7.6 mm	11.1 mm	3.4 mm	9.5 mm	______ mm
Week 4	4.8 mm	20.6 mm	7.3 mm	6.4 mm	______ mm

3. Draw ⟷ to connect numbers you would add together first. Then write the answer.

a. 14.6 + 3.5 + 12.4 + 6.5 = ______

b. 21.2 + 5.7 + 11.8 + 4.3 = ______

c. 30.5 + 16 + 11.5 + 14 = ______

d. 16.4 + 21.1 + 18.9 + 7.7 = ______

Exploring the Area of Irregular Shapes

1. Estimate the area of each leaf sketch in square centimetres.

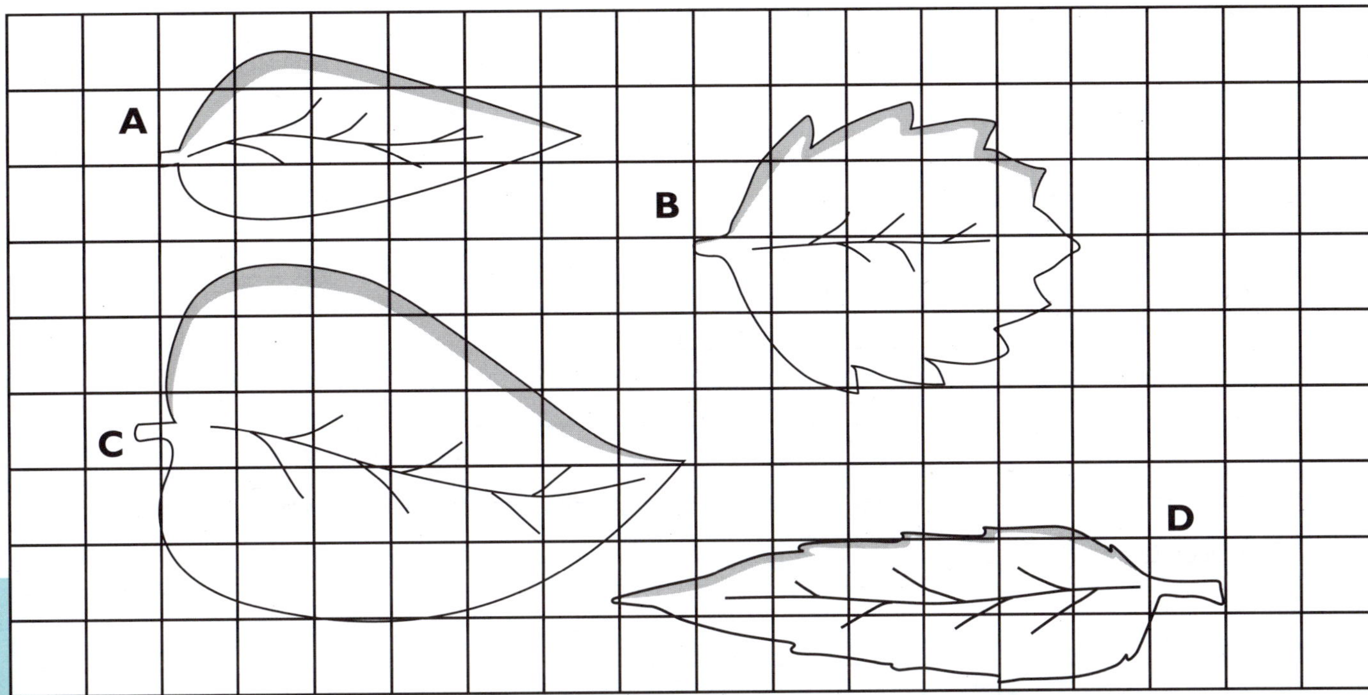

Leaf	A	B	C	D
Estimated area	______ cm^2	______ cm^2	______ cm^2	______ cm^2

2. Find 2 different leaves. Trace the leaves on this grid. Estimate the area of each leaf.

Leaf A: Area is about ______ cm^2

Leaf B: Area is about ______ cm^2

Look at Question 1. Does the longest leaf have the greatest area? Does the shortest leaf have the smallest area?

Creating Shapes with Equivalent Area

Worksheet 118

1. For each of these shapes, calculate the area in square centimetres.
Then draw two more different shapes that have the same area.

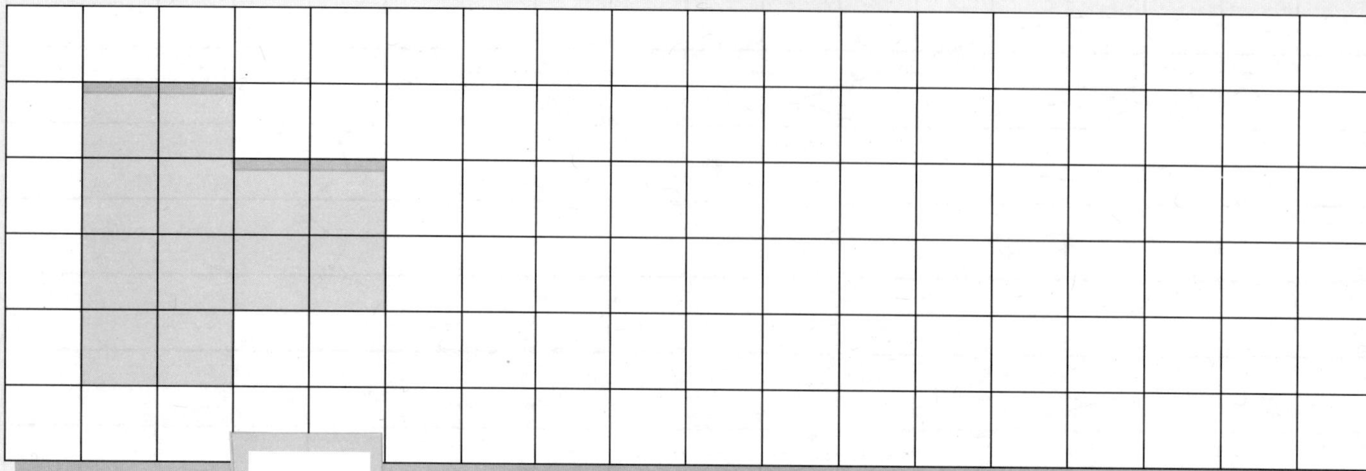

a. The area is _______ cm².

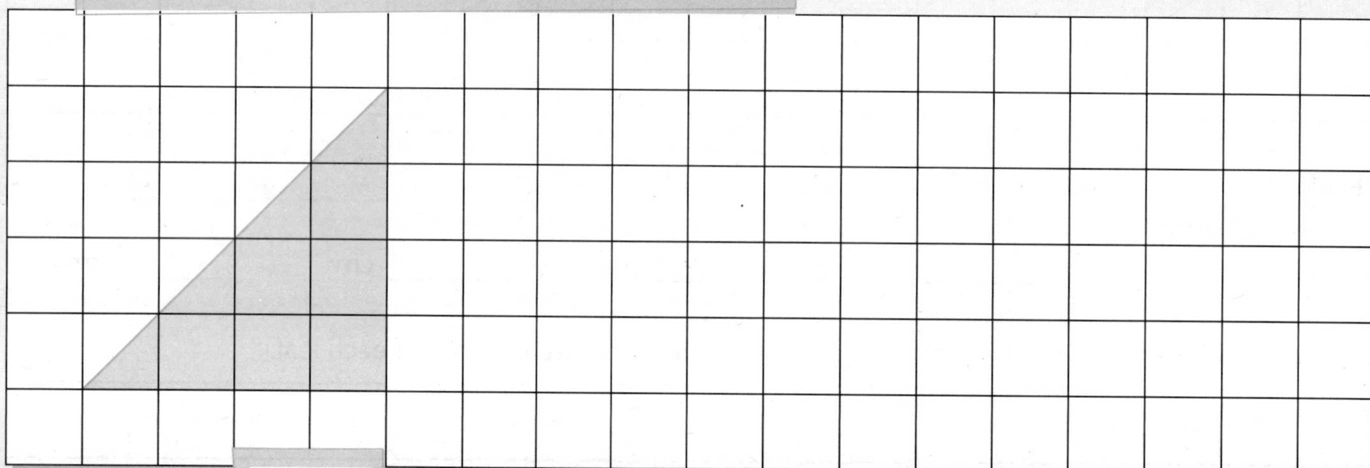

b. The area is _______ cm².

c. The area is _______ cm².

Use grid paper to draw two different shapes that have an area of 17 square centimetres.

Comparing Areas of Polygons

1. Calculate the area of each shape. Try using the area of the rectangle to help you.

a.

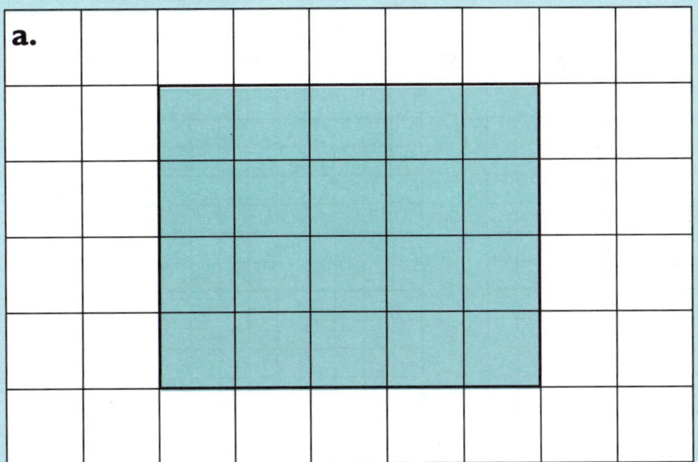

Area = ______________ cm^2

b.

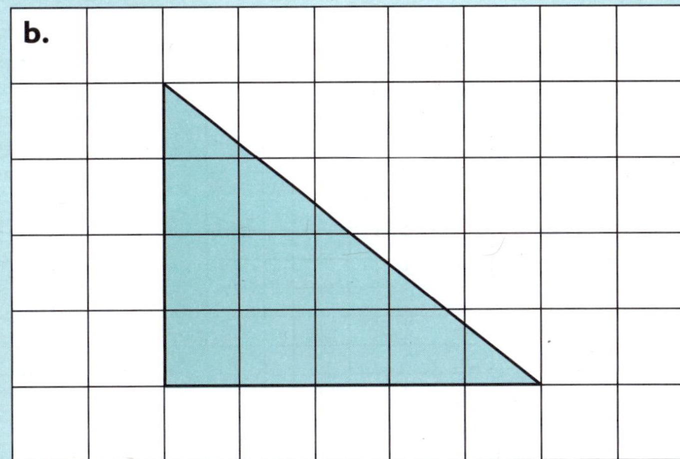

Area = ______________ cm^2

c.

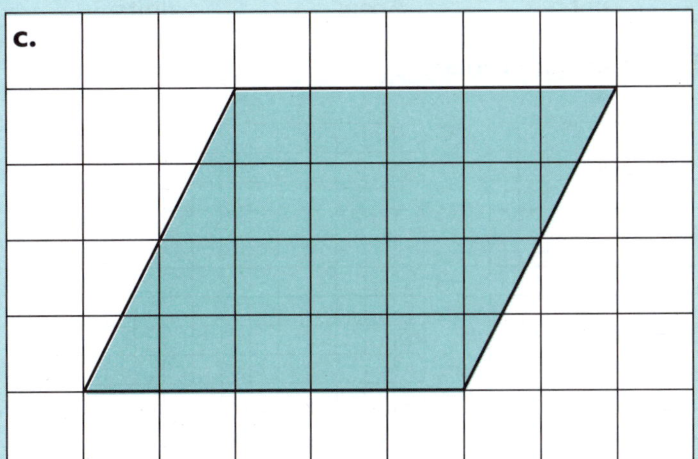

Area = ______________ cm^2

d.

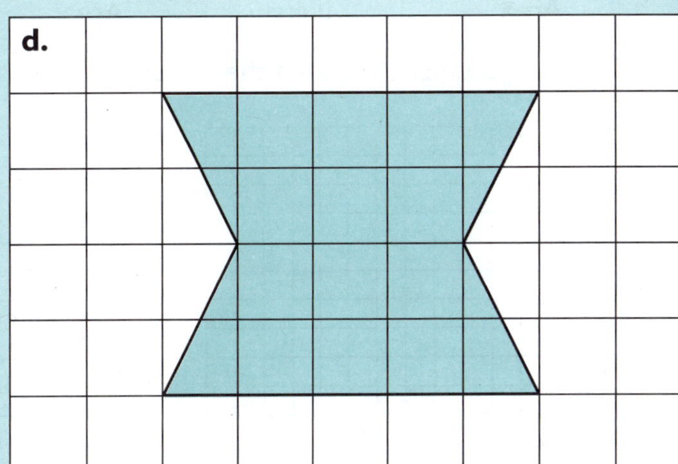

Area = ______________ cm^2

e.

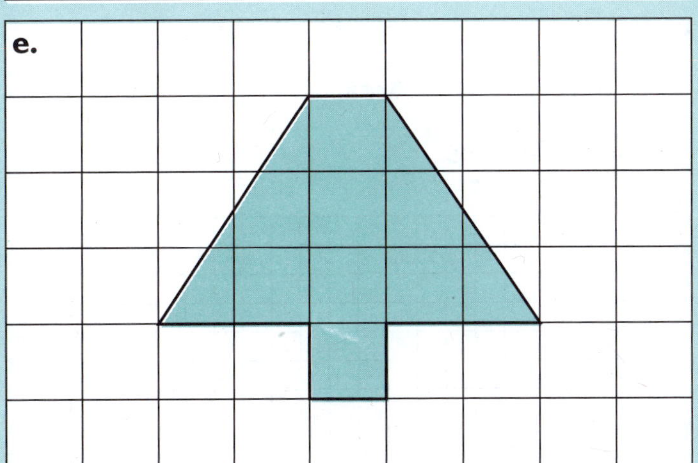

Area = ______________ cm^2

f.

Area = ______________ cm^2

How does the rectangle above help you find the area of the triangle and the parallelogram?

1. Calculate the area of each shaded rectangle.

a. 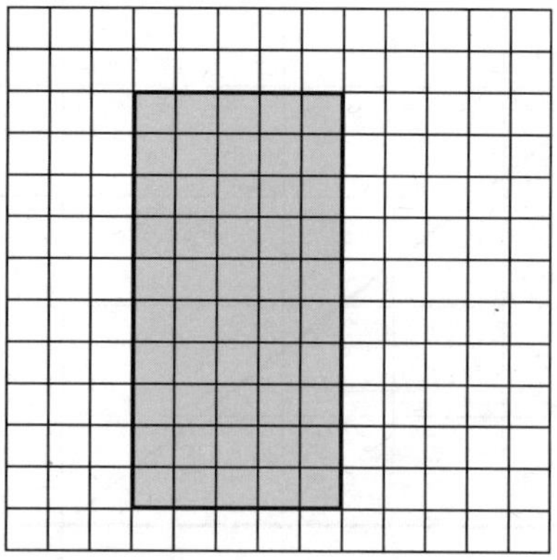

Length: ______ units

Width: ______ units

Area: ______ units

b. 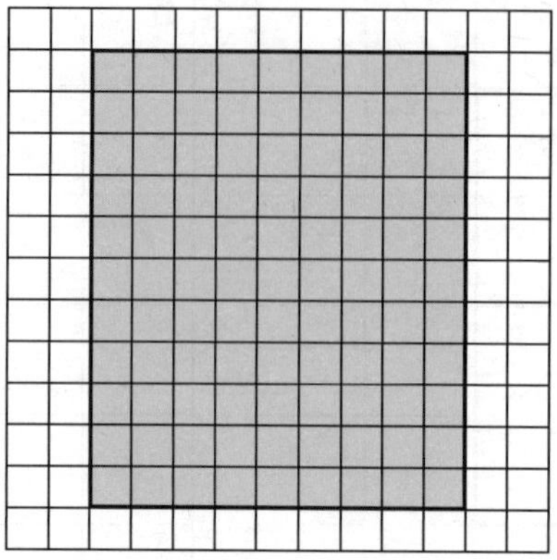

Length: ______ units

Width: ______ units

Area: ______ units

c. 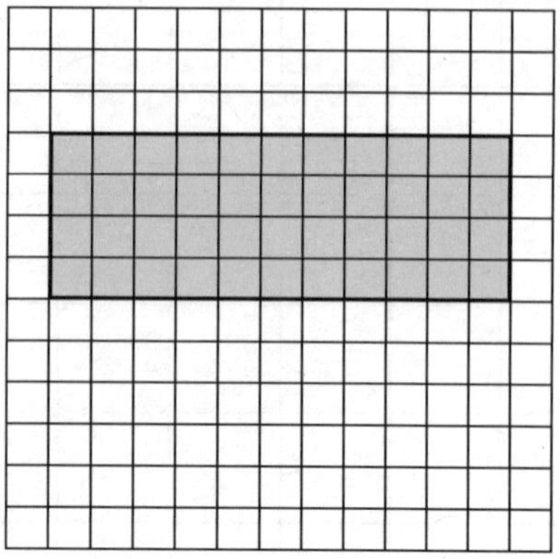

Length: ______ units

Width: ______ units

Area: ______ units

2. Draw a rectangle to match the dimensions given. Then calculate the area.

a.

Length: 13 units

Width: 6 units

Area: ______ units

b.

Length: 12 units

Width: 7 units

Area: ______ units

c.

Length: 12 units

Width: 9 units

Area: ______ units

3. Draw a rectangle to match the area given. Then write the dimensions.

a.

Area: 48 units

Length: ____ units Width: ____ units

b.

Area: 72 units

Length: ____ units Width: ____ units

What are the dimensions of the different rectangles you can draw that have an area of 72 units?

Calculating the Area of Rectangles

1. Calculate the area of these rectangles.

a.

80 m, 150 m

80 m, 300 m

150 × 80 = ________ m^2

300 × 80 = ________ m^2

b.

60 m, 250 m

60 m, 500 m

250 × 60 = ________ m^2

500 × 60 = ________ m^2

2. Calculate the area of these rectangles. Draw a ✓ on the rectangles greater than one hectare.

a.

350 m, 30 m

30 × 350 = ________ m^2

b.

300 m, 52 m

52 × 300 = ________ m^2

c.

115 m, 90 m

____ × ____ = ________ m^2

d.

210 m, 50 m

____ × ____ = ________ m^2

e.

110 m, 80 m

____ × ____ = ________ m^2

f.

50 m, 50 m

____ × ____ = ________ m^2

Write the dimensions of a rectangle that has an area of one hectare.

Calculating the Area of Rectangles

Worksheet 122

1. Imagine you wanted to lay grass in this garden. Write how you would calculate the area.

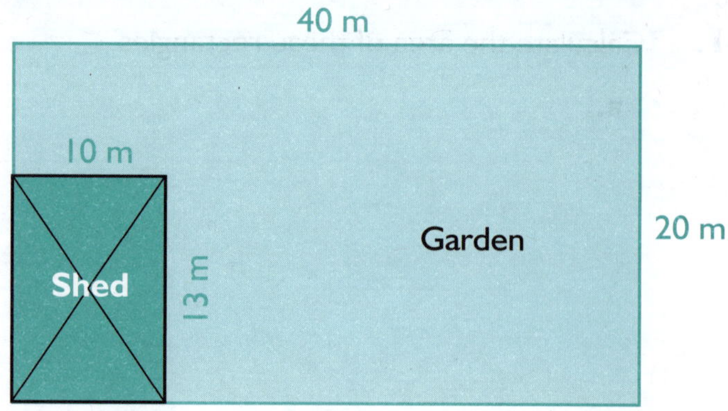

____

____

____

____

2. Use your method to calculate the area of the white part.

a.

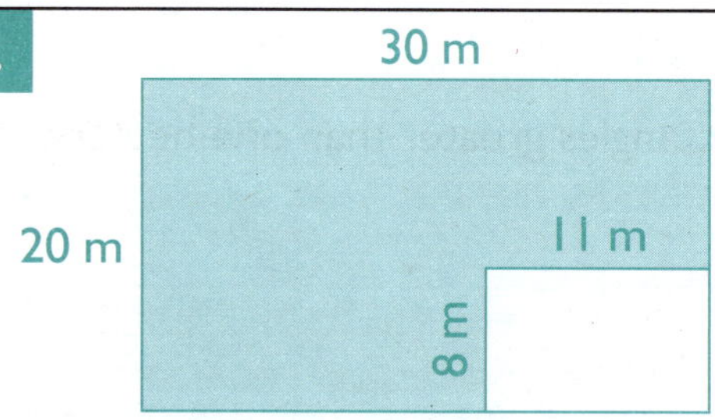

Area = ________ m^2

b.

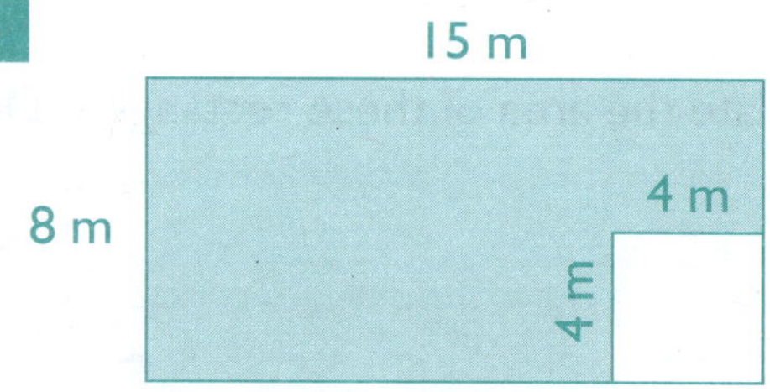

Area = ________ m^2

c.

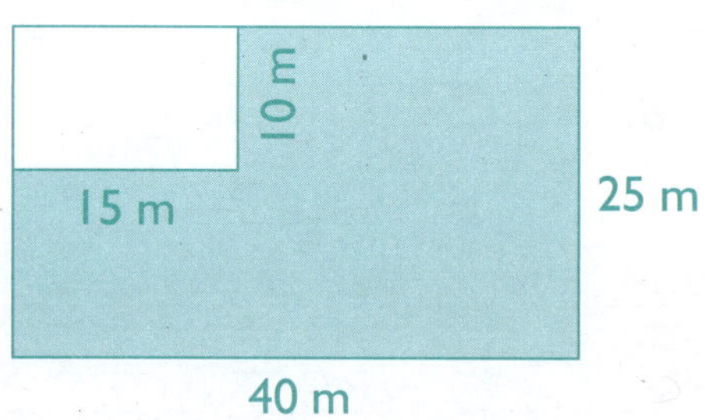

Area = ________ m^2

d.

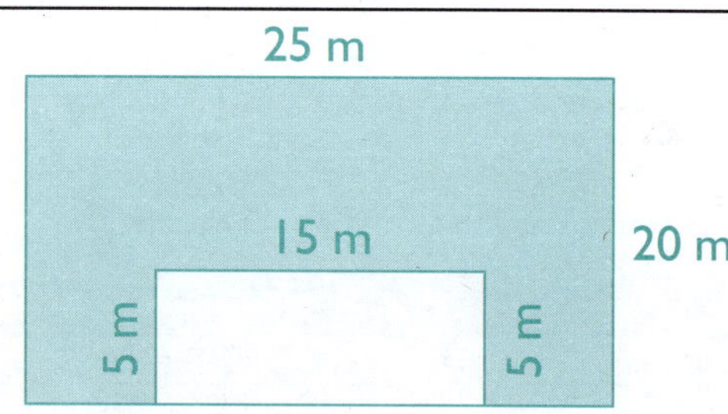

Area = ________ m^2

e.

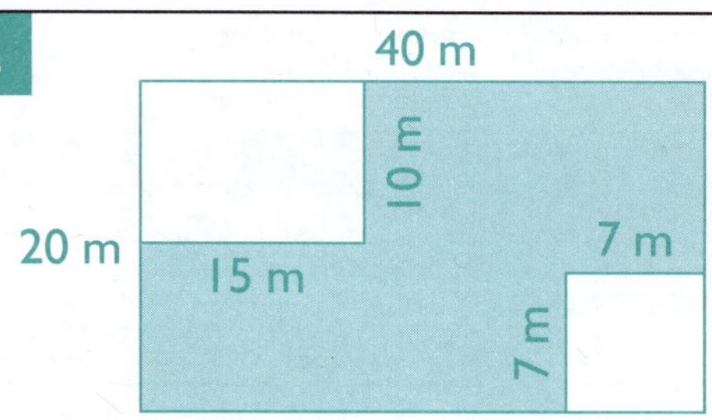

Area = ________ m^2

f.

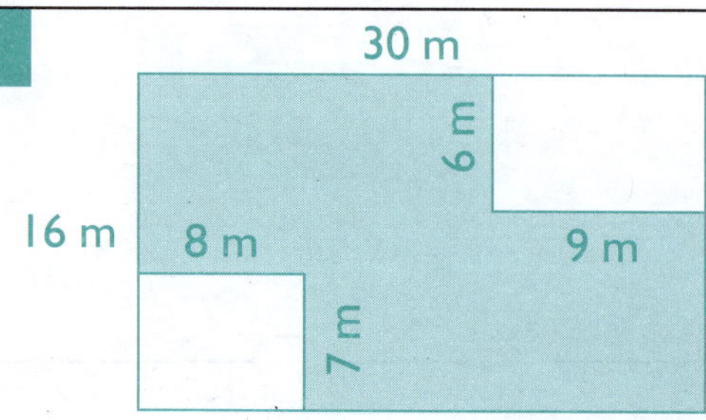

Area = ________ m^2

Draw a garden in the corner of the yard in Question 1. Label the dimensions and calculate the area of the garden.

Calculating the Area of Rectangles

1. Round the dimensions to estimate the total area. Write whether the exact area will be **more** or **less** than your estimate.

a. 1.8 m × 1.7 m

Estimated area ______ m^2

The exact area will be ________________.

b. 4.8 m × 2.9 m

Estimated area ______ m^2

The exact area will be ________________.

c. 5.2 m × 1.7 m

Estimated area ______ m^2

The exact area will be ________________.

d. 3.5 m × 2.8 m

Estimated area ______ m^2

The exact area will be ________________.

e. 7 m × 4.8 m

Estimated area ______ m^2

The exact area will be ________________.

f. 4.5 m × 2.5 m

Estimated area ______ m^2

The exact area will be ________________.

g. 6.1 m × 4.6 m

Estimated area ______ m^2

The exact area will be ________________.

h. 5.4 m × 2.7 m

Estimated area ______ m^2

The exact area will be ________________.

Draw a ✓ on the examples for which you could calculate the exact area mentally.

City Apartment Living

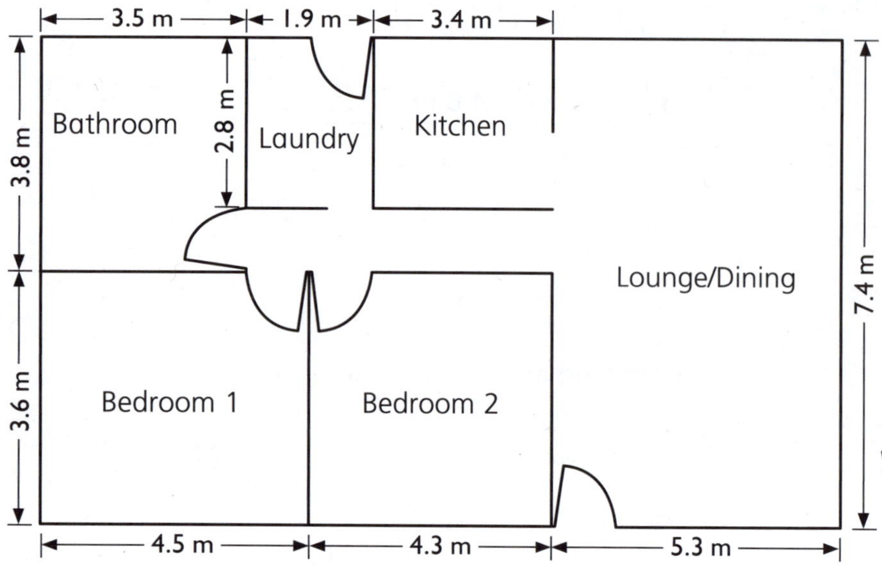

1. Use the plan above to calculate the area of each room.

a. Bedroom 1

_________ m^2

b. Kitchen

_________ m^2

c. Bathroom

_________ m^2

d. Bedroom 2

_________ m^2

e. Lounge/Dining

_________ m^2

f. Laundry

_________ m^2

2. Calculate the area of each of these.

a. Balcony 8.6 m × 1.9 m

_________ m^2

b. Carport 5.4 m × 3.2 m

_________ m^2

c. Living area 14.1 m × 7.4 m

_________ m^2

Figure out the area of the hallway.

Relating Perimeter and Area

1. This is a sketch of a large paddock.

a. Complete this table.

Length	Width	Area	Perimeter
______ m	______ m	______ m^2	______ m

b. Write the dimensions of the rectangular paddocks you can make that have the same area. Then write the perimeter.

Length	Width	Area	Perimeter
______ m	______ m	______ m^2	______ m
______ m	______ m	______ m^2	______ m
______ m	______ m	______ m^2	______ m

c. Write the dimensions of other rectangular paddocks you can make that have the same perimeter. Then write the area.

Length	Width	Area	Perimeter
______ m	______ m	______ m^2	______ m
______ m	______ m	______ m^2	______ m
______ m	______ m	______ m^2	______ m
______ m	______ m	______ m^2	______ m

What is the length of a paddock that is one metre wide and has an area of one hectare? How long is the fence around it?

You have learnt that:

- There are 24 hours in a day.
- There are 60 minutes in an hour.
- There are 60 seconds in a minute.

Conversion of time from one unit to another

- To convert minutes to seconds, multiply by 60.
- To convert seconds to minutes, divide by 60.

Example: Convert 345 seconds into minutes.

Solution: Divide 345 by 60

$$\begin{array}{r@{\,}l} & \underline{5} \longrightarrow \text{minutes} \\ 60\,) & 345 \\ & \underline{300} \\ & \underline{45} \longrightarrow \text{seconds} \end{array}$$

345 seconds is 5 minutes and 45 seconds

- To change hours into minutes, multiply by 60.
- To change minutes into hours, divide by 60.

- To change days into hours, multiply by 24.
- To change hours into days, divide by 24.

Example: Convert 3 hours 25 minutes into seconds.

Solution:

I hour = 60 minutes and I minute = 60 seconds

Therefore, I hour = 60 × 60 seconds = 3600 seconds

3 hours	= 3 × 3600 seconds
	= 10,800 seconds
25 minutes	= 25 × 60 seconds
	= 1,500 seconds
3 hours 25 minutes	= 10,800 + 1,500 seconds
	= 12,300 seconds

The 24-hour Clock

There are two ways to show the time: 12-hour clock (am/pm) or 24-hour clock.
With the 24-hour clock, the time is shown as how many hours and minutes since midnight.
With 12-hour clock the day is divided into 12 hours from midnight to noon (the am hours) and another 12-hours from noon to midnight (the pm hours).

24-hour clock

	Midnight to Noon	Noon to Midnight
12-hour clock	am	pm
24-hour clock	0:00 to 11:59	12:00 to 23:59

Converting from 12-hour time to 24-hour time

- For the first hour of the day (12 midnight to 12:59 am), subtract 12 hours
  Examples: 12 midnight = 0:00, 12:35 am = 0:35

- From 1:00 am to 12:59 pm, no change.
  Examples: 10:20 am = 10:20, 12:35 pm = 12:35

- From 1:00 pm to 11:59 pm, add 12 hours.
  Examples: 6:30 pm = 18:30, 10:50 pm = 22:50

Converting from 24-hour time to 12-hour time

- For the first hour of the day (0:00 to 0:59), add 12 hours, make it 'am'.
  Examples: 0:10 = 12:10 am, 0:40 = 12:40 am

- From 1:00 to 11:59, no change just add 'am'.
  Examples: 1:15 = 1:15 am, 11:25 = 11:25 am

- From 12:00 to 12:59, no change- just add 'pm'.
  Examples: 12:10 = 12:10 pm, 12:55 = 12:55 pm

- From 13:00 to 23:59, subtract 12 hours, add pm
  Examples: 14:55 = 2:55 pm, 23:30 = 11:30 pm

Here is a chart comparing the 24-hour clock and 12-hour clock:

24-hour clock	12-hour clock
0:00	**12 midnight**
0:59	12:59 am
1:00	1:00 am
2:00	2:00 am
3:00	3:00 am
4:00	4:00 am
5:00	5:00 am
6:00	6:00 am
7:00	7:00 am
8:00	8:00 am
9:00	9:00 am
10:00	10:00 am
11:00	11:00 am

24-hour clock	12-hour clock
12:00	**12 noon**
12:59	12:59 pm
13:00	1:00 pm
14:00	2:00 pm
15:00	3:00 pm
16:00	4:00 pm
17:00	5:00 pm
18:00	6:00 pm
19:00	7:00 pm
20:00	8:00 pm
21:00	9:00 pm
22:00	10:00 pm
23:00	11:00 pm
23:59	11:59 pm

1. A train leaves Central Station at 3 o'clock. Look at each watch below. For how many minutes does a person need to wait for the train?

a. b. c. d.

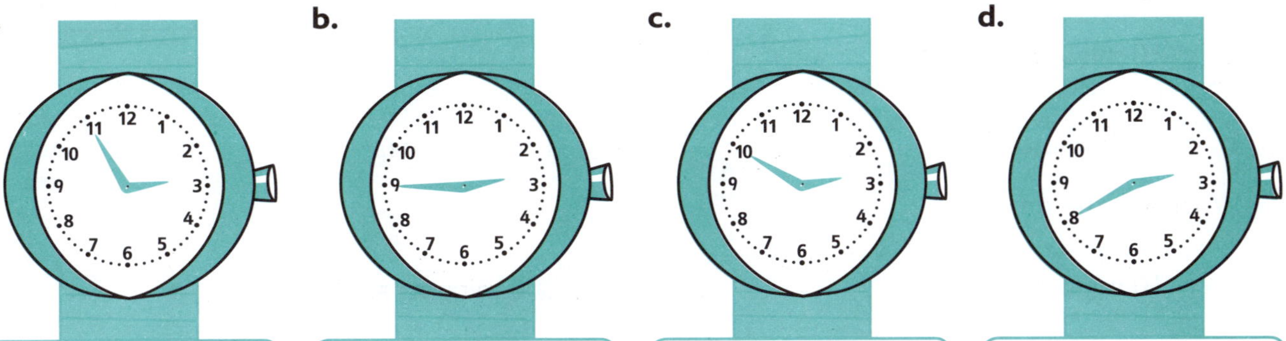

a. ________ minutes
b. ________ minutes
c. ________ minutes
d. ________ minutes

2. Write the time on each watch using 'minutes to'.

a. b. c. d.

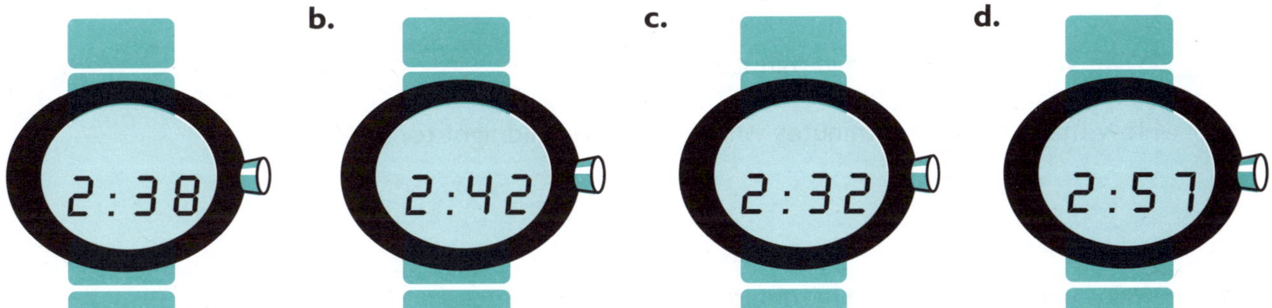

a. _____ minutes to ____
b. _____ minutes to ____
c. _____ minutes to ____
d. _____ minutes to ____

3. Show the time on the analogue and digital clocks.

a. 15 minutes to 3
b. 20 minutes to 5
c. 17 minutes to 6
d. 7 minutes to 9

A train trip took 15 minutes. Write four possible starting and finishing times.

Working with Units of Time

1. Write the current time on this clock. Use this time to answer Questions 2–5.

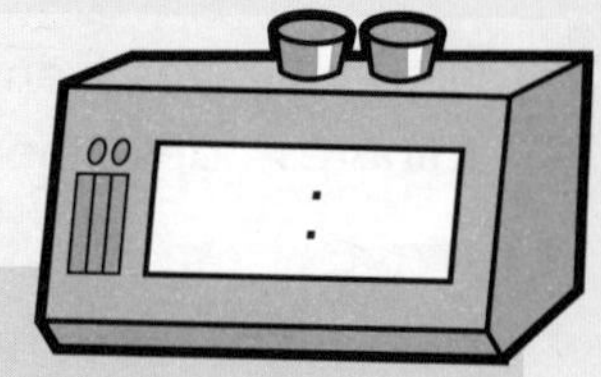

2. What time will it be in
   - a. 10 minutes?
   - b. 100 minutes?
   - c. 1,000 minutes?

3. What was the time
   - a. 10 minutes ago?
   - b. 100 minutes ago?
   - c. 1000 minutes ago?

4. a. How many hours and minutes have passed since midnight last night?

   b. Write your answer again in minutes.

5. a. How many hours and minutes will pass before midnight tonight?

   b. Write your answer again in minutes.

6. Write the missing times.

10 hours before						
Time	10:35 am	11:09 pm	11:40 am	7:20 pm	3:50 am	6:15 pm
10 hours after						

7. a. Write today's date on the desk calendar.

   b. Which date is exactly
   - 100 days from now?
   - 150 days from now?
   - 200 days from now?

FF Figure out how many days old you are.

Relating Units of Time

1. Complete these facts.

a. In 1 minute there are ______ seconds.

b. In 1 hour there are ______ minutes.

c. In 1 hour there are ______ seconds.

d. In 1 day there are ______ hours.

e. In 1 day there are ______ minutes.

f. In 1 day there are ______ seconds.

2. List things that would take about **1 second**, **1 minute** and **1 hour** to do.

1 second	1 minute	1 hour
sneeze		

3. Write **true** or **false**.

a. 1,000 seconds is more than 1 hour. ______

b. 100 hours is less than 1 week. ______

c. 10,000 minutes is less than 1 week. ______

d. 1,000 hours is less than 1 month. ______

4. Imagine it is 1 January. What will the date be

a. 100 hours later? ______

b. 1,000 hours later? ______

5. How old would you be if you were

a. 10,000 seconds old? ______

b. 10,000 minutes old? ______

Figure out how old you would be if you were: a. 10,00,000 seconds old b. 10,00,000 minutes old c. 10,00,000 hours old? d. 10,00,000 days old?

This display shows departure times for trains leaving Central Station.

Departs Central Station to:

Raj Nagar	4:03	Model Town	11:51
Uttam Nagar	1:32	Ambedkar Nagar	1:40
Janakpuri	8:27	Gurgaon	3:26
Inderlok	10:42	Noida	4:08
Civil Lines	11:15	Azadpur	5:45
Race Course	12:47	Rajinder Nagar	5:12

Draw hands on the clocks to show the departure times from Central Station to these stations.

a.
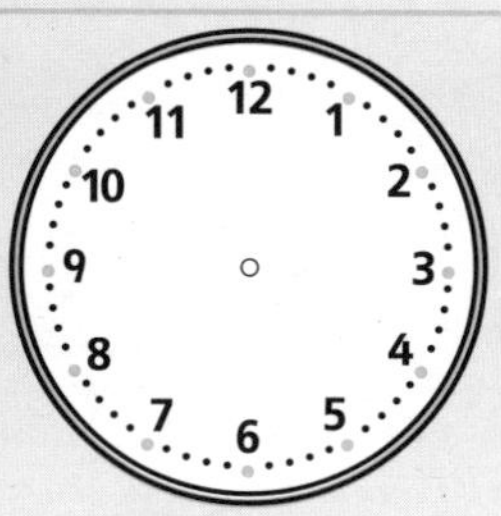
Azadpur

b.
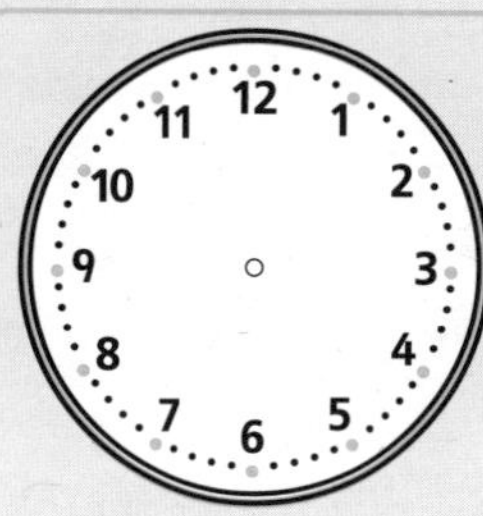
Race Course

c.

Noida

d.

Uttam Nagar

e.

Civil Lines

f.

Gurgaon

g.

Janakpuri

h.

Model Town

i.

Raj Nagar

j.
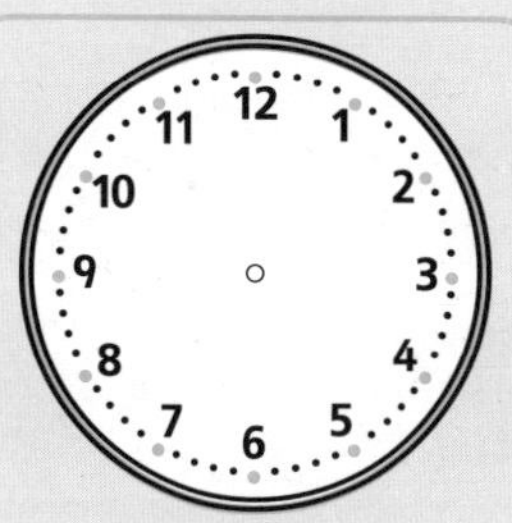
Inderlok

k.

Ambedkar Nagar

l.

Rajinder Nagar

The trains to Azadpur, Race Course, Noida and Uttam Nagar were 30 minutes late. Write the new departure times in digital form.

24-hour Clock

1. Convert the following into the 24-hour format.

12:55 pm		7:10 pm		3:35 am	
6:45 am		10:00 pm		9.50 pm	
8:05 am		11:40 am			

2. Write the time using am and pm.

thirty-five minutes after midnight	
twenty-four minutes after seven in the morning	
five minutes after three in the afternoon	
nine-fifteen in the evening	
seven minutes to midnight	
seventeen minutes after noon	
eight minutes after six in the morning	
eight-fifty in the morning	

3. Convert the following.

How many hours in 480 minutes?	
What is 500 minutes expressed in hours and minutes?	
What is 2 hours and 35 minutes expressed in minutes?	
What is 80 minutes expressed in hours and minutes?	
What is 7 hours 20 minutes added to 8 hours and 30 minutes?	
How much is 30 minutes added to 6 hours and 30 minutes?	
What is 10 hours 20 minutes take away from 5 hours 40 minutes?	

1. Solve the word problems.

a. Amita started drawing a picture of her garden at 11:55 am. She finished at 12:05 pm. How much time has passed?

b. Harry started putting together a 100-piece puzzle at 2:45 pm. He worked on it until 3:17 pm. How much time had passed?

c. Asha called her friend at 8:49 pm. She hung up the phone at 9:10 pm. How long did she talk on the phone?

d. School ends at 2:35 pm. Akul has to stay back for his football coaching class. If the class lasts for 2 hours and 39 minutes after school, what time will the practice end?

e. Anmol's mother allows Anmol to play a video game for 2 hours and 10 minutes. If Anmol starts playing at 1:10 am, when should he stop?

Time Word Problems

Worksheet 132

1. Timetable

Yoga	8:43 am to 9:27 am
Science	9:29 am to 10:15 am
Maths	10:17 am to 10:57 am
Lunch	10:59 am to 12:12 pm
Social studies	12:14 pm to 1:01 pm
Art	1:03 pm to 1:50 pm
English	1:52 pm to 2:46 pm

a.	How long is the English class?	
b.	Your teacher would prefer to eat lunch one period earlier. How many minutes earlier would she prefer to eat?	
c.	How long is the day at school?	
d.	My sister's maths class is one period before mine. What time does my sister's maths class begin?	

CHAPTER 12

Data Handling

Data means information. Information can be organised in different ways. Information can be shown in tables, charts and graphs to make the information easier to read.
Data can be collected on any subject including the height of students in a class or the number of people in an office who wear glasses.

A **survey** is conducted to collect information. Information can be collected by asking questions.
If many people are interviewed, the data is collected in a tally table. A tally table is a chart used to keep a record of something in groups of fives and ones.
Tally marks are used for counting things. For every one score, a vertical line, |, is used. When the number is five, a slanted stroke is placed through the four strokes. So 5 would look like this 卌.
Frequency tables show the totals of the tally marks.

Example:

A group of 70 people were interviewed. Their choice of favourite fast food item were recorded.

Food Item	Tally	No. of people
Burger	卌 卌 卌 卌 |	21
Hotdog	卌 ||||	9
Sandwich	卌 卌 卌 |||	18
Pizza	卌 卌 卌 卌 卌 ||	27

Every time someone chose an item, a tally mark, |, was used in that row.
The tally marks for each item are counted to get the frequency.
In the example, 21 people said that their favourite food item was burger, 9 chose hotdog, 18 chose sandwich and 27 chose pizza.

The picture graph for the above data is:

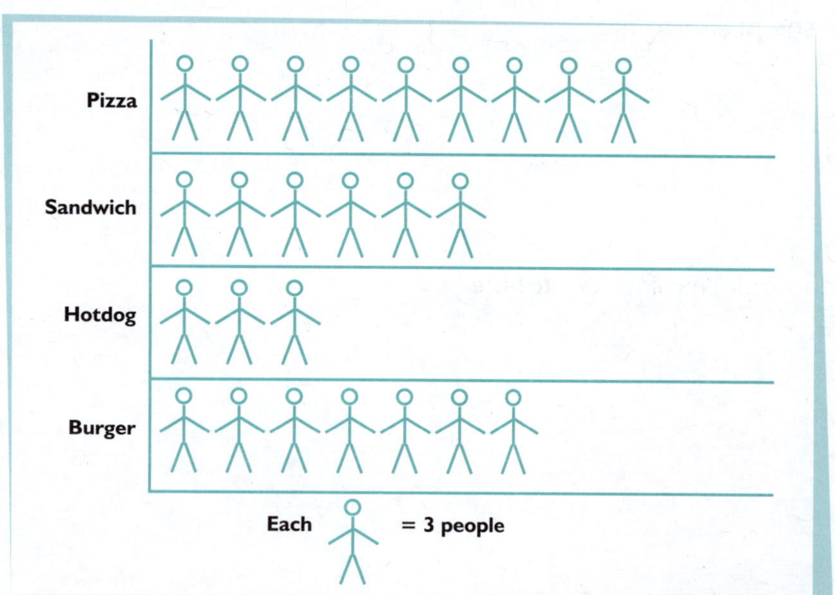

Bar Graphs

A bar graph is a graph which displays amounts or frequencies as bars. A bar graph helps us to easily compare data.

Drawing and Labelling a Bar Graph

1. Decide on a title for the graph (favourite food item).
2. Draw a horizontal line OX. Draw OY perpendicular to it. OX is called the X-axis and OY the Y-axis.
3. Label the X-axis (food items).
4. Write the names of food items against each bar (burger, hotdog, sandwich, pizza).
5. Label the Y-axis (number of people).
6. Decide on the scale. The numbers along the side of the bar graph are called the scale.
7. Consider the least and the greatest number shown on the graph. The range of numbers is from 9 to 27.
8. So, begin at 0 and count by 3s up to 30.
9. For drawing the bar for burger, draw a rectangle reaching up to a height of 21. The hot dog bar should reach up to 9 and so on.
10. All the bars should have equal width.
11. Leave space between the bars.

The bar graph for the favourite food item is shown below:

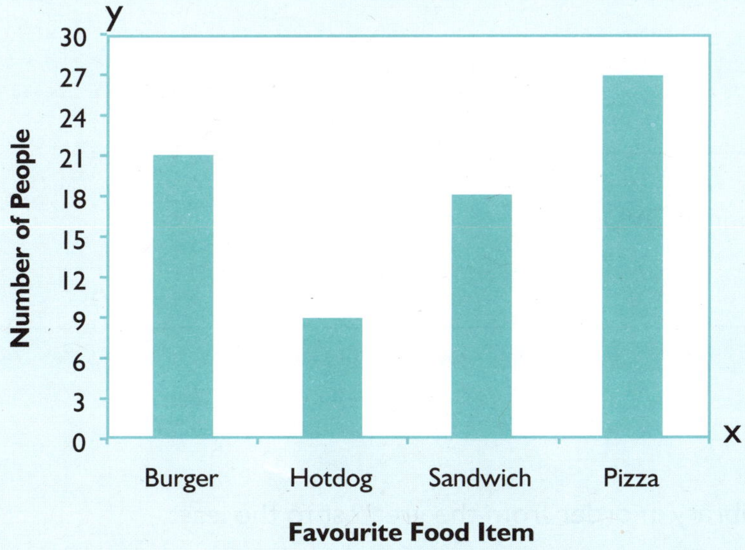

This picture graph shows the number of DVDs in the libraries of some students.

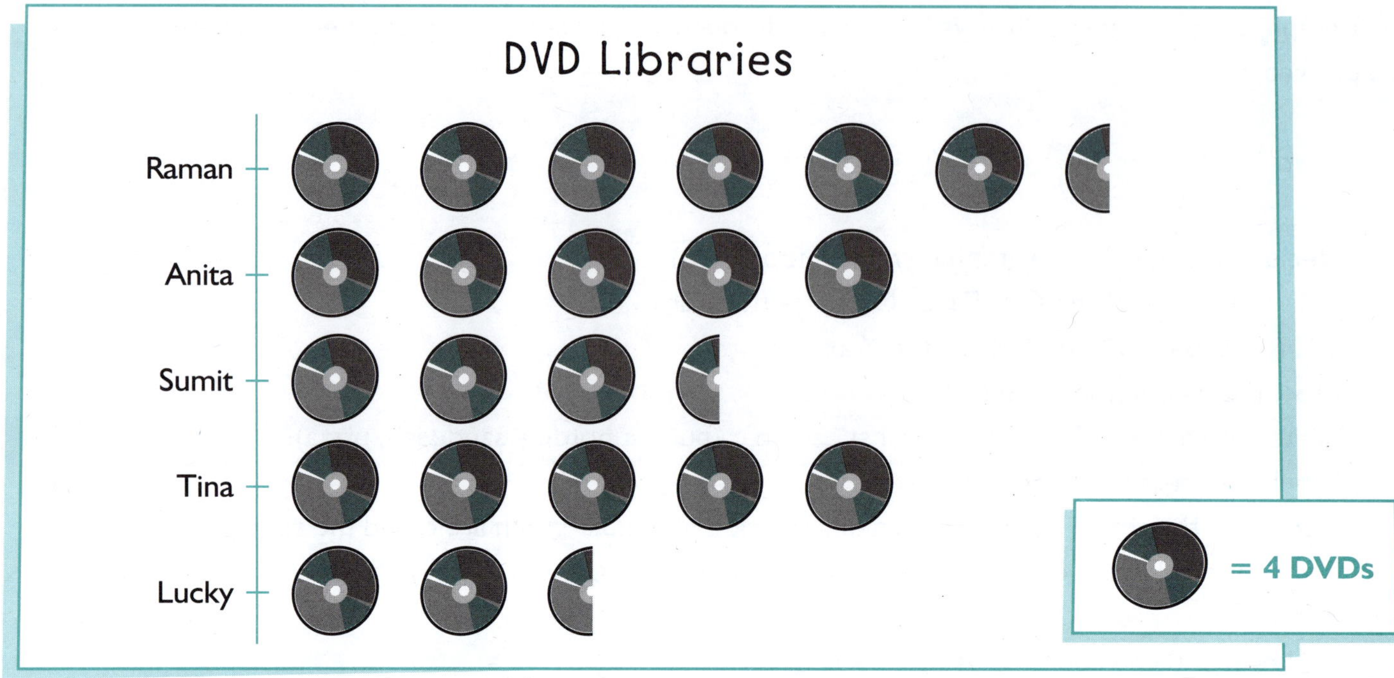

1. What does each represent? ________________

2. How many DVDs does the student with the greatest number have? ________

3. How many DVDs are in Sumit's library? ________

4. Which student has exactly 10 DVDs? ____________

5. **a.** Which students have the same number of DVDs?

____

b. How many do they each have? ____________

6. **a.** Write the number of DVDs in each library in order from the greatest to the least.

______ ______ ______ ______ ______

b. Draw a ✓ on the number in the middle.

Brady's family has 48 DVDs. How would you show this data in the picture graph above?

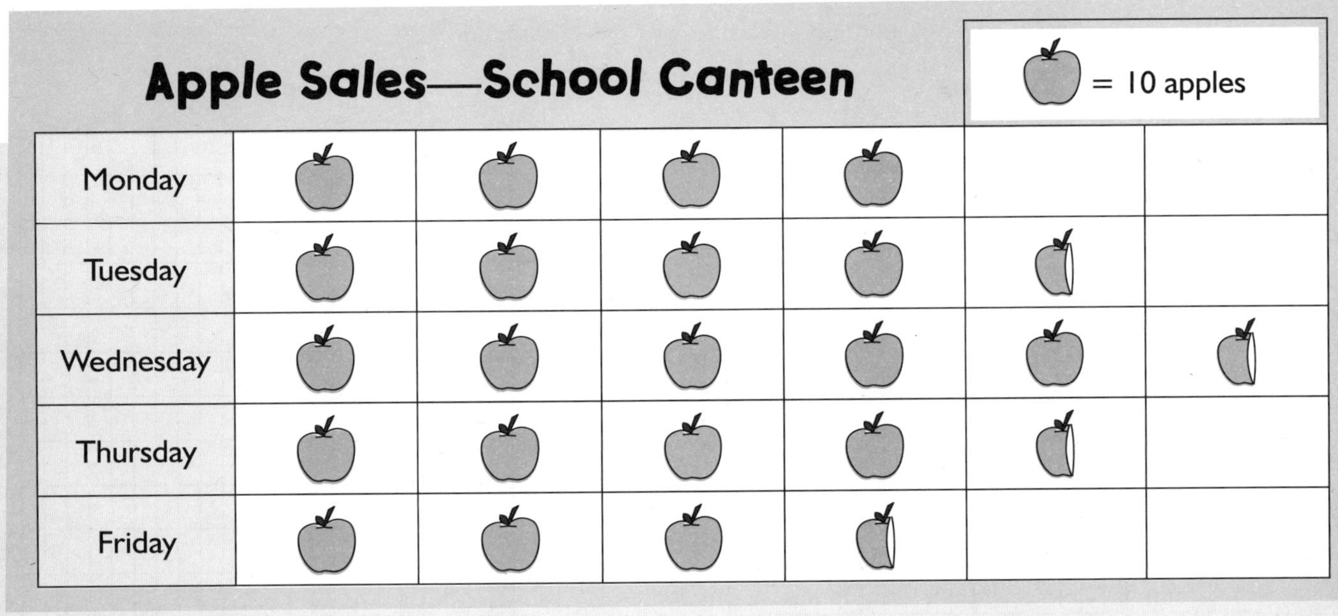

1. What does each (apple) represent? ______________________

2. a. How many apples were sold on Monday? ______

   b. How many apples do you think were sold on Friday? ______

3. a. On which day were the most apples sold? ______________

   b. How many apples were sold? ______

4. a. On which two days were the same number of apples sold?

   ______________ ______________

   b. How many apples were sold altogether on those two days? ______

5. How many **more** apples were sold on Wednesday than on Monday? ______

6. How many apples were sold during the school week? ______

7. a. What scale would you use if the greatest number of apples sold on one day was 17? (apple) = ______ apples

   b. How many whole apples would you show for that day? ______

Look at your answer to Question 1. Why do you think this scale was chosen for this graph?

Monthly Rainfall

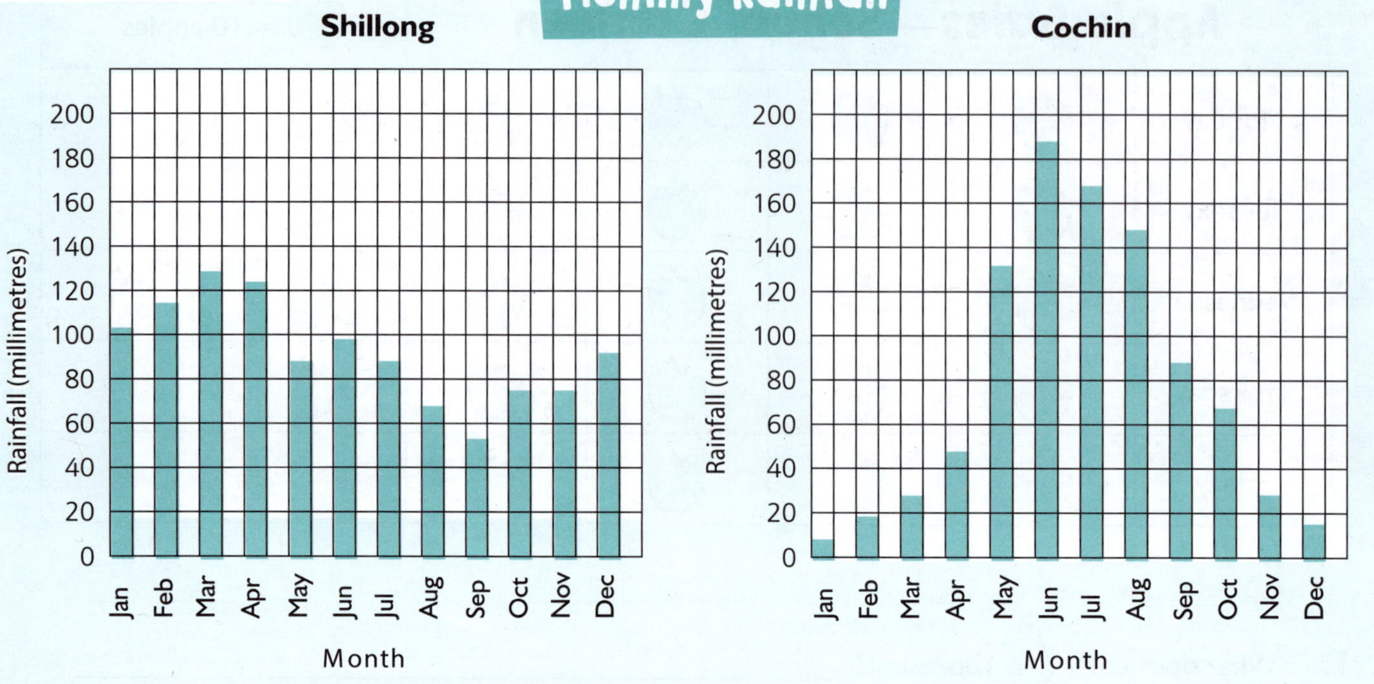

1. Compare the data in the graphs. Write two generalisations.

a. ______________________________

b. ______________________________

2. Which month had the greatest and least amount of rain?

	Shillong	
	Greatest	Least
Month		

	Cochin	
	Greatest	Least
Month		

3. Which month(s) in Shillong had

a. 100 mm of rainfall? ______________

b. more than the rainfall for January? ______________

c. the same amount of rainfall? ______________

4. Look at Cochin's data. How much rainfall (in cm) was received in the following months

a. January ________ cm **b.** September ________ cm **c.** May ________ cm

Calculate the total rainfall for each city.

Interpreting a Column Graph

Paper Plane Flights

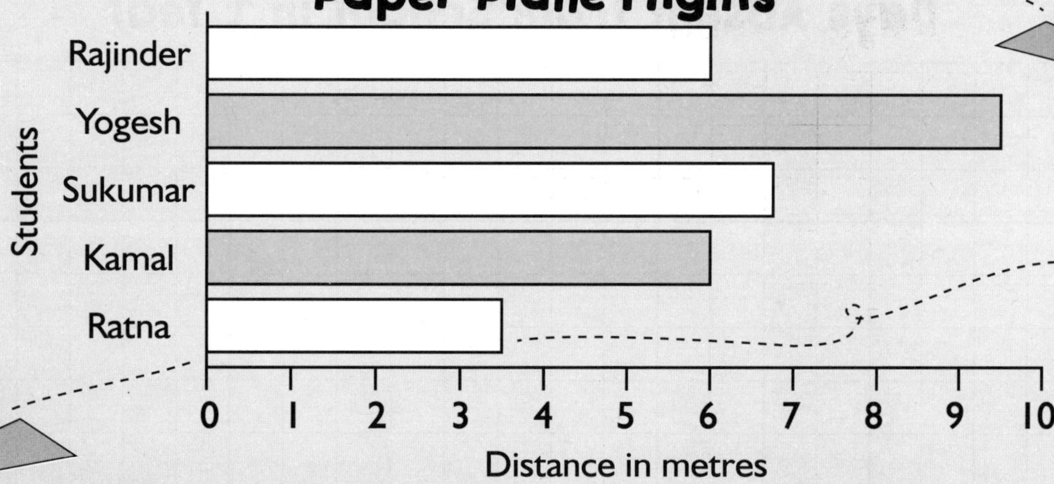

1. Whose plane flew a little more than 3 m?

2. Whose plane flew a little less than 7 m?

3. Whose planes flew the same distance?

4. The previous record was 6.1 m. Whose planes broke the record?

5. How much further do you think Yogesh's plane flew than Ratna's?

6. Construct a horizontal column graph to show this plane flight data:
   - Seema 9.1 m
   - Vimal 5.5 m
   - Shivneet 7.9 m

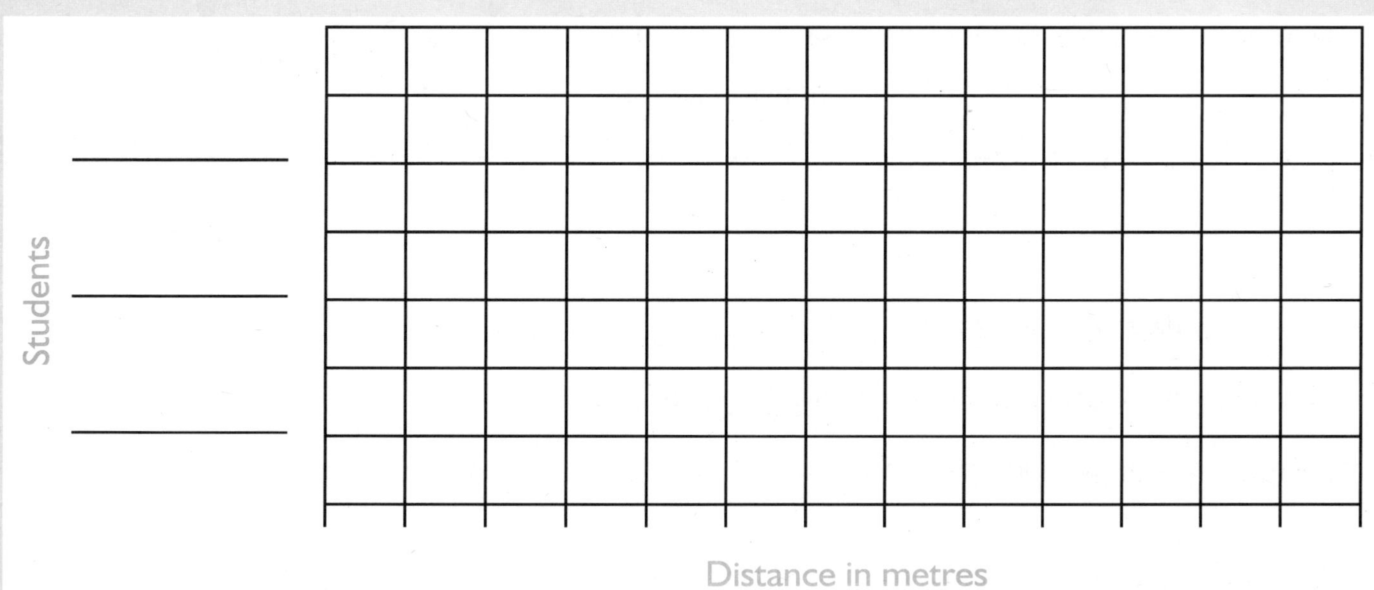

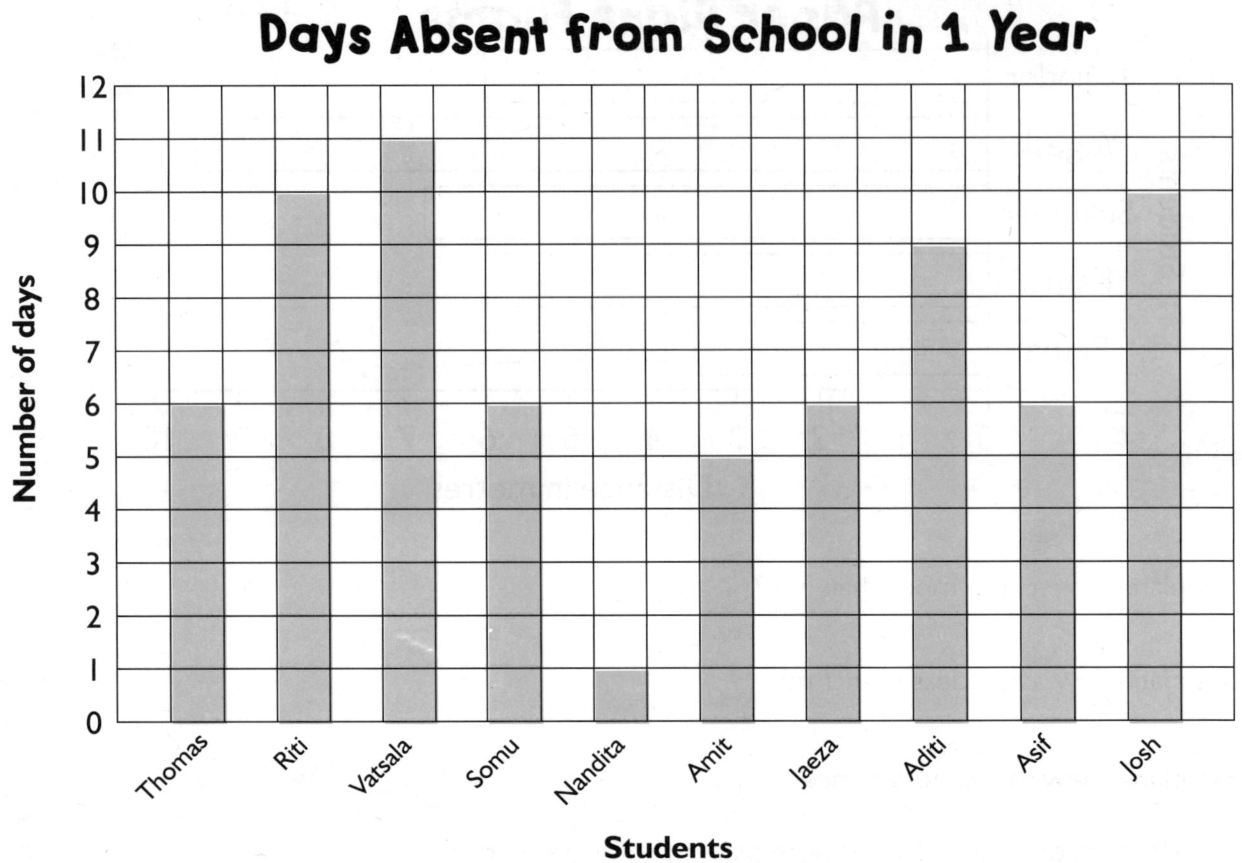

1. What is the greatest number of days any one student was absent? ______

2. What is the least number of days any one student was absent? ______

3. Draw one tally in this table for each student in the graph.

Number of Days Absent

0	1	2	3	4	5	6	7	8	9	10	11
						|					

4. How many days was Vatsala absent? ______

5. How many more days was Riti absent than Nandita? ______

6. Who was absent for more days—Thomas or Amit?

______

1. Write the number of cups in each batch. Then write the total.

Batch	Number of cups: Sugar	Number of cups: Flour	Total
	____	____	____
	____	____	____
	____	____	____

2. Complete this table.

Cups of sugar	1	2	3	4	5	6	7
Cups of flour	4						
Total cups	5						

3. Write a rule you can use to figure out the number of cups of flour for any given number of cups of sugar.

____

4. Write a rule you can use to figure out the total numbers of cups for any size batch.

____

Write a different rule you can use to answer Question 4.

1. Write the number of squares in each part. Then write the total.

	Picture	Number of squares in each part	Total
a.	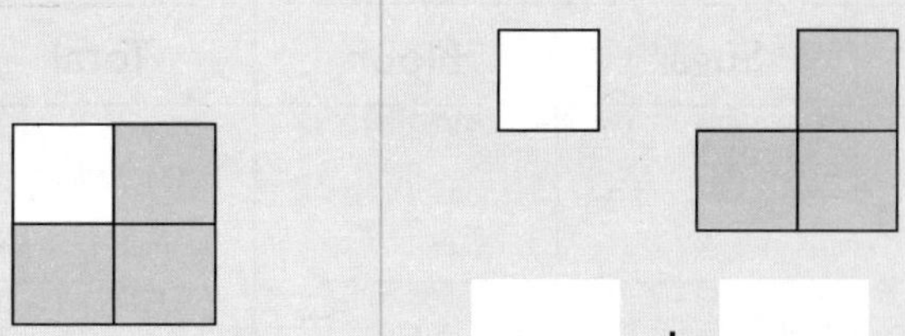	___ + ___	___
b.	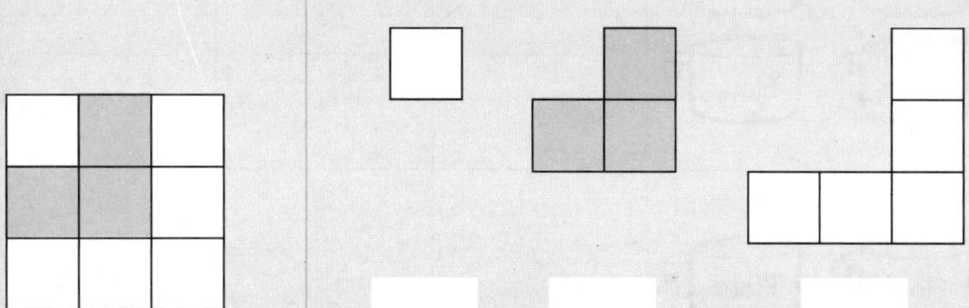	___ + ___ + ___	___
c.	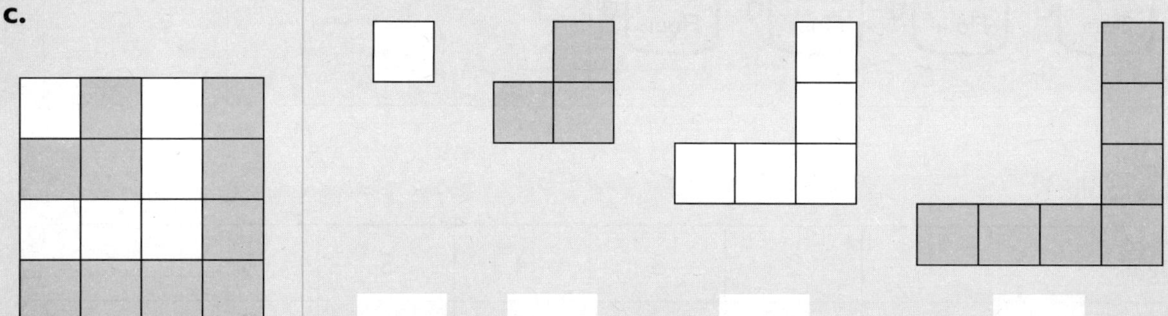	___ + ___ + ___ + ___	___

2. Complete this table to show the sequence of square numbers.

Length of side	1	2	3	4	5	6	7
Total number of squares	1						

3. Write a rule you can use to figure out the number of squares in any picture like those shown in Question 1.

____

FF **Use your rule from Question 3 to calculate the number of squares in a picture that is 20 squares wide.**

Relating Data to Rules

1. Complete the chart to show the number of crosses and squares for each picture.

Picture	Number of crosses	Number of squares
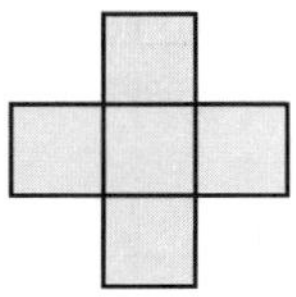	1	______
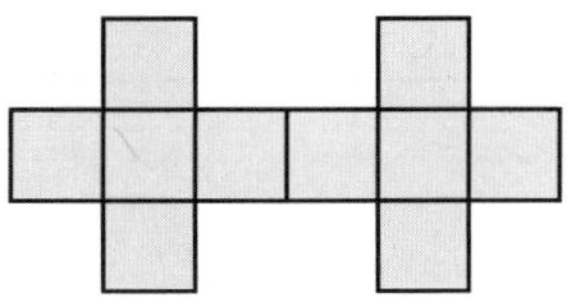	2	______
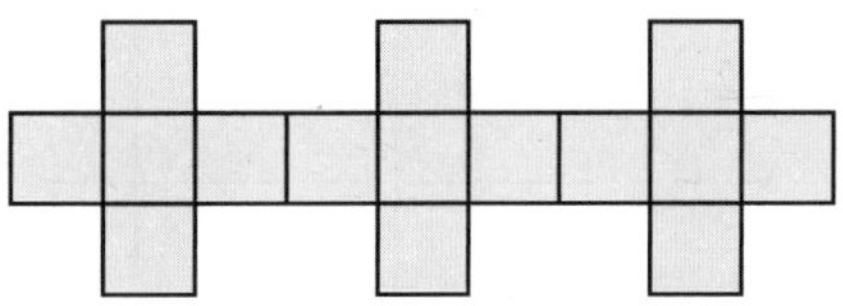	______	______
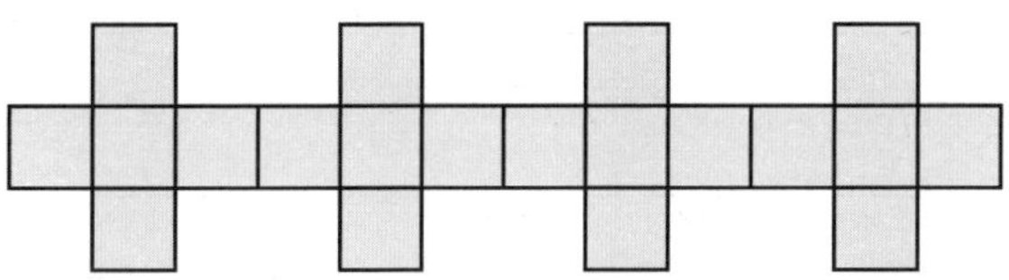	______	______
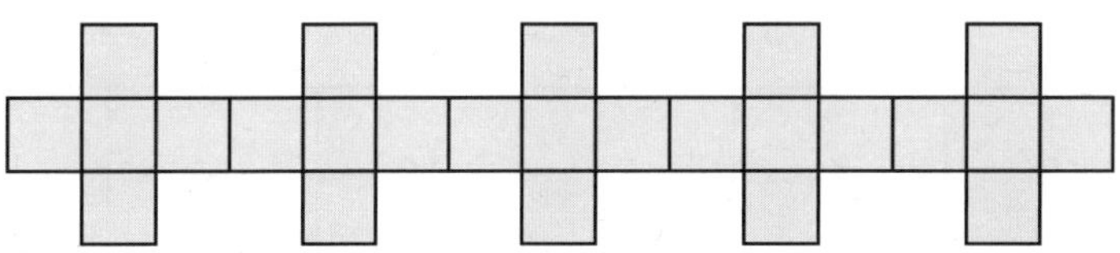	______	______

2. Write how you can figure out the number of squares when you know the number of crosses.

____

____

3. Figure out the number of squares there are in a picture that has

a. 10 crosses ______ **b.** 15 crosses ______

4. How many squares would you draw to make a picture in this pattern that has

a. 100 crosses? ______ **b.** 120 crosses? ______

Try abbreviating the rule you wrote for Question 2.

Working with Tables

Worksheet 141

1. Use the pattern to help you complete each table. Then write the rule.

a.

Books bought	6	7	8	10	15	19	23	26
Books received	8	9	10	12				

Rule: ______________________________

b.

Old price	Rs 16	Rs 21	Rs 29	Rs 36	Rs 42	Rs 48	Rs 57	Rs 63
New price	Rs 11	Rs 16	Rs 24	Rs 31				

Rule: ______________________________

c.

Tables	1	2	3	4	5	10	12	15
Chairs	4	8	12	16				

Rule: ______________________________

d.

Crayons	8	16	24	32	40	88	120	160
Boxes	1	2	3	4				

Rule: ______________________________

For each table above, what is the second number if the first number is 200?

Revision 1

1. Fill in the blank columns.

	Standard Form	Expanded Form	Words
a.			Six crore fifty lakh ninety three thousand four hundred and seventy-eight
b.		16,00,000 + 80,000 + 3,000 + 400 + 80 + 4	
c.	3,10,20,500		
d.			Five crore three lakh seven thousand nine hundred and ninety
e.		5,00,000 + 500 + 50 + 5	

2. Arrange the following numbers in decreasing order.

a. 123.984   129.986   123.905   129.968

b. 7,34,23,047   7,34,13,047   7,34,33,047   7,34,03,047

c. $\frac{1}{2}$ $\frac{5}{4}$ $\frac{13}{2}$ $\frac{3}{4}$

3. Solve the following.

a. 81,16,82,389 + 15,908 + 6,11,62,929

b. $1\frac{3}{5} + \frac{2}{5}$

c. $3\frac{12}{17} \times 1\frac{11}{34}$

d. 6.8 – 5.034

e. 34,829 × 805

f. 73,56,44,192 – 25,58,14,663

g. 30,022 ÷ 34

h. 77.743 + 98.6

i. 4.16 ÷ 600

4. Fill in the blanks.

Decimal	Fraction	Percent
0.8		
		65%
0.012		
	$\frac{36}{100}$	
		87.5%

5. An empty basket weighs $\frac{1}{6}$ kg. Shalini put $2\frac{1}{4}$ kg apples in it. What is the total weight of the basket and apples?

6. Kiran wanted to buy a skirt and a shirt for her birthday. Her mother took her shopping. The price of the skirt was Rs 1,234.60 and the price of the shirt was Rs 421.50. How much did Kiran's new outfit cost?

7. Colour the numbers that are factors of the number in the centre. Then, divide the number by the factors you shaded and write the answers.

9. Use the factor tree in Question 8 to help you list all the factors of 80.

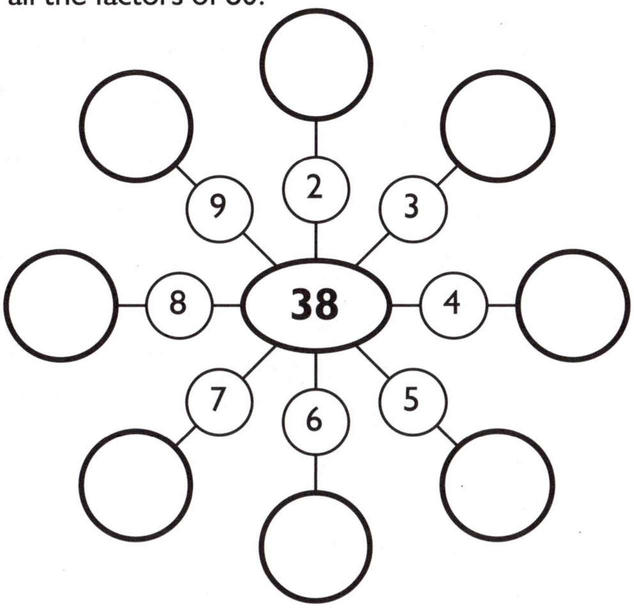

8. Make a factor tree for 80.

10. **a.** Circle the multiples of 3.

43 51 75 82 87 121 133 152 183

Write how you decided.

b. Circle the multiples of 4.

48 56 73 84 96 146 164 170 188

Write how you decided.

c. Circle the multiples of 9.

72 84 99 153 162 167 171 184 199

Write how you decided.

11. Complete each of these to show equivalent fractions.

a. $\frac{1}{4} = \frac{\_\_\_}{20}$ (× ___ , × ___)

b. $\frac{3}{5} = \frac{\_\_\_}{100}$ (× ___ , × ___)

c. $\frac{2}{5} = \frac{\_\_\_}{100}$ (× ___ , × ___)

d. $\frac{8}{20} = \frac{\_\_\_}{100}$ (× ___ , × ___)

12. Shade the decimal fraction. Then write the common fraction.

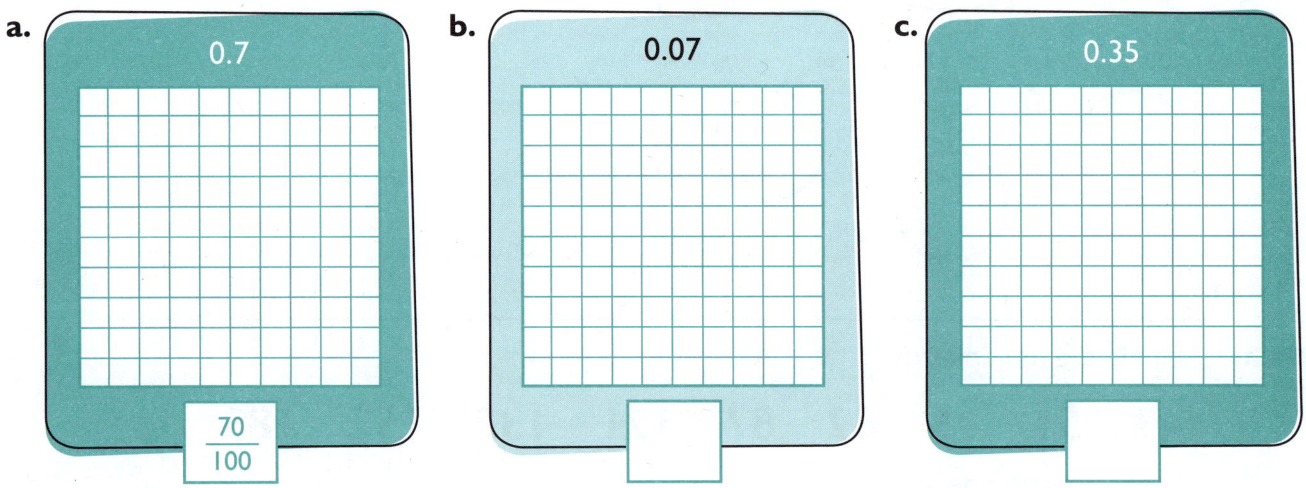

13. Complete the pieces to match.

a.

b.

14. Write the fraction or write the number word.

a. 4.15 ______________________

b. ______ four and fifty-hundredths

c. 4.51 ______________________

d. ______ four and five-hundredths

15. Draw arrows to show where these numbers are located on the number line. Then write how far away each number is from the nearest whole number.

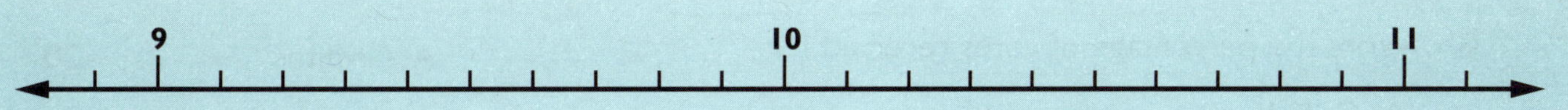

a. 8.9 ______

b. 9.45 ______

c. 9.89

d. 10.3

e. 10.71

16. Write these numbers in order from the greatest to the least.

3.14 3.40 4.03 4.13 3.41 4.30

______, ______, ______, ______, ______, ______

17. Colour the square to show the fraction. Then express the fraction as a percentage and as a decimal.

a. Colour $\frac{2}{5}$

$\frac{2}{5}$ is the same as $\frac{\quad}{100}$

$\frac{2}{5}$ is the same as 0.____

b. Colour $\frac{1}{4}$

$\frac{1}{4}$ is the same as $\frac{\quad}{100}$

$\frac{1}{4}$ is the same as 0.____

18. Each arrow is pointing to a number. Write it as a **common fraction** above the line and as a **decimal fraction** below the line.

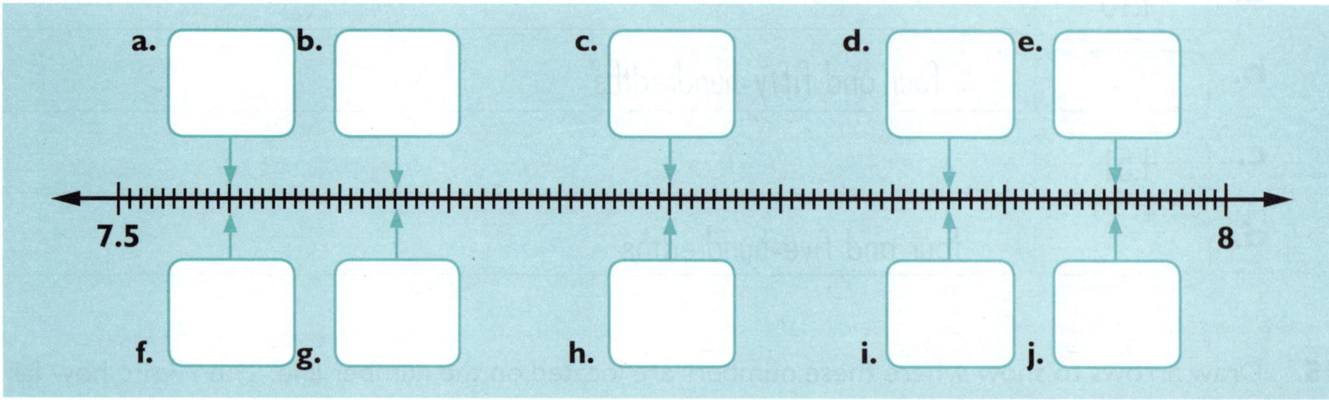

19. **a.** Write the total number of votes

b. Write the percentage of votes received for

A. Griffiths

J.K. Rowling

c. Which author received less than 20% of the votes?

d. What percentage of people voted for E. Rodda and A. Griffiths altogether

Favourite authors (votes)

A. Griffiths	20
P. Jennings	25
E. Rodda	15
J.K. Rowling	40

20. Complete the pieces to match.

a.

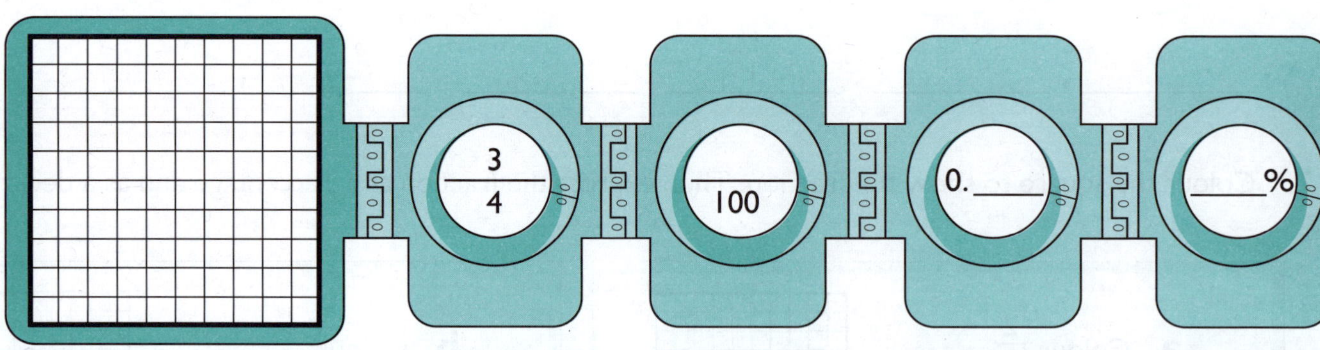

b.

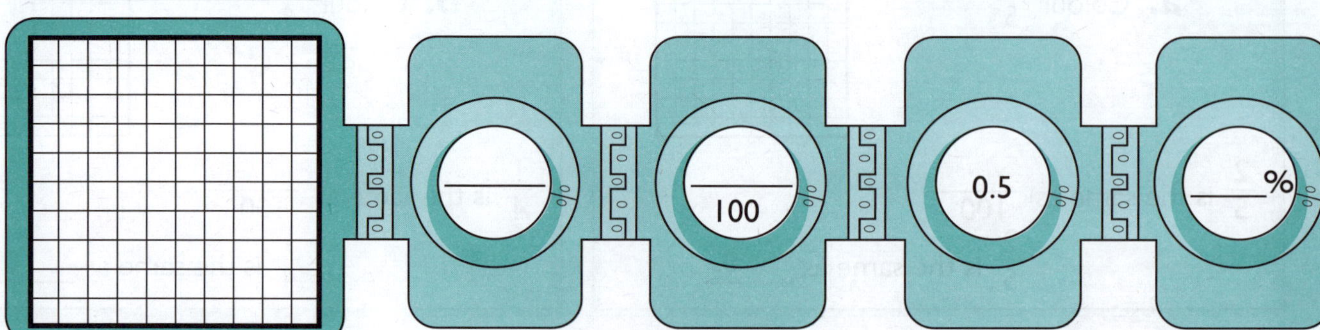

Revision 2

1. The graph below shows the percentage obtained by Alka from Classes I to V. Study the graph and answer the questions.

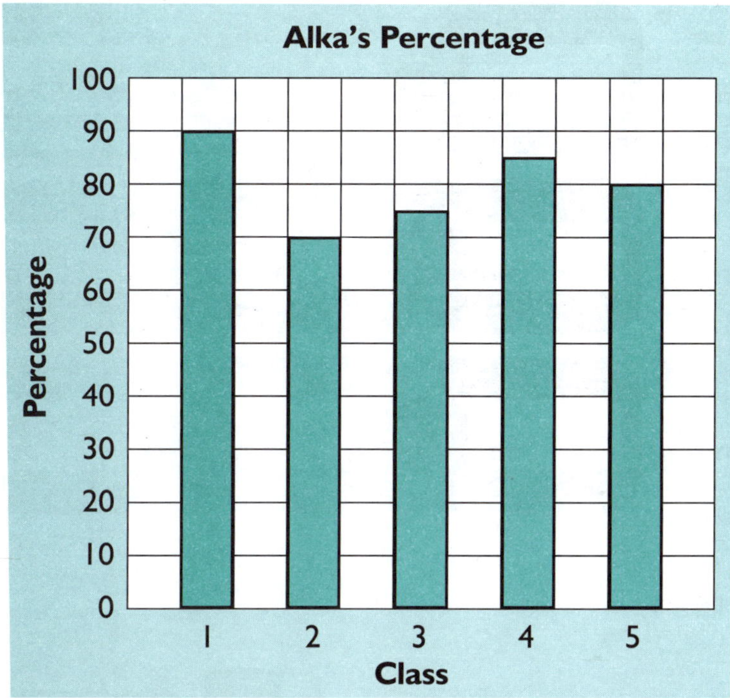

a. In which class did Alka score the highest?

b. What was Alka's percentage in Class III?

c. In which class/classes did Alka score more than 80%?

2. A group of students were asked what their favourite colour was. The data is shown below. Draw a picture graph for the data.

Colour	Number of students
Purple	4
Red	10
Green	8
Blue	14
Yellow	6

3. Shown below is a cube of side 40 cm. A smaller cube with side 6 cm has been cut out of the larger cube.

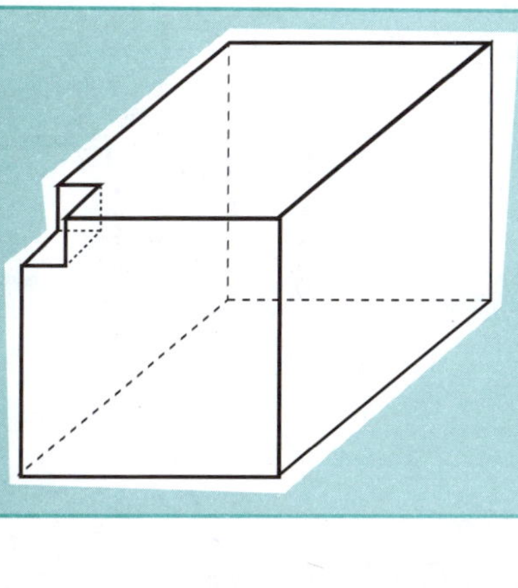

a. What was the volume of the larger cube before the smaller cube was cut out?

b. What is the volume of the smaller cube?

c. What is the volume of the shape that is left?

4. Write numbers to show equal lengths.

	mm	cm	m
a.	345 mm	cm	m
b.	mm	cm	1.75 m
c.	mm	65 cm	m
d.	mm	120 cm	m
e.	mm	cm	.85 m
f.	17 mm	cm	m

5. Write each volume as a decimal fraction of 1 litre.

a.

b.

c.

6. Write each capacity as a decimal fraction of 1 litre.

a.

b.
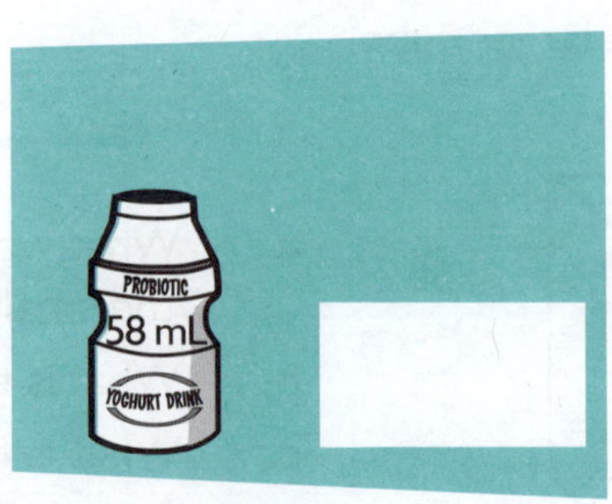

c.

7. a. Use a blue pencil to show the perimeter of this shape.

   b. Use a red pencil to show the area of this shape.

   c. Write how you would explain perimeter and area to a Class 4 student.

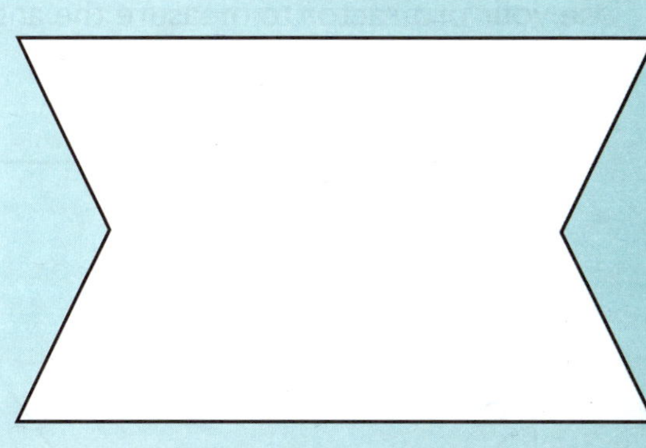

Perimeter ________________________________

Area ________________________________

8. Calculate the perimeter and area of these shapes.

a.

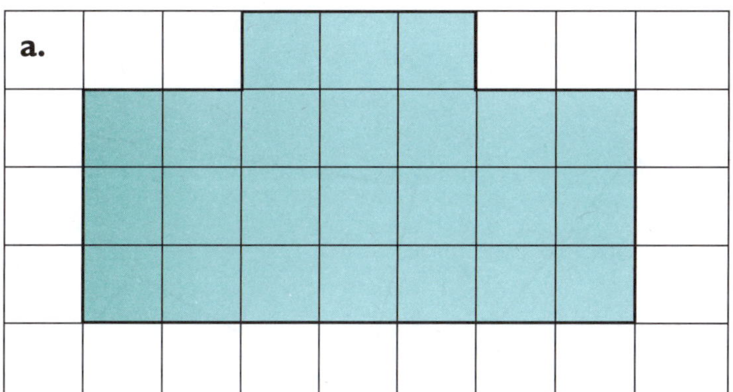

Perimeter = ______________ centimetres

Area = ______________ square centimetres

b.

Perimeter = ______________ centimetres

Area = ______________ square centimetres

9. Draw a rectangle to match the dimensions given. Then, calculate the area.

Length: 12 squares Width: 8 squares

Area: ________ squares

10. Draw a rectangle to match the area given. Then, write the dimensions.

Area: 64 squares

Length: ___ squares Width: ___ squares

Revision 2

11. Use your protractor to measure the angles in this shape. Write the measurements in the table.

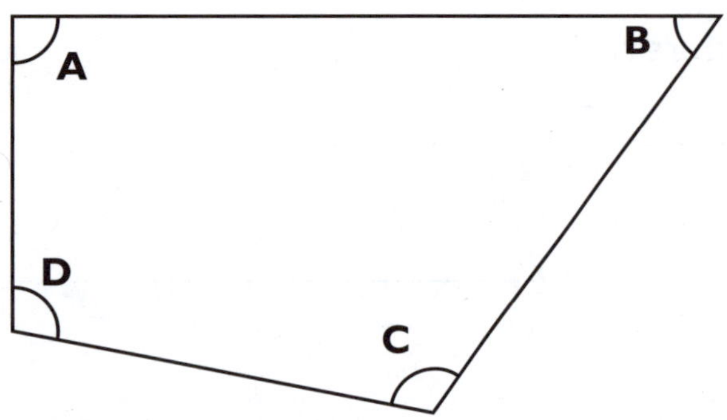

Angle	Measure
A	
B	
C	
D	

12. Look at each interior angle in the shapes below. Mark each angle with a

- Blue arc if it is an acute angle
- Red arc if it is a right angle
- Green arc if it is an obtuse angle
- Yellow arc if it is a reflex angle

13. Draw lines to connect the triangles to a label that matches. There may be more than one match for each triangle.

right-angled triangle | **isosceles triangle** | **equilateral triangle** | **scalene triangle**

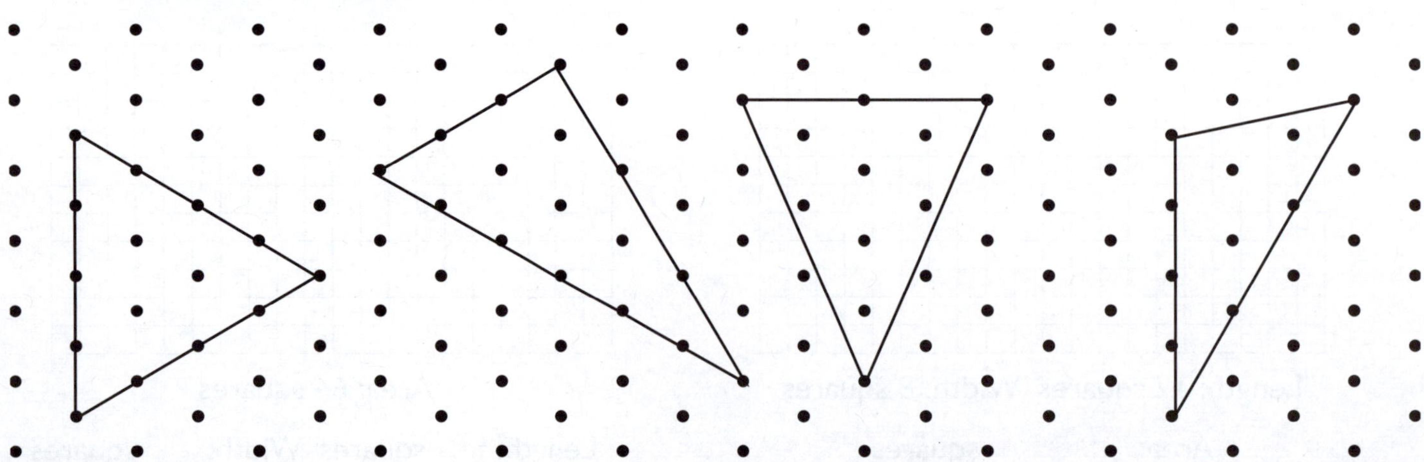

14. Complete the missing parts.

a.

b.

c.

15. Complete these facts.

a. 1 minute = ______ seconds

b. 1 hour = ______ minutes

c. 1 hour = ______ seconds

d. 1 day = _______ hours

e. 1 day = _______ minutes

f. 1 day = _______ seconds

16. Use this timetable to answer the questions below.

Trains from Raja Garden to Central Station									
Raja Garden	6:45	7:15	7:45	8:25	8:40	9:15	9:45	10:15	10:30
Gurgaon	6:49	7:18	7:48	8:28	8:43	–	9:48	10:18	10:35
Lodhi Road	6:50	7:20	7:50	8:31	8:45	–	9:50	10:20	10:40
Sant Nagar	6:52	7:22	7:52	8:36	8:47	–	9:52	10:22	10:45
Rampur	6:56	7:26	7:56	8:40	8:51	9:23	9:56	10:26	10:49
Central Station	6:58	7:28	7:58	8:42	8:53	9:25	9:58	10:28	10:51

a. If you take the 9:45 train from Raja Garden, how long will it take to get to

- Lodhi Road ☐
- Central Station ☐

b. If you live at Raja Garden, what are the times of the trains you could catch to get to Central Station by 8:00? ☐

c. Between 8:00 and 10:00, how many trains leave

- Raja Garden? ☐
- Sant Nagar? ☐
- Rampur? ☐

17. Look at the interior angles of these quadrilaterals.

a. Draw red arcs to mark the angles that are less than a right angle.

b. Draw blue arcs to mark the right angles.

c. Draw green arcs to mark the angles that are greater than a right angle.

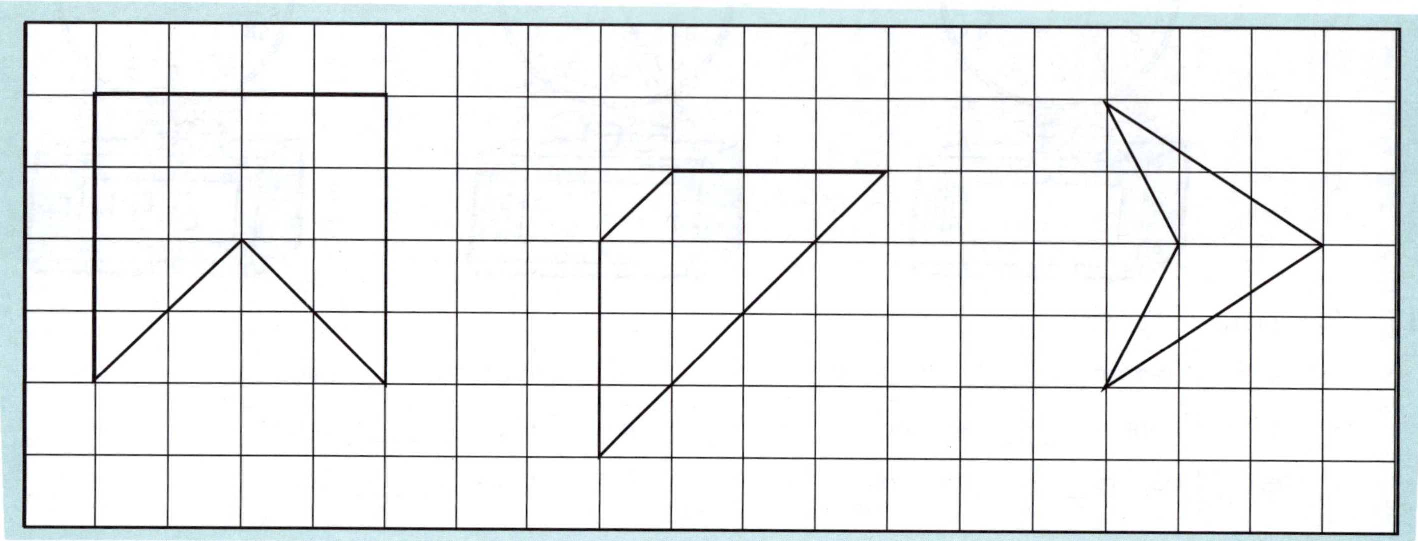

18. Look at the triangles below.

a. Place a red ✓ inside the triangles with exactly two sides of equal length.

b. Place a blue ✓ inside the triangles with all sides of equal length.

c. Place a green ✓ inside the triangles with all sides of different lengths.

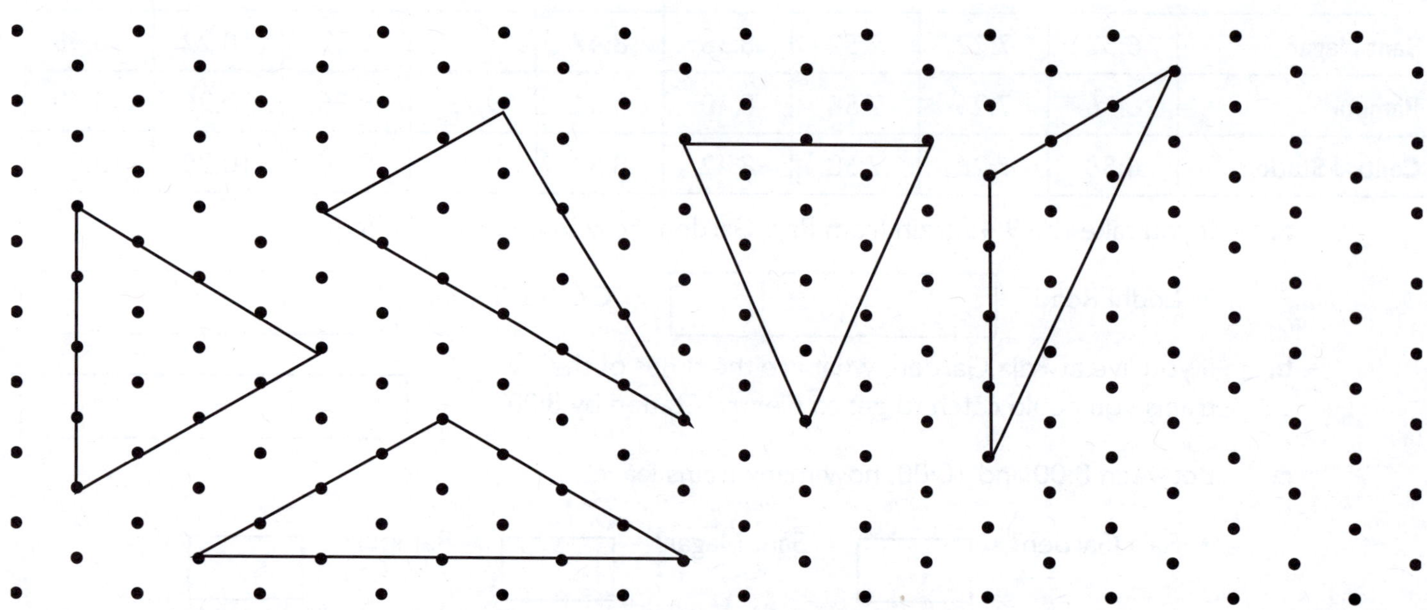

Self Assessment—How I Feel About Maths

1. Draw a ☺ or ☹ below to show how you feel about

a. doing maths at school
b. solving maths problems with others
c. doing mental maths

2. **a** What do you like most about maths?

____

____

b. How do you think you could improve at maths?

____

____

3. For each of these, circle the hand sign that reflects your level of understanding.

a.

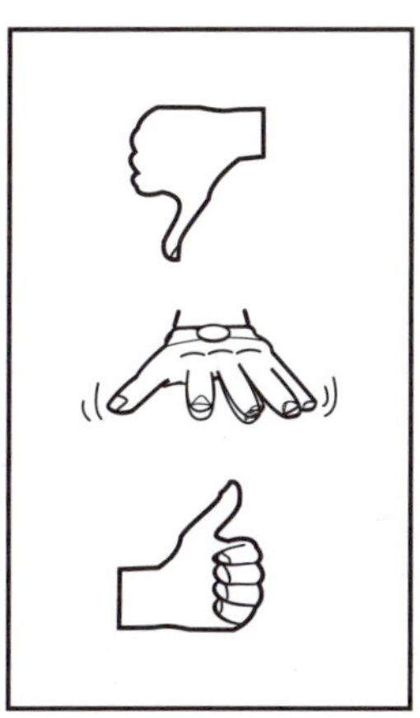

3-D Objects

b.

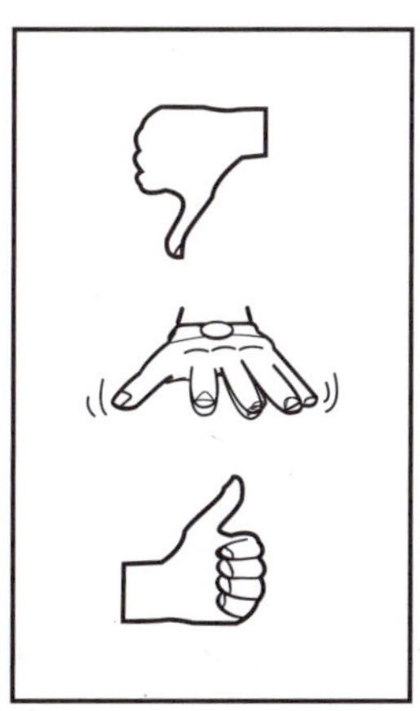

Timetables and Timelines

c.

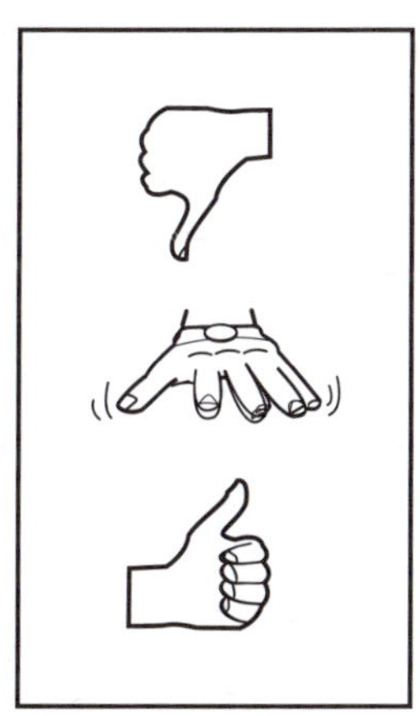

Percentages

d.

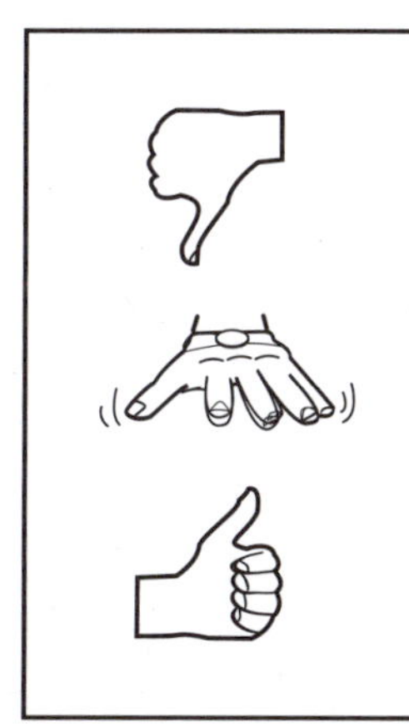

Area and Perimeter

Self Assessment—How I Feel About Maths

1. Draw a ✓ on the number line to show how you feel about

a. playing maths games	unhappy ——— ok ——— happy
b. doing maths at home	unhappy ——— ok ——— happy
c. doing maths word problems	unhappy ——— ok ——— happy

2. Complete these sentences.

a Maths is fun when ______________________________

____

b. Maths is a pain when ______________________________

____

3. For each of these, circle the hand sign that reflects your level of skill.

a.

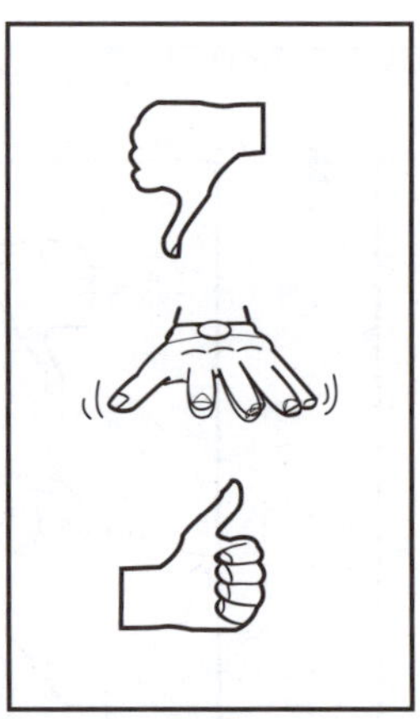

Adding and subtracting mentally

b.

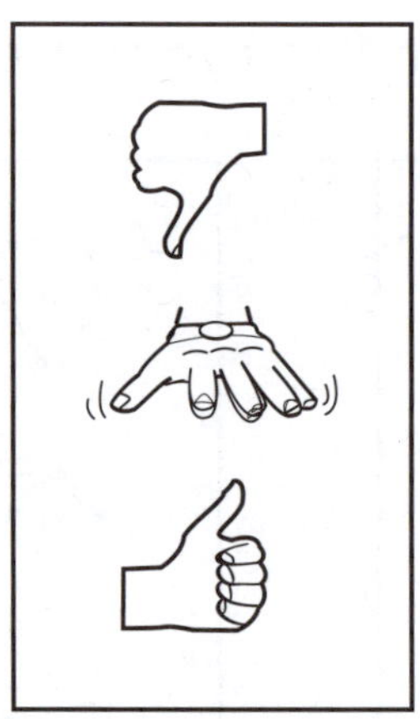

Multiplying and dividing mentally

c.

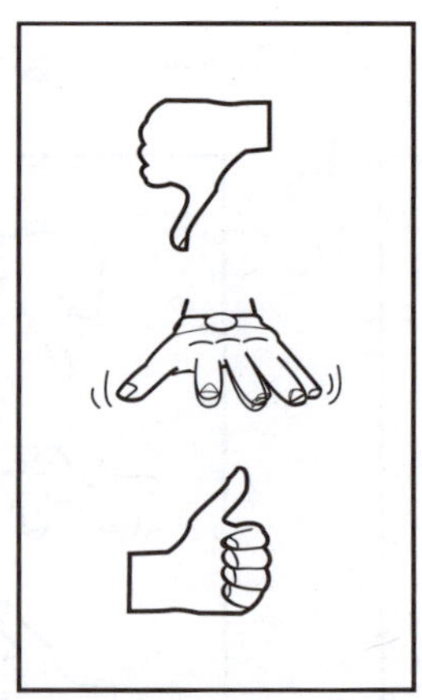

Reading and writing decimal fractions

d.

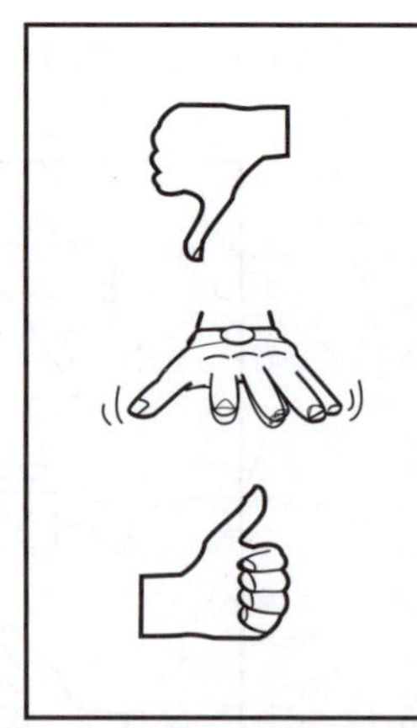

Constructing graphs

Answers

Worksheet 1
1 a. 21,000; b. 25,000; c. 31,000; d. 35,000; e. 39,000; f. 22,000; g. 24,000; h. 29,000; i. 33,000; j. 38,000
2 a. 21,000; b. 21,600; c. 21,900; d. 22,500; e. 22,900; f. 21,300; g. 21,700; h. 22,100; i. 22,400; j. 22,800
3a. 21,100; b. 21,170; c. 21,190; d. 21,240; e. 21,290; f. 21,120; g. 21,150; h. 21,210; i. 21,260; j. 21,280
4 a. 21,111; b. 21,114; c. 21,119; d. 21,124; e. 21,129; f. 21,112; g. 21,117; h. 21,121; i. 21,126; j. 21,128

Worksheet 2
1a. 6,10,000; b. 6,50,000; c. 7,10,000; d. 7,50,000; e. 7,90,000; f. 6,20,000; g. 6,40,000; h. 6,90,000; i. 7,30,000; j. 7,80,000
2 a. 6,10,000; b. 6,10,000; c. 6,10,900; d. 6,20,500; e. 6,20,900; f. 6,10,300; g. 6,10,700; h. 6,20,000; i. 6,20,400; j. 6,20,800
3 a. 6,11,100; b. 6,11,700; c. 6,11,900; d. 6,12,400; e. 6,12,900; f. 6,11,200; g. 6,11,500; h. 6,12,100; i. 6,12,600; j. 6,12,800
4 a. 6,11,110; b. 6,11,140; c. 6,11,190; d. 6,11,240; e. 6,11,290; f. 6,11,120; g. 6,11,170; h. 6,11,210; i. 6,11,260; j. 6,11,280

Worksheet 4
1 a. 619 thousands, 342 ones; six lakh nineteen thousand three hundred and forty-two; b. 703 thousands, 415 ones; c. two lakh sixty-one thousand five hundred and eight; d. 318 thousands, 24 ones.

Worksheet 5
1 a. 10 ones; b. 10 tens, 100 ones; c. 1 hundred, 10 tens, 100 ones
2a. 10 thousands, 100 hundreds, 1,000 tens, 10,000 ones
2b. 10 ten thousands, 100 thousands, 1,000 hundreds, 10,000 tens, 1,000,000 ones
2c. 100 lakh, 1000 ten thousands, 10,000 thousands, 100,000 hundred, 1,000,000 tens, 10,000,000 ones

Worksheet 6
1 a. 98,17,439 > 45,80,544; b. 42,16,268 > 34,49,879; c. 42,16,268 < 42,92,223; d. 34,49,879 > 13,76,950; e. 42,16,268 < 45,80,544; f. 25,40,069 < 45,80,544; g. 22,07,340 < 42,16,268; h. 98,17,439 > 23,24,319
2 a. 13,76,950; b. 22,07,340; c. 23,24,319; d. 25,40,069; e. 34,49,879; f. 42,16,268; g. 42,16,268; h. 42,92,223; i. 45,80,544; j. 98,17,439

Worksheet 7

1a. 4,07,15,029; b. 6,03,80,201; c. 21,00,56,930; d. 9,201,08,005; e. 18,00,06,488; f. 30,00,14,097
2a. 6,08,03,000; b. 16,08,33,402; c. 61,00,18,342; d. 6,01,00,83,420

Worksheet 8
1a. 6,57,08,526; b.1,16,63,971; c. 16,40,84,498; d. 9,95,47,709; e. 8,94,88,818; f. 8,10,34,065
2a. 1,03,13,306; b. 14,45,490; c. 7,77,886; d. 8,56,80,519; e. 34,95,112; f. 7,23,32,379

Worksheet 9
1a. 1,45,996; b. 5,75,361; c. 3,08,61,309; d. 17,42,832; e. 24,79,887; f. 14,148
2a. 1,88,960; b. 5,37,57,556; c. 1,15,308; d. 4,34,80,896; e. 3,54,50,435
3a. 14,501; b. 5,228; c. 10,411; d. 12,741

Worksheet 10
83,087,357; 2. Rs 1,956,114; 3. 97,763,217 kilos; 4. Rs 192,663; 5. Rs 3,3624,112; 6. 4,523,110; 7. 33,253,783; 8. 16,577,681; 9. 429,286

Worksheet 11
1a. 471 mm; b. 518 mm; c. 734 mm
2a. 597mm; b. 667 mm; c. 1,136 mm
3a. 253 mm; b. 127 mm; c. 276 mm

Worksheet 12
1a. 5200; b. 6,500; c. 8,100; d. 2,500; e. 1,300; f.1,600
2a. 3,300; b. 3,500; c. 3,100; d. 1,500; e. 1,300; f. 900

Worksheet 13
2a. 3,600; b. 1,700; c. 3,200; d. 2,100; e. 1,400; f.1,550
4a. 600; b. 400; c. 700; d. 1,100; e. 300; f. 900

Worksheet 14
1a. No; b. 180
2a. 120; b. 360; c. 210; d. 300; e. 450; f. 490; g. 480; h. 720; i. 720

Worksheet 15
1a. 384; b. 492; c. 253; d. 403; e. 143; f. 588
2a. 483; b. 288; c. 451; d. 372
3a. 276; b. 341; c. 286

Worksheet 16
1a. 210
2a. 660; b. 2,700; c. 3,000; d. 420; e. 840; f. 720
3a. 450; b. 1,200; c. 1,200; d. 3,000; e. 1,100; f. 1,500

Worksheet 17
1a. 434; 651; 868; 4,340; 6,510; 8,680
1b. 776; 1,164; 1,552; 7,760; 11,640; 15,520
2a. 9,168; b. 836; c. 15,960; d. 8,800; e.8,910; f. Rs 10,854

Worksheet 18
1a. 12,896; b. 2,108; c. 18,055; d. 7,776; e. 18,128; f. 8,602
2a. 12,558; b. 23,456; c. 26,565; d. 5,136; e. 11,288; f. 9,960

Worksheet 19
1a. 5,248; b. 8,635; c. 11,092; d. 11,508; e. 32,472; f. 2,875; g. 27,300; h. 26,010; i. 7,650; j. 8,190; k. 18,576; l. 19,038

Worksheet 20
1a. 109; b. 106; c. 107; d. 921; e. 920; f. 607
3a. 206; b. 103; c. 208; d. 106; e. 102; f. 307

Worksheet 21
1a. 100 + 96; b. 200 + 92; c. 300 + 72; d. 200 + 56
2a. 2,400 + 120; b. 1,200 + 1,620; c. 3,000 + 150; d. 4,500 + 6
3a. 270; b. 1,170; c. 460; d. 650
4a. 82; b. 33; c. 76; d. 14; e. 32; f. 36

Worksheet 22
1a. 32, 40, 48, 56, 64
1b. 8 X number of minutes
1c. 80; 240; 480
2a. 36, 48, 5, 7, 10, 15
2b. 4 X number of minutes
2c. 80; 100; 128

Worksheet 24
1a. 60; b. 72; c. 90; d. 42; e. 60
2a. 70 days; b. 24 minutes; c. 8 inches

Worksheet 25
1a. 14; b. 1; c. 6; d. 4; e. 2; f. 3
2a. 18 inches; b. 30

Worksheet 27
1a. 2 X 2 X 3 X 3; b. 3 X 5 X 2 X 2; c. 2 X 2 X 3 X 2 X 2; d. 2 X 2 X 2 X 3 X 3
2a. 2 X 2 X 3 X 7; b. 2 X 2 X 2 X 3 X 5

Worksheet 28
1a. 3 X 5; 1 X 15; b. 5 X 5; 1 X 25; c. 2 X 7; 1 X 14; d. 2 X 8; 4 X 4; 16 X 1; e. 2 X 14; 4 X 7; 14 X 2; f. 2 X 9; 3 X 6; 1 X 18; g. 2 X 12; 3 X 8; 4 X 6; 8 X 3; h. 2 X 32; 4 X 16; 8 X 8; 1 X 64; i. 2 X 15; 3 X 10; 5 X 6; 1 X 30; j. 2 X 18; 3 X 12; 4 X 9; 6 X 6; 1 X 36; k. 2 X 40; 4 X 20; 5 X 16; 8 X 10; 20 X 4; l. 2 X 50; 4 X 25; 5 X 20; 10 X 10; 20 X 5

Worksheet 29
1a. 4 X 4; 8 X 2; b. 2 X 14; 4 X 7; c. 2 X 9; 3 X 6; d. 6 X 4; 2 X 12; 3 X 8; e. 2 X 21; 6 X 7; 14 X 3; f. 2 X 15; 3 X 10; 5 X 6; g. 2 X 50; 4 X 25; 5 X 20; 20 X 5; h. 2 X 40; 4 X 20; 5 X 16; 8 X 10; i. 2 X 24; 3 X 16; 4 X 12; 6 X 8; j. 2 X 30; 3 X 20; 4 X 15; 5 X 12; 6 X 10; k. 2 X 42; 3 X 28; 4 X 21; 6 X 14; 7 X 12; l. 2 X 48; 3 X 32; 4 X 24; 6 X 16; 8 X 12

Worksheet 30
1a. 270; b. 600; c. 220; d. 800
2a. 540; b. 770; c. 270; d. 990; e. 540; f. 720
3a. 400; b. 420; c. 1,080; d. 810; e. 630; f. 550

Worksheet 31
1a. 81
2a. 42; b. 71; c. 82; d. 61; e. 21; f. 41
3a. 43; b. 11; c. 31; d. 121; e. 71; f. 92

Worksheet 33
1a. 25; b. 99; c. 55; d. 39; e. 28; f. 28; g. 66; h. 42

Worksheet 36
1a. $\frac{4}{6}$; b. $\frac{3}{12}$; c. $\frac{6}{8}$; d. $\frac{4}{12}$; e. $\frac{4}{10}$; f. $\frac{3}{9}$; g. $\frac{1}{4}$; h. $\frac{2}{6}$
2a. $\frac{1}{3}$; b. $\frac{2}{5}$; c. $\frac{1}{3}$; d. $\frac{2}{4}$; e. $\frac{2}{8}$; f. $\frac{2}{3}$; g. $\frac{1}{3}$; h. $\frac{3}{4}$

Worksheet 37
1a. $\frac{2}{10}$; b. $\frac{60}{100}$; c. $\frac{25}{100}$; d. $\frac{30}{100}$; e. $\frac{75}{100}$; f. $\frac{70}{100}$

Worksheet 38
2 a. $\frac{20}{100}$; b. $\frac{40}{100}$; c. $\frac{50}{100}$; d. $\frac{75}{100}$; e. $\frac{20}{100}$;
f. $\frac{36}{100}$; g. $\frac{60}{100}$; h. $\frac{80}{100}$

Worksheet 39
3a. $1\frac{7}{8}$; b. $1\frac{1}{4}$; c. $1\frac{9}{8}$; d. $2\frac{3}{4}$
3b. $\frac{11}{8}$; b. $\frac{7}{4}$; c. $\frac{23}{8}$; d. $\frac{13}{4}$

5 a. $1\frac{5}{10}$; b. $2\frac{6}{10}$; c. $1\frac{15}{100}$; d. $1\frac{26}{100}$; e. $1\frac{8}{10}$;
f. $7\frac{10}{10}$; g. $1\frac{90}{100}$; h. $2\frac{70}{100}$

Worksheet 41
1a. $\frac{7}{8}$; b. $\frac{4}{6}$; c. $\frac{7}{10}$; d. $\frac{5}{8}$; e. $\frac{4}{5}$; f. $\frac{11}{12}$
2a. $\frac{3}{6}$; b. $\frac{3}{10}$; c. $\frac{2}{8}$; d. $\frac{4}{12}$; e. $\frac{2}{8}$; f. $\frac{3}{12}$

Worksheet 42
1a. $\frac{6}{8}$; b. $\frac{4}{8}$; c. $\frac{7}{8}$; d. $\frac{4}{8}$; e. $\frac{6}{8}$; f. $\frac{12}{8}$
2a. $\frac{7}{5}$; b. $\frac{8}{5}$; c. $\frac{10}{5}$; d. $\frac{4}{5}$; e. $\frac{3}{5}$; f. $\frac{4}{5}$
3a. $\frac{15}{8}$; b. $\frac{64}{8}$; c. $\frac{30}{5}$; d. $\frac{29}{5}$; e. $\frac{4}{8}$; f. $\frac{14}{8}$; g. $\frac{3}{8}$; h. $\frac{4}{5}$; $\frac{9}{5}$

Worksheet 43
1a. $\frac{7}{8}$; b. $\frac{7}{8}$; c. $\frac{3}{6}$; d. $\frac{9}{16}$; e. $\frac{7}{12}$; f. $\frac{1}{8}$; g. $\frac{2}{10}$; h. $\frac{1}{6}$; i. $\frac{3}{10}$

Worksheet 44
1a. $\frac{5}{6}$; b. $\frac{7}{8}$; c. $\frac{6}{8}$
2a. $\frac{16}{20}$; b. $\frac{22}{24}$; c. $\frac{16}{24}$; d. $\frac{18}{24}$; e. $\frac{18}{24}$; f. $\frac{14}{16}$

Worksheet 45
1a. $\frac{3}{6}$; b. $\frac{2}{12}$; c. $\frac{3}{8}$
2a. $\frac{6}{16}$; b. $\frac{2}{24}$; c. $\frac{4}{24}$; d. $\frac{6}{24}$; e. $\frac{8}{24}$; f. $\frac{2}{16}$

Worksheet 46
1a. $\frac{3}{8}$; b. $\frac{24}{117}$; c. 9; d. $\frac{7}{36}$; e. $\frac{25}{88}$; f. $\frac{49}{2}$; g. $\frac{8}{39}$; $\frac{56}{9}$

Worksheet 47
1a. 219 acres; b. 4; c. $\frac{9}{39}$

Worksheet 49
1a. 0.50; b. 0.10; c. 0.20; d. 0.80
2a. 0.25; b. 0.75

Worksheet 51
1 a. 0.7; b. 1.1; c. 1.6; d. 1.9; e. 2.2; f. 0.9; g. 1.0; h. 1.4; i. 2.0; j. 2.4
2 a. 8.8; b. 9.2; c. 9.5; d. 9.8; e. 10.3; f. 8.9; g. 9.3; h. 9.6; i. 10.1; j. 10.5
3 a. 22.4; b. 22.8; c. 23.3; d. 23.7; e. 23.9; f. 22.6; g. 22.9; h. 23.2; i. 23.6; j. 24.2

Worksheet 53
1a. 4.9; b. 5.3; c. 5.8; d. 6.1; e. 6.4; f. 5.1; g. 5.4; h. 5.7; i. 6.2; j. 6.6
2a. 3.44; b. 3.48; c. 3.51; d. 3.54; e. 3.59; f. 3.46; g. 3.49; h. 3.52; i. 3.56; j. 3.61
3a. 5.87; b. 5.91; c. 5.96; d. 5.98; e. 6.02; f. 5.89; g. 5.92; h. 5.95; i. 5.99; j. 6.03

Answers

Worksheet 58
1a. 1.217; b. 1.221; c. 1.226; d. 1.229; e. 1.232; f.1.219; g. 1.222; h. 1.224; i.1.228; j. 1.234
2a. 1.488; b. 1.492; c. 1.497; d. 1.498; e. 1.503; f. 1.489; g. 1.493; h. 1.496; i. 1.501; j. 1.505
3a. 2.054; b. 2.058; c. 2.063; d. 2.067; e. 2.069; f. 2.056; g. 2.059; h. 2.062; i. 2.066; j. 2.071

Worksheet 59
1a. 3.457; b. 3.461; c. 3.466; d. 3.469; e. 3.472; f. 3.459; g. 3.462; h. 3.464; i. 3.468; j. 3.474
2a. 0.888; b. 0.892; c. 0.895; d. 0.898; e. 0.903; f. 0.889; g. 0.893; h. 0.896; i. 0.901; j. 0.905
3a. 0.064; b. 0.068; c. 0.073; d. 0.077; e. 0.079; f. 0.066; g. 0.069; h. 0.071; i. 0.076; j. 0.081

Worksheet 63
1a. 3.87 m; b. 4.27 m; c. 3.5 m; d. 3.86 m; e. 4.51 m
2a. 3.86 > 2. 97; b. 3.5 > 3.42
3a. 3.87, 3.45, 3.18; b. 4.27, 4.15, 4.06; c. 3.5, 3.42, 3.38; d. 3.86, 3.21, 2.97; e. 4.51, 4.3, 4.04
4a. Akul; b. Vani

Worksheet 67
1a. 28.47 kg; b. 42.28 kg; c. 32.55 kg; d. 50.26 kg; e. 39.29 kg; f. 52.78 kg; g. 41.95 kg; 43.15 kg; 42.38 kg

Worksheet 68
1a. 372.5 km; b. 209.5 km; c. 267.1 km; d. 167.2 km
2a. 167.8 km; b. 98.8 km; c. 210.1 km; d. 110.2 km
3a. 52.7 km per hour; b. 93.8 km per hour; c. 7.5 km per hour; d. 96.9 km per hour

Worksheet 69
1a. 0.36 m; b. 0.34 m; c. 0.32 m; d. 0.24 m; e. 0.17 m
2a. 0.07 m; b. 0.05 m; c. 0.14 m; d. 0.11 m; e. 0.06 m
3a. 0.21 m; b. 0.13 m; c. 0.54 m; d. 0.33 m
4a. 0.17 m; b. 0.03 m; c. 0.07 m; d. 0.11 m
5a. 3.26 m; b. 3.2 m; c. 3.13 m; d. 2.63 m; e. 2.14 m

Worksheet 70
1a. 8.2 kg; b. 2.6 kg; c. 5.6 kg; d. 2.45 kg; e. 8.9 kg; f. 4.35 kg; g. 13.75 kg; h. 6.35 kg; i. 8.55 kg

Worksheet 71
1a. 205.8; b. 326.65; c. 244.85; d. 207.8; e. 186.35; f. 379.3
2a. 118.75; b. 13.3; c. 56.8

Worksheet 72
1a. 5.097 kg; b. 3.756 kg; c. 2.209 kg; d. 5.453 kg; e. 3.062 kg; f. 3.726 kg
2a. 1.178 kg; b. 1.68 kg; c. 1.663 kg; d. 1.471 kg; e. 0.152 kg; f. 2.342 kg

Worksheet 73
2a. 96, 9.6, 0.96; b. 192, 19.2, 1.92; c. 232, 23.2, 2.32; d. 144, 14.4, 1.44; e.120, 12, 1.2; f. 70, 7, 0.7

Worksheet 74
1a. 3.4; b. 7.6; c. 10.8; d. 7.2
2a. 25.2; b. 59.2; c. 28.8

Worksheet 75
2a. 24.6; b. 13.6; c. 25.2; d. 28.4; e. 22; f. 32.2; g. 41.2; h. 48.8; i. 61

Worksheet 76
1c. 20
2a. 30; b. 26; c. 18; d. 35; e. 44
3a. 35; b. 27; c. 35; d. 33; e. 63; f. 66
4a. 40, 48, 56; b. 12.5, 15, 17.5; c. 22.5, 27, 31.5

Worksheet 77
1a. 34.4; b. 22.4; c. 50.4; d. 33.5; e. 27.6; f. 52.5; g. 42.9; h. 51.6
2a. 19.2; b. 11.4
3a. 22.4; b. 36; c. 40.8

Worksheet 78
1a. 3.9; b. 0.59; c. 4.16; d. 0.42; e. 0.33; f. 0.17; g. 21.83; h. 15.16; i. 8.85

Worksheet 79
1.942; 2. Rs 339.88; 3. 0.078; 4. Rs 11.08

Worksheet 80
2a. 66%; b. 50%; c. 87%; d. 33%; e. 83%; f. 25%; g. 41%; h. 75%

Worksheet 81
1a. 50%; b. 60%; c. 150%; d. 175%

2a. $\frac{75}{100}$, 0.75, 75%; b. $\frac{120}{100}$, 1.2, 120%; c. $\frac{80}{100}$, 0.8, 80%; d. $\frac{20}{100}$, 0.2, 20%; e. $\frac{250}{100}$, 2.5, 250%; f. $\frac{110}{100}$, 1.1, 110%

Worksheet 82
1a. $\frac{4}{10}$, $\frac{40}{100}$, 0.4, 40%; b. $\frac{4}{100}$, 0.04, 4%; c. $\frac{6}{25}$, $\frac{24}{100}$ 0.24, 24%; d. $\frac{4}{20}$, $\frac{20}{100}$, 0.2, 20%; e. $\frac{3}{5}$, $\frac{60}{100}$; 0.60, 60%

Worksheet 84
1a. 5, 25, 10, 5, 2.5, 1.25; b. 20, 100, 40, 20, 10, 5; c. 25, 125, 50, 25, 12.5, 6.25; d. 40, 200, 80, 40, 20, 10

Worksheet 85
1a. 20%; b. 25%; c. 10%
2a. 60%; b. 30%; c. 3%
3a. 10%; b. 20%; c. 50%; d. 2%

Worksheet 86
1. 100
2a. $\frac{30}{100}$; b. $\frac{15}{100}$; c. $\frac{20}{100}$; d. $\frac{35}{100}$
4a. 30 %; b. 15 %; c. 20 %; d. 35 %
5a. sports, soaps; b. movies, cartoons
6a. 50 %; b. 35 %; c. 50 %
7a. 20 %; b. 35 %; 30 %

Worksheet 88
1a. Rs 81; b. Rs 415; c. Rs 13.85; d. Rs 274.05; e. Rs 954

Worksheet 89
1a. Loss Rs 225; b. Profit Rs 72.1; c. Profit Rs 269; d. Profit Rs 91; e. Loss Rs 53.75

Worksheet 90
Rs 3,333; 2. Rs 28, 975; 3. Loss Rs 180; 4. Rs 3,225

Answers

Worksheet 102
1a. chord; b. radius; c. diameter; d. centre; e. diameter; f. chord
2a. 16 cm; b. 20 m; c. 70 cm; d. 4.8 cm; e. 12 mm; f. 16.4 cm
3a. 11 cm; b. 135 m; c. 8 mm; d. 7.4 cm; e. 17 mm; f. 55 cm

Worksheet 103
1a. 2 cm, 3 cm; b. 3 cm, 4 cm; c. 2 cm, 4 cm; d. 3 cm, 3.5 cm; e. 2.5 cm, 3.5 cm; f. 2.5 cm, 3 cm
2a. 33 mm, 28 mm; b. 18 mm, 32 mm; c. 42 mm, 32 mm; d. 27 mm, 22 mm; e. 28 mm, 24 mm; f. 22 mm, 32 mm

Worksheet 104
1a. 6000 mm; b. 9000 mm; c. 4000 mm; d. 11000 mm; e. 15000 mm; f. 7500 mm

Worksheet 105

	Length	Width	Height
1a.	150 mm	90 mm	15 mm
	15 cm	9 cm	15 cm
	0.15 m	0.09 m	0.015 m
1b.	860 mm	750 mm	1750 mm
	86 cm	75 cm	175 cm
	0.86 m	0.75 m	1.75 m
1c.	415 mm	380 mm	270 mm
	41.5 cm	38 cm	27 cm
	0.415 m	0.38 m	0.27 m
1d.	400 mm	230 mm	6 mm
	40 cm	23 cm	0.6 cm
	0.4 m	0.23 m	0.006 m

2a. 21.5 cm, 0.215 m; b. 650 mm, 0.65 m; c. 3750 mm, 375 cm; d. 5000mm, 500cm; e. 50 mm, 0.05 m; f. 0.5 cm, 0.005 m

Worksheet 107
Kavita 3.158 m; Rita 4.901 m; Deepak 4.473 m; Chintu 4.755 m
1. Convert all measurements into one unit
2. Kavita 3.1586 m, 315.86 cm, 3158.6 mm; Rita 4.901 m, 490.1 cm, 4901 mm; Deepak 4.473 m, 447.3 cm, 4473 mm; Chintu 4.255 m, 425.5 cm, 4255 mm
3. Rita
4. Kavita
5a. Deepak; b. Rita

Worksheet 108
1a. 134 cm; b. 196 cm; c. 182 cm
3a. 246 cm; b. 218 cm; c. 156 cm

Worksheet 109
1a. 0.1; b. 0.01; c. 0.001
2a. 0.375; b. 0.062; c. 0.625; d. 0.270; e. 0.310; f. 0.080; g. 0.850; h. 0.008; i. 0.720
3a. 0.340; b. 0.220; c. 0.180; d. 0.400

Worksheet 111
1. 1 cm^3

2a. Container A	72 cm^3
Container B	120 cm^3
Container C	64 cm^3
Container D	400 cm^3
Container E	1000 cm^3

Worksheet 113
1a. 24; b. 24; c. 30; d. 28
2a. 22; b. 22; c. 22 (Even though parameter is same shapes and area is not the same)

Worksheet 114
1a. 5.93 m; b. 5.95 m; c. 9.45 m; d. 15.3 m; e. 20.3 m; f. 14.93 m; g. 37.55 m; h. 51.05 m; i. 30.15 m

Worksheet 115
1a. 10.5 cm; b. 6.5 cm; c. 9.2 cm; d. 9.8 cm; e. 7.6 cm; f. 7.5 cm
2. Hemali 10 km; Sonali 13.8 km; Yudi 13.3 km; Chitra 12.5 km
3a. 11; b. 16; c. 15; d. 12

Worksheet 116
1a. 15 m; b. 17 m; c. 22 m; d. 24.9 cm; e. 16.1 cm; f. 17.7 cm
2. Week1 32 mm; Week2 30 mm; Week3 31.6 mm; Week4 39.1 mm
3a. 37; b. 43; c. 72; d. 64.1

Worksheet 120

	Length	Width	Area
1a.	10 units	5 units	50 units
b.	11 units	9 units	99 units
c.	11 units	4 units	44 units

Worksheet 121
1a. 12,000, 24,000; b. 15,000, 30,000
2a. 10,500; b. 15,600; c. 10,350; d. 10,500; e. 8,800; f. 2,500

Worksheet 122
2a. 88; b. 16; c. 150; d. 75; e. 601; f. 370

Worksheet 123
1a. 3.06 m^2; b. 13.92 m^2; c. 8.84 m^2; d. 9.8 m^2; e. 33.6 m^2; f. 11.25 m^2; g. 28.06 m^2; h. 14.58 m^2

Worksheet 124
1a. 16.2 m^2; b. 9.52 m^2; c. 13.3 m^2; d. 15.48 m^2; e. 39.22 m^2; f. 5.32 m^2;
2a. 16.34 m^2; b. 17.28 m^2; c. 104.35 m^2

Worksheet 125
1a. Length 250m; Width 40m; Area 1000 m^2; Perimeter 580 m

Worksheet 126
1a. 5; b. 15; c. 10; d. 20
2a. 22 minutes to 3; b. 18 minutes to 3; c. 28 minutes to 3; d. 3 minutes to 3
3a. 2:45; b. 4:40; c. 5:43; d. 6:53

Worksheet 128
1a. 60; b. 60; c. 3600; d. 24; e. 1440; f. 86400
3a. False; b. True; c. True; d. False
4a. 5th January; b. 11th February
5a. 2 hrs 77 mins 78 sec; b. 166 hrs 66 min 67 sec

Worksheet 130
1. 1255, 0645, 0805, 1910, 2200, 1140, 1535, 2150
2. 12:35 am, 7:24 am, 3:05 pm, 9:15 pm, 11:53 pm, 12:17 pm, 6:08 am, 8:50 am
3. 8 hours, 8 hours 20 minutes, 155 minutes, 1 hour 20

Answers

minutes, 15 hours 50 minutes, 7 hours, 5 hours 20 minutes

Worksheet 131
1a. 10 minutes; b. 32 minutes; c. 21 minutes; d. 5:14 pm; e. 3:20 am

Worksheet 132
1a. 54 minutes; b. 42 minutes; c. 6 hours 3 minutes; d. 9:29 am

Worksheet 133
1. 4 DVDs
2. 26
3. 14
4. Lucky
5a. Anita and Tina; b. 20
6a. 26, 20, 20, 14, 10

Worksheet 134
1. 10 apples
2a. 40; b. 35
3a. Wednesday; b. 55
4a. Tuesday, Thursday; b. 90
5. 15
6. 220
7a. 8.5; b. 2

Worksheet 135
1a. In Shillong it rains throughout the year;
b. In Cochin it rains heavily in May, June, July, August
2. March, September; June, January
3a. June; b. February, March, April; c. May, July
4a. 1 cm; b. 9 cm; c. 13.5 cm

Worksheet 136
1. Ratna
2. Sukumar
3. Kamal, Rajinder
4. Sukumar, Yogesh
5. 6 m

Worksheet 137
1. 11
2. 1
4. 11
5. 9
6. Thomas

Worksheet 138
1.

Sugar	Flour	Total
1	4	5
2	8	10
3	12	15

Worksheet 139
1a. 4; b. 9; c. 16

Worksheet 140
1.

Number of crosses	Number of squares
5	
10	
3	15
4	20
5	25

2. Each cross is made up of 5 squares
3a. 50; b. 75
4a. 500; b. 600

Worksheet 141
1a. 17, 21, 25, 28; b. Rs 37, Rs 43, Rs 52, Rs 58; c. 20, 24, 28, 32; d. 5, 11,15, 20

Revision 1

Standard Form	Expanded Form	Words
1a. 6,50,93,478	60000000 + 5000000 + 30000 + 400 + 70 + 8	
b. 16,83,484		sixteen lakh eight three thousand four hundred and eight four
c.	30000000 + 1000000 + 20000 + 500	three crore ten lakh twenty thousand and five hundred
d. 5,03,07,999	50000000 + 300000 + 7000 + 900 + 90 + 9	
e. 5,00,555		Five lakh five hundred and fifty five

3a. 872861226; b. $\frac{8}{5} + \frac{2}{5} = \frac{10}{5} = 2$; c. $\frac{63}{17} \times \frac{45}{34} =$
4.9048; d. 1.766; e. 28037345; f. 479829529; g. 883; h. 176.343; i. 0.0069
5. 2.46 kg
6. Rs 1656.1
16. 4.30, 4.13, 4.03, 3.41, 3.40, 3.14
19a. 100; b. 20%, 40%; c. E.Rodda; d. 35%

Revision 2
1a. 1; b. 75%; c. 1 and 4
4a. 34.5 cm, 0.345 m; b. 1750 mm, 175 cm; c. 650 mm, 0.65 m; d. 1200 mm, 1.2 m; e. 850 mm, 85 cm; f. 1.7 cm, 0.017 m
5a. 0.375 l; b. 0.062 l; c. 0.625 l
6a. 0.6 l; b. 0.058 l; d. 0.589 l
15a. 60; b. 60; c. 3600; d. 24; e. 1440; f. 86400
16a. 5 minutes, 13 minutes; b. 7:15 and 7:45; c. 4, 3, 4